Theories of Counseling

Guidance, Counseling, and Student Personnel in Education

WALTER F. JOHNSON, *Consulting Editor*

McGraw-Hill Book Company

New York
St. Louis
San Francisco
Toronto
London
Sydney

Theories of Counseling

Editor BUFORD STEFFLRE
Michigan State University

Theories of Counseling

Preface

The purpose of this book is to assemble descriptions of the major positions with regard to counseling, as distinguished from psychotherapy, that are now determining the form that this expanding activity is taking. With the advent of the National Defense Education Act and the growing interest in the provision of counseling services in schools and agencies, it seems important that the student of counseling have an acquaintance with current theoretical positions. The authors feel that a contribution might be made to the field by having the various theories presented by those who are intimately acquainted not only with the counseling process but also with its theoretical background. A special effort is made to indicate the place —including the value and limitations—of theoretical structure as it influences the behavior of counselors in high schools and colleges.

The book is designed to serve as a textbook in classes with such titles as "Counseling Theory," "Introduction to Counseling," and "Practice in Counseling." It is also assumed that the book might be assigned as supplementary reading in other courses in guidance, counseling, and pupil and student personnel services. Such a book, we would hope, might be useful at both the master's and doctoral level as well as in those few institutions which teach introductory courses at the undergraduate level.

Chapter 1 deals with the function and nature of counseling theory. A discussion of the definition and necessity of theory is followed by an examination of its function in practical situations. Next counseling is defined, and an attempt is made to distinguish it both from therapy on the one hand and instruction on the other. Having defined theory and counseling, the chapter lists what we consider to be the important substantive elements of a counseling theory.

The remainder of the book deals with specific counseling theories and their place in given counseling settings. Chapter 2 treats the client-centered adaptation of counseling. This chapter is concerned with self-theory as it applies to counseling and discusses the substantive elements listed above as they apply in this theory. Because this theory has been so well presented by Rogers, Patterson, and others, it is of special importance to students in training to be counselors. Chapter 3 discusses adaptations of the psychoanalytic theory and examines their relevancy for counseling. Although this theory has previously been primarily concerned with psychotherapy, it will be shown that it has certain usefulness for counseling too. Chapter 4 attempts an adaptation of neobehavioral learning theory to the counseling process. Again, here we have a major psychological position applied to counseling. Chapter 5 may have largely a historical interest to many since it is essentially an examination of the trait-and-factor theory, but to most practicing counselors, particularly at the high school level, this is the theory which fits best and explains best what they are doing. Chapter 6 discusses the place of theory in high school counseling and makes specific conclusions regarding its relevance to those workers. Chapter 7 performs a like function for the college counselor. Chapter 8 attempts an overall evaluation and synthesis of what has previously been discussed.

Because the authors have had their training in a variety of settings, represent several points of view, and have had experience in different professional contexts, we hoped to escape the parochialism which sometimes results in presenting a theory of counseling in a manner that resembles an invitation to join a cult. We leave to the reader's judgment and mercy the answer as to whether we have achieved this goal.

Buford Stefflre

About the Authors

Leonard D. Goodstein is professor of psychology at the University of Cincinnati. He was formerly director of the University Counseling Service at the University of Iowa. He received his bachelor's degree cum laude in psychology from the City College of New York. His graduate degrees are from Columbia University in Psychological Services. Before going to the University of Iowa he served as an instructor in psychology at Hofstra College. Professor Goodstein is a diplomate in clinical psychology of the American Board of Examiners in Professional Psychology. He is the author of several articles in the professional literature on counseling and clinical psychology and serves as a consulting editor for the *Journal of Applied Psychology* and *Psychological Reports*. He is a fellow of the American Psychological Association.

Donald L. Grummon is professor of psychology and director of the Counseling Center at Michigan State University. His bachelor's degree is from DePauw University, his master's from Ohio State University and his doctorate from the University of Chicago. He served for two years as a psychologist at the Cheltenham School for Boys (a training school for court-committed delinquents) and then was at the University of Chicago where he was an assistant professor of psychology, a counselor, and administrative and research coordinator in the Counseling Center. He has written in the fields of both counseling and clinical psychology. While at Ohio State University and at the University of Chicago, Dr. Grummon worked closely with Carl Rogers.

Paul T. King is director of the Counseling Center and a counseling psychologist at the University of Missouri. His bachelor's degree is in journalism from the University of Kentucky where he also received his master's degree. His doctorate is from Pennsylvania State University. Dr. King is a diplomate of the American Board of Examiners in Professional Psychology in counseling psychology. He has served as a psychologist in child guidance clinics, speech pathology clinics, and psychological clinics. For the last ten years he worked as a counseling psychologist in the Counseling Center at Michigan State University and at the University of Missouri.

William Ratigan is Director of Personnel and Guidance Services at Charlevoix, Michigan. His bachelor's degree is from the University of Chattanooga and his graduate degrees are from Michigan State University. He has held a number of writing and reporting assignments and is the author of eleven books concerned chiefly with the history of the Great Lakes region.

Buford Stefflre is a professor in the College of Education at Michigan State University. His bachelor's degree was in English from the University of California and his graduate degrees are from the University of Southern California in guidance. He worked for fifteen years with the Los Angeles City Schools as a teacher, counselor, and supervisor of counseling. He has been at Michigan State University since 1955 in the Department of Guidance and Pupil Personnel Services. He is presently editor of the *Personnel and Guidance Journal* and was issue chairman of the "Guidance and Pupil Personnel" issue of the *Review of Educational Research* which was published in April, 1963. He is the author of numerous articles in professional psychological and educational journals and two school guidance texts.

Edmund G. Williamson is professor of psychology and dean of students at the University of Minnesota. His bachelor's degree is from the University of Illinois and his doctorate from the University of Minnesota. Dean Williamson was the recipient of the research award in 1953 and the Nancy C. Wimmer award in 1962 from the American Personnel and Guidance Association. He was a Fulbright visiting lecturer at Tokyo University in 1955. From 1950 to the present he has been chairman of the Veterans Administration Advisory Committee on Counseling Services for Vocational Rehabilitation and Education. Dean Williamson is the author of numerous books and articles in the field of psychology and education and has been active in a number of organizations in these fields.

Contents

chapter 1

BUFORD STEFFLRE | *Function*

and Present Status

of Counseling Theory

As counseling becomes a more recognized service of educational institutions, it is necessary to make an effort to conceptualize this process so
that its purposes and methods are more amenable to study and understanding. The experienced counselor may need to make a more systematic effort to look at what happens in the counseling interview so
that he may understand it within a framework which makes sense in
the light of his knowledge about human behavior. The inexperienced
counselor, or the counselor in training, may need to develop some
guidelines regarding what he should do during the counseling interview—guidelines which logically evolve from overarching theories.
This chapter will attempt to define theory and show its values and
limitations. It will also attempt to define counseling and distinguish it
both from psychotherapy on the one hand and instruction on the
other. Subsequent chapters will show the place of counseling theory in
school settings and will delineate four of the most important theories
currently in use.

What Is a Theory?

Scientists and philosophers have given us many definitions of theory.
One has called it a human convention for keeping data in order. This
philosopher points out that if human memories were better than they
are, we should have no need for theory since we could simply refer to
raw data whenever we wanted to consider a problem. Because our
memories are fallible, theories are not only convenient but necessary
since they enable us to reduce complexities to manageable proportions
so that we can deal with an otherwise overwhelming amount of information. To perform this function, a theory must consist of data plus
an interrelating structure which tell us how one piece of information

has relevance for another (Pepper, 1961, p. 72) . Another definition says that a theory is a provisional systemization of events. Again, we are being told that a theory is a device which enables us to see relationships between one event or fact and another (McCabe, 1958, p. 49) . Currently it seems fashionable to think of theories as models. A theory, then, may be called a conceptual model—for example, the id—which is postulated to explain a process inferred from observed behavior. This definition says that we see certain happenings and that we strive to have them make sense. They make sense only if we are able to postulate some process which if it operated, would result in the behavior (McCabe, 1958, p. 49). In a widely used discussion of theory in the field of psychology, the definition evolved indicates that theory is a cluster of relevant assumptions systematically related to each other and a set of empirical definitions (Hall & Lindzey, 1957, p. 10) . Here again are the elements of data—empirical definitions, postulates or conventions, and relevant assumptions—which have appeared in previous definitions. Finally, we come to a most usable and memorable definition which states merely that a theory is a possible world which can be checked against the real world (Pepinsky & Pepinsky, 1954, p. 18).

What these definitions have in common are the elements of reality and belief. Reality is the data or behavior which we see and strive to explain. Belief is the way that we try to make sense out of the data by relating what we see to conceivable explanations of it. Theory building, then, grows out of our need to make sense of life. A theory is a map on which a few points are known, and the road between them is inferred. Good maps can be filled in as we learn more about the world, and, poor ones will need to be thrown away when we find that they are leading us astray.

Do We Need Theory?

Often the experienced counselor, and even the trainee, is scornful of theory and questions its value to him. Students frequently say that they want more practical courses and "not all this theory." A dichotomy between theory and practicality is often assumed. In reality, however, nothing is as practical as a good theory. Like a good map, it tells us what to look for, what to expect, and where to go. The use of theory can be analogous to the learning about life that helps the neonate make sense out of the booming, buzzing confusion which is his world. The phenomena of nature are not in themselves necessarily ordered. But to operate, we must impose order on them, and this ordering is a function of theory.

Those who feel that they can operate entirely without theory and even assume an antitheoretical position are usually basing their behavior on vaguely defined but implicit theory. There is no other way that they can decide what to do. Intuition, often advanced as a substitute for theory, is itself but a crude type of hypothesizing (McDaniel, Lallas, Saum, & Gilmore, 1959, p. 148). "The views of the 'practical men' are usually derived from assumptions and arguments no less complex than those on which theory is based; they are more and not less liable to error because they are less openly expressed" (Campbell, 1953, p. 289). The real question then is not whether we shall operate from theory since we have no choice in this matter, but rather what theories shall we use and how shall we use theories. Specifically, in a counseling situation when a client says "I hate my mother," the counselor's reactions are limited only by his biological status. He can slap the client, he can run out of the room, he can jump up on his chair, he can reply "It makes you bitter just thinking about her," or he can do any of a number of things. When he makes a choice among the responses open to him, he must act from theory. That is, he must act from some notion as to what the client means by his statement, what his statement means in the life of the client, what the proper goals of counseling are, what the function of the counselor is, what techniques are successful in moving toward the determined goals, and the other elements which taken together constitute for him a theory of counseling.

What Underlying Bases Do Theories Have?

Just as phenomena which we observe can be seen in many ways, so countless theories can possibly be constructed. To explain why we have the theories which we do, we must look at the bases of theory.

Personal basis. One of the underlying sources of theory is the personal need structure of the theory builder or user. This dimension of theory has been pointed up by Shoben (1962, p. 619), who says that since there is little in the way of research evidence that points to one theory as being superior to another in the field of counseling, we must look within the counselor who uses a given theory to determine why he is attracted to that particular one. Certainly this same personal element would seem to be present in theory building. The character, the genius, the personality of the theory constructor is expressed in the theory which he develops.

Historical basis. A good example of the influence of history on the possibility of theory building is given by Theobald:

> The stated aims of the physical and social sciences are indeed very similar. Their object is to reduce the overwhelming diversity and complexity of reality to simple theoretical regularities so that events can be understood, and, if possible, the future predicted on the basis of the laws discovered. Two steps are generally considered necessary in the evolution of a theory. First, observations of the facts of phenomena to be described, and, second, the formulation of a theory that will cover all the observed facts. It can then be tested by using it for the purposes of prediction: as long as it gives valid results, it remains useful. However, if exceptions are found, it should be modified so that it will cover all the observed facts (1961, p. 40).

Theobald goes on to point out that up to about five hundred years ago theory building in the physical sciences was bound by emotional attachment and belief. The examples of the difficulties of Copernicus are known to us. People could not build and believe in a theory which did not put the earth at the center of the universe.

The social sciences are today, and perhaps forever, in the position of the physical sciences of five hundred years ago in the limits placed upon them. It is impossible to be completely free of emotional and value elements as theory builders in the social science. The social sciences are such that we must always consider "ends," and at least at this time in history desirable ends, or goals, are apt to be "given" and so not subject to investigation. We cannot escape ethical theory which points toward what should be, even though it may limit the acceptance of psychological theories regarding what is or what can be. Psychological theory may tell us the relative distance and the type of surface of several roads, but only ethical theory can tell us which one is worth taking. For example, we cannot meaningfully and freely construct theories to answer the question "Which is more efficient, communism or free enterprise?" because we must first ask a prior ethical question "Which is right?"

Still another limitation on theory building in social science is the fact that research itself, at least with our present techniques, may alter objective reality. In the physical science this influence of the researcher on his data is called "the principle of indeterminancy." In social science it is quite clear that in many contexts as soon as we begin to do research, the situation we wanted to understand vanishes. A good example of this principle is shown by the recent discussion of the placebo effect in counseling. When a client changes his behavior after counseling, it is difficult to determine whether the change is associated with the personality of the counselor, the technique of counseling, or the attention given him. This last factor—sympathetic attention—has been likened to the physician's placebo. An extension to another area is illustrated by some research on causes of leaving school which was done in a large school system. A group of potential dropouts was identified and randomized into two groups. One group—the experimental—got all kinds of special treatment and attention and the other—the control group—did not. True, the experimental group began to behave in a more desirable fashion, but unfortunately for science, the control group began to respond in much the same way. In other words, as soon as research was done in the school, it altered the reality of the situation. The classrooms were different, the halls were different, and objective reality was not what it was when the research began. We must conclude then that theories in the social sciences are bound by space and bound by time. The theories that explain behavior in 1850 may not explain it in the year 2000. The theory that seems reasonable in America may not be useful in Vietnam.

Sociological basis. Theories are influenced not only by the personal context but by the cultural context in which the theory builder and user lives. Americans are said to live in a world which is orderly, and so we are attracted to theory in general and particularly to theories which attempt to make sense of natural phenomena. We believe that it is a man's job to discover the order in the universe and build models (theories) which reflect it (Hall, 1961, p. 133). In such an orderly universe we are apt to look for causality and assume that it is present. The usual arguments against complete causality (determinism) include the belief that the individual is unique and complex, that causality may imply teleology, and finally that if behavior is caused, we are left without the concept of guilt. On the other hand, those arguing for the acceptance of causality would reply first that uniqueness is relative in psychology if not in etymology and that in the history of science many previously complex problems now seem understandable. With regard to teleology the espousers of a position assuming causality would say that perhaps it is the present expectation and not the future goal which motivates. Finally, they would say that we may still punish antisocial behavior, but our motives would be to affect the future and not to correct the past. Regardless of the logic of the position, most counselors behave "as if" behavior is both caused and to some extent free. Logical contradictions notwithstanding, we believe that there is sufficient order in the psychological universe so that we can to some extent understand and predict behavior, but sufficient freedom in an individual that he has some choices which are relatively free of genetics and of history. We ask not "Is man free?" but "How free is man?" The sociological base of theory in America, then, is an orderly one. We look for order in the world, and we find it.

Americans are also concerned with recent times rather than with remote history, and therefore our theories are apt to explain behavior in terms of relatively recent events. Because of this point of view, we may sometimes slip into the error of thinking that since *A* happened after *B*, *B* must have caused *A*. Instruction in formal logic will not always free us of this fallacy because the culture within which we operate tends to value such explanations. A good example of the American concern with the present as opposed to the concern of some other peoples with the past was given recently by an American researcher working in Florence, Italy. The researcher was trying to discover the effects of university services on community life in small villages. His research designs always called for counting and analyzing the relationships among events that were happening or had just happened. His Italian colleagues, however, who were also interested in the problem were more apt to approach the hypotheses through a discussion of what the Etruscans did and how this influenced the Romans, what the Romans did and how this influenced the Goths, and so on to the present. The theories built and held by Americans are apt to be time-bound in the sense that they look not very far in the past and not very far in the future, for Americans are most comfortable in "possible worlds" of this kind.

Still another sociological influence in American theory building and theory holding is the English language itself.

> The categories and types that we isolate from the world of phenomena we do not find there because they stare every observer in the face; on the contrary, the world is presented in a kaleidoscopic flux of impressions which has to be organized by our minds. We cut nature up, organize it into concepts, and ascribe significance as we do, largely because we are parties to an agreement organized in this way—an agreement that holds throughout our speech community and is codified in the patterns of our language . . . no individual is free to describe nature with absolute impartiality . . . (From *The Silent Language* by Edward T. Hall. Copyright © 1959 by Edward T. Hall. Reprinted by permission of Doubleday & Company, Inc.)

Perhaps the best known example of the influence of language on perception is that some Eskimo dialects have as many as twenty different words for snow in its various forms and stages. A language like English with its relative lack of concern for snow would not lend itself to the same kinds of theory about snow as an Eskimo theorist might build. It has been further suggested that even such a seemingly objective phenomenon as the color spectrum itself is sliced up arbitrarily and differently by different languages. Therefore, there would be people who would be incapable of developing a theory involving, for example, "purple," for purple is not *seen* by the speakers of the language.

Purple would not be seen because it could not be isolated and labeled. Our language, too, by arbitrary designations forbids us to see what others may see or to think thoughts that others might think.

Philosophical basis. Although there would seem to be a logical connection between philosophy and practice, it does not yet seem clear whether a given philosophical position will necessarily lead to a specific counseling theory. Perhaps Wrenn (1959) in the *NSSE Yearbook* has made the most ambitious attempt to relate philosophy to counseling. Essentially, however, Wrenn pointed to the several philosophical bases which could justify the various school personnel activities which have evolved rather than starting from philosophical positions and drawing conclusions about the type of services they would consistently suggest. Curriculum theorists have largely given up trying to show necessary bonds between philosophical positions and classroom experiences. Many of them rather postulate a series of principles between the philosophy and the practice. These principles might stem from a number of different philosophical positions, but they tend to narrow the field of practice if we assume them to be sound principles.

In the counseling field such guiding principles—halfway between philosophy and practice—might come from the area of mental health. In other words, regardless of the basic philosophy which we hold, perhaps we can agree that mental health is a desirable goal and come to some conclusion as to what constitutes desirable mental health and then construct a theory of counseling which we hope will lead toward desirable mental health. Unfortunately, however, there is not agreement on what constitutes mental health (Jahoda, 1958, p. 23). Jahoda summarizes current concepts of mental health and says that there are six criteria which seem most fruitful in considering this concept. The six criteria which she lists are (1) attitudes of an individual toward his own self; (2) growth, development, or self-actualization; (3) integration; (4) autonomy; (5) perception of reality; and (6) environmental mastery. One or more of these criteria would probably be accepted by most theorists in the counseling field as a legitimate goal of their activity. If we accept the first criterion as the best indicator of mental health, certain counseling theories might be suggested, while the last criterion might suggest quite different ones. Our theory building and use are guided, if not by our philosophy, at least by our acceptance of basic principles which are near philosophy in sweep and depth. It is only after such a goal has been clarified and accepted, however, that a reasonable theory can be built. If we operated from other principles or philosophical bases, we should have to construct other theories.

In summary, then, theories do not appear at random. If we are to understand why certain theories are constructed and accepted, we need to know something about the philosophical assumptions that the theory builders and the theory holders operate from. We need to know something about the historical context in which the theory appears. We need to understand the sociocultural milieu in which the theory developed. In this milieu we should want to pay particular attention to the language and to the life view which the inhabitant held. Finally, we can only understand the genesis of a theory by knowing something about the personality, needs, strengths, and genius of the theory builder.

What Do Theories Do?

Theories once constructed and accepted perform a variety of functions. A theory may lead us to observe relationships which we had previously overlooked. The germ theory pointed out relationships which had long been present in fact but made no sense until a theory was built which related one fact to another. The relationship between sleeping with the windows open in the malaria-ridden South and getting sick with malaria only became apparent after the theory regarding the disease was constructed.

Theories help us to incorporate our data because theories predict laws just as laws predict events (Campbell, 1953, p. 300). From theories we may define operational truths because theories involve assertions which lead to prediction which can be tested and verified (McCabe, 1958, p. 51). Theories focus our attention on relevant data by telling us what to look for and lead us to the use of consistent terminology. It was only after the construction and acceptance of self-theory that such matters as warmth and friendliness in the classroom received systematic attention from researchers. Theories may help us construct new methods of behaving in a counseling situation and point to ways of evaluating the old ones (Brammer & Shostrom, 1960, p. 6). Recently, a doctoral student indicated that he was interested in studying the problem of college students who did not have a declared academic major. When he asked what he should look for in doing research on these students, there was obviously no way to give him an answer until there was some clarification as to what theory he was holding about them. Without a theory he might have studied their intelligence, their blood types, the color of their hair, their height, or the names of their uncles. After the student had considered the problem, he decided that the most meaningful theory for his investigation was that developed by Super, who suggests that a selection of an occupation constitutes the implementation of a self-concept. It would seem to follow from this theory that a student who was unable to tentatively select an occupation would have a very unclear self-concept. Starting from this theoretical basis, the doctoral student was able to proceed with his research. The theory told him what to look for. At the end of his investigation it helped him incorporate his findings and make sense from them.

A special problem in the use of theory is its application to individual cases. Theories essentially lead to generalizations about averages, but for dealing with an individual, we often feel that we need principles which explain the unique personality. In dealing with an individual, we need to remember that laws are probability statements and that the more classes for which we have explanatory laws, the more effectively we can deal with an individual. It would seem that as we narrow the reference cases, we can become more explicit and helpful in explaining individual behavior (Phillips, 1956, p. 75; Pepinsky & Pepinsky, 1954, p. 20). The previously quoted article by Shoben (1962) refers to this problem and points out that the use of theory with an individual case both facilitates and inhibits our behavior. Theory facilitates by helping us see sense and meaning in the client's behavior, but it may inhibit us by blinding us to his uniqueness. We may force him to fit on the Procrustean bed of a theory applicable to the many.

We need, then, not only theory to help us see what is happening within an individual but skepticism stemming from the realization that present theories in social science will rarely, if ever, completely explain the behavior of a given individual.

How Do We Know a Good Theory?—Formal Attributes

There are pigs and pigs; there are theories and theories. A good theory may be said to have five formal attributes. *A good theory is clear* in that there is agreement among its general principles (philosophy), and agreement of its consequences with observation (science). It is clear in that it is communicable, and those who read it will understand what is meant. It is an easily read map.

A good theory is comprehensive in that it has scope and accounts for much behavior. It will explain what happens to many people in many situations. It approaches all-purpose utility.

A good theory is explicit, that is, it has precision. While it may make use of evocative statements such as "psychological warmth," and "fully functioning," these concepts will be translatable into denotative statements so that they can be checked against clear referents in the real world (Frank, 1949, p. 27). It is not the mystical or obscure talk of the theorist that spoils his theory, but it is his failure to translate his poetry into science.

A good theory is parsimonious and does not overexplain phenomena. A theory which explains a given event in five different ways is apt not to explain it at all.

Finally, *a good theory generates useful research*. Some theories may stand for decades untested because they lack this formal attribute. Other theories more heuristic may be excellent theories simply because they stimulate much research which itself proves them false.

In summary, then, a theory is always a map in the process of being filled in with greater detail. We do not so much ask is it true, but is it helpful.

How Do We Use Theory?

Among counselors we may find attitudes toward the value of various types of theory on a continuum from the dogmatically theoretical to the dogmatically antitheoretical. Six steps or gradations have been identified (Bone, 1959, p. 99). One person may see psychology as exactly the same as physical science in both goals and methods. He would search for the most rigorous behavioristic theories and attempt to find them apart from the influence of society, history, and personality. A second person may believe that the above position is true in principle but not completely so in fact, and he will temper his "rigor" with the realization that what is good for physical science may not be good for counseling. A third person would value the ideographic but press, to the extent that he could, toward the nomothetic. Such a person would attempt to wed the values of the physical science with the peculiarities of the social science. A fourth person might use both approaches but really feel that the ideographic is the best for his purposes. A fifth might make use of clinical insight in his work but try when possible to check it by an approximation of the scientific method. Such a person would have a basic commitment to the ideographic but some sense of responsibility for using the nomothetic. Finally, there are counselors who would use the completely clinical method and feel that attempts at theory building and rigorous research were inappropriate as well as impossible.

As we examine counseling theories, we may be appalled by the fact that they do not seem to be very soundly based on empirical data or always skillfully constructed to illuminate the relationships among the facts that we do have. Such a realization may tend to immobilize a new counselor. He may say, "How can I act when our theories are so poorly supported?" This dilemma seems best resolved by making a distinction between action and belief. We may have to act on less evidence than we can demand for belief since the basis of action is ethical and the basis of belief is cognitive. We cannot wait until theories are perfected but must operate on what evidence we have. As we choose among the approaches open to us, we may have to take the best of what appears to be a very poor lot. We may have to act "as if" we know, when, in fact, we know we do not know.

Conflicting theories also may be somewhat traumatizing to the student. Closer examination, however, may in some cases indicate that theories complement each other rather than contradict (McCabe, 1958, p. 50). The use of more than one theory may point to the same facts and give clarity where previously we had confusion. The analogy might be made of the use of a variety of stage lights in a theatrical production. Sometimes the overhead light will give us the view we want; sometimes the red spotlight or blue will illuminate what we are looking for.

A philosopher has suggested that we strive for rational clarity in theory and reasonable eclecticism in practice (Pepper, 1961, p. 330). This advice would permit us to be as rigorous as we should like in a cognitive area but as humane as we should be in action. "Rational clarity" demands that we hold our theory explicitly if we should make the best use of it because only then can we correct for our biases in theory selection and valuation. It is the theory we use without knowing we are using it that is dangerous to us and our clients. Just as personality defects and emotional problems in the counselor need not preclude the possibility of effective work if they are taken into account and corrected for, so theory may be better used in counseling if we are aware that the theory is held and acknowledge its limitations and some of the sources of its attraction to us.

Finally, it has been suggested that we make best use of theories in social science by remembering that they will not long remain useful. Since they are bound by space and time and the present level of our knowledge, the best of theories will not long serve. If we should accept this limitation, we should teach our students not only presently held theories but ways of building new ones (Theobald, 1961, p. 100). Theory building will need to be a constant process for those who remain in counseling. It is for this reason that there may be value in examining as we have the structure, function, and genesis of theory.

What Is Counseling?

Having considered the nature and function of theory, we must now discuss the activity to which it will be applied in this book—counseling. Defining counseling and distinguishing it from both psychotherapy and instruction is the next task which must be performed to enable us to consider various theories of counseling.

In defining counseling, we are again faced with the fact that various authorities have seen it in different lights. These differences are due not only to differences in point of view and philosophy among the specialists in this field but are due to historical changes in the perceptions which have been held of this art.

In 1945, the educational dictionary maker, Good, defined counseling as the "individualized and personalized assistance with personal, educational, vocational problems, in which all pertinent facts are studied and analyzed, and a solution is sought, often with the assistance of specialists, school and community resources, and personal interviews in which the counselee is taught to make his own decisions" (1945, p. 104). This older definition would now be seen as merely a statement supporting one point of view or theory of counseling. Its strong emphasis on cognitive material, immediate decision making, and use of external resources was characteristic of the views of counseling commonly held at that time and still held by certain proponents.

A more recent definition is that of English and English (1958, p. 127) in their dictionary in which they say that counseling is "a relationship in which one person endeavors to help another to understand and solve his adjustment problems. The area of adjustment is often indicated: educational counseling, vocational counseling, social counseling, et cetera." They go on to point out that "counseling is a two-way affair involving both counselor and counselee. Unfortunately, both noun and verb counsel retain an older meaning of advice giving, which is now conceived as only part of the counseling process."

Still another of the more modern and psychologically oriented definitions is the one by Pepinsky and Pepinsky in which they say that counseling is seen as "(a) diagnosis and treatment of minor (nonimbedded, nonincapacitating), functional (nonorganic) maladjustment and (b) as a relationship, primarily individual and face-to-face, between counselor and client" (1954). A middle-of-the-road definition much valued and used is that given by Wrenn when he says that "counseling is a dynamic and purposeful relationship between two people in which procedures vary with the nature of the student's need, but in which there is always mutual participation by the counselor and the student with the focus upon self-clarification and self-determination by the student" (1951). It will be seen that Wrenn's definition is sufficiently broad to encompass both the activities of the earlier proponents of counseling and those of the more modern practitioners. Hahn (1953) points out that the reason for these different perceptions in the counseling process is that counseling itself seems to have three different bodies of supporters. He identifies the social welfare advocates who have primarily an ideographic interest. Typical of these would be Coombs and the others in the phenomenological school. A second group would be those who are more medically oriented and more nomothetic in their position. Foremost among these would be such men as Thorne. The final and third movement identified by Hahn would be those people who are primarily concerned with student personnel administration and who have great interest in measurement. Typical of this group would be Strong, Bingham, and probably Williamson (Hahn, 1953, p. 234). Because counseling practitioners approach the process from a variety of directions and backgrounds, it should not seem unusual that they view and define counseling in a variety of ways. Although they may be each patting the same elephant, they are getting quite different notions of what the beast is like.

A common element in many current definitions of counseling is the notion that counseling is aimed at helping people make choices and act on them—helping them answer the question, "What shall I do?" Perhaps the clearest advocate of this point of view is Tyler: "Counseling is one kind of psychological helping activity, the kind that concentrates on the growth of a clear sense of ego identity and the willingness to make choices and commitments in accordance with it" (1958, p. 8). Others have agreed that this element of choice is the key factor in counseling. Moore (1961, p. 63) in making the point that high school counselors should not do psychotherapy defines counseling in the high school setting as help with choice making. Traube says

> A counselor's task is helping the student to examine and analyze his own problem; to gather, evaluate, and organize pertinent data in regard to it; to think through the probable consequences of various possible solutions; to choose and try out the solution that seems to fit the known facts and and needs most adequately; and to modify his plan of solution when it proves to be out of harmony with the facts and needs of the situation (1950, p. 932).

Shostrom and Brammer quote a definition which tells us that counseling is "a purposeful, reciprocal relationship between two people in which one, a trained person, helps the other to change himself or his environment" (1952, p. 1). And finally, Wolberg tells us that counseling is "a form of interviewing in which the client is helped to understand himself more completely in order to correct an environmental or adjustment difficulty" (1954, p. 12). An important element in any understanding of counseling is a recognition that many people see it as an aid in choice making prior to acting.

Learning is another element which is often used in defining counseling. Gustad says that

> counseling is a learning-oriented process, carried on in a simple, one-to-one social environment, in which a counselor, professionally competent in relevant psychological skills and knowledge, seeks to assist the client by methods appropriate to the latter's needs and within the context of the total personnel program, to learn more about himself, to learn how to put such understanding into effect in relation to more clearly perceived, realistically defined goals to the end that the client may become a happier and more productive member of his society (1953).

This concern with learning which we have seen was an element in earlier definitions of counseling has again come to the fore with research and study on the behavioral aspects of the counseling process. Indeed, most theorists in the field now would agree that counseling is a learning process, although they might have some sharp differences as to what facilitates learning and how learning occurs.

Still another element frequently found in definitions of counseling is that of personality development. Bordin says "The psychological counselor is a psychological practitioner who aids people with these problems of behavior in which the critical issues have to do with their emotions and motivations. . . . Counseling . . . involves interactions . . . where the counselor . . . has taken responsibility for making his role in the interaction process contribute positively to the other person's personality development" (1955, p. 3). Again, although almost all theorists might agree that counseling involves personality development, there might be relatively little agreement as to how personality development is best furthered.

One of the more promising conceptions of counseling that is currently being discussed involves its effect on role clarification. Tyler (1961, p. 21) says that counseling is much concerned with role problems as opposed to psychotherapy with its emphasis on intrapersonal conflict. A recent authoritative report by the Division of Counseling Psychology of the American Psychological Association (1961) defines counseling as being involved primarily with role problems. This report points out that three trends merge in counseling psychology—vocational guidance, psychometrics, and personality development. The fact that these three streams have different sources may indicate some of the reasons for differences of opinion with regard to what counseling is or should be. The report goes on to say that the present emphasis in counseling embraces such goals for the client as clear self-perception and harmony with environment and such goals for society as the encouragement of society to recognize individual differences and encouragement of the full development of all people. This report would suggest that there will remain some differences in the specifics of what counseling should be but that there might be general agreement that one of the purposes of counseling is to help an individual understand one of his role commitments and carry it out more successfully.

The attempts at definitions that are quoted here have had in common the primarily instrumental character of counseling. Although some of them would suggest that counseling is basically concerned with dynamic problems, the bulk of counseling theorists seem to believe that counseling deals with such problems as choice, action, and role definition. It has been seen that many writers have attempted to define counseling without, on the one hand, succeeding to everyone's satisfaction, or, on the other hand, seriously damaging themselves or the profession. Thus encouraged, this author joins the line with his definition: "Counseling denotes a professional relationship between a trained counselor and a client. This relationship is usually person-to-person, although it may sometimes involve more than two people, and it is designed to help the client understand and clarify his view of his life space so that he may make meaningful and informed choices consonant with his essential nature in those areas where choices are available to him." This definition like many quoted above indicates that counseling is a process, that it is a relationship, that it is designed to help people make choices, that underlying better choice making are such matters as learning, personality development, and self-knowledge which can be translated into better role perception and more effective role behavior.

Distinctions between Counseling and Psychotherapy

Efforts to distinguish counseling from psychotherapy have not met with universal approval. Some people think that such a distinction should not be made and that the two terms should be used synonymously. Others, however, particularly those training secondary school counselors, are of the opinion that such a distinction *must* be made. If it is not present in nature, it must be invented. If no distinction is possible, then certainly all master's level counselor education pro-

grams should stop at once and twenty thousand secondary school counselors who are presently employed to do "counseling" should be dismissed, for few would hold that these people are properly trained
psychotherapists. A distinction, then, must be found even though the
edges of the distinction may blur and agreement on all particulars is
unlikely. The problem is clearly posed by Hahn who writes,

> I know of few counselors or psychologists who are completely satisfied
> that clear distinctions (between counseling and psychotherapy) have been
> made.... Perhaps the most complete agreements are: 1- that counseling
> and psychotherapy cannot be distinguished clearly, 2- that counselors
> practice what psychotherapists consider psychotherapy, 3- that psychothera-
> pists practice what counselors consider to be counseling, and 4- that despite
> the above they are different (1953, p. 232).

The difficulty of distinction was recognized by English and English
in their previously quoted definition which goes on to say of counseling that "while usually applied to help the normal counselee it
merges by imperceptible degrees into psychotherapy" (1958).

Before trying to make a distinction between counseling and psychotherapy, we might find it helpful to pause and define psychotherapy
itself. Wolberg defines psychotherapy as "a form of treatment for problems of an emotional nature in which a trained person deliberately
establishes a professional relationship with a patient with the object of
removing, modifying or retarding existing symptoms, of mediating disturbed patterns of behavior, and of promoting positive personality
growth and development" (1954, p. 1). Eysenck quotes an amusing
definition which says that psychotherapy is "an unidentified technique
applied to unspecified problems with unpredictable outcomes. For this
technique we recommend rigorous training" (1961, p. 698). Eysenck
then more seriously defines psychotherapy as containing such elements
as (1) a prolonged interpersonal relationship, (2) the involvement of
trained personnel, (3) a self-dissatisfaction with emotional and/or interpersonal adjustment on the part of the client, (4) the use of psychological methods, (5) an activity based on a theory of mental disorders,
and (6) an aim through this relationship of ameliorating self-dissatisfaction.

To see some of the differences between counseling and psychotherapy,
we shall look at their respective goals, clients, practitioners, settings, and methods. Although we shall examine these differences, no
completely satisfactory, defensible, and clear distinctions are expected.
It seems more likely that a continuum may exist from one activity to
the other in regard to each of these elements. Just as first aid may
shade into the practice of medicine so counseling may shade into psy-

chotherapy, but no one thinks that it is impossible to distinguish the application of a band-aid from brain surgery. Or as Goldman (1964) writes, "True, there are times, around dusk, when one is uncertain about turning on the lights.... Do these borderline decisions mean that there is no value in differentiating between day and night...?"

This notion of a continuum of counseling to psychotherapy has been well expressed by Brammer and Shostrom who indicate that the two activities may overlap, but that in general counseling would be characterized by such terms as "educative, supportive, situational, problem solving, conscious awareness, and emphasis on normal," whereas therapy would be characterized by such terms as "reconstructive, depth emphasis, analytic, focus on unconscious and emphasis on neurotic or other emotional problems" (1960, p. 6). Patterson, in reviewing the literature on counseling, indicates that the counseling end of a counseling-psychotherapy continuum would be characterized by such elements as "normal, preventive, developmental, not severe, area versus total, reality oriented, positive, non-imbedded" (1959, p. 4). This emphasis on distinction by relative position on several continua provides a useful framework from which to attempt more specific differences with regard to goals, clients, practitioners, settings, and methods.

Goals. In looking at the goals of counseling as distinguished from the goals of psychotherapy, it would seem that frequently a goal of counseling is to help an individual deal with the developmental tasks which are appropriate to his age. The adolescent who is being helped with the problems of sexual definition, emotional independence from parents, preparation for an occupation, and the other tasks typical of his age and our culture would be receiving counseling. On the other hand, a middle-aged person who is grappling with these same problems might be closer to the appropriate concern of a psychotherapist.

The previously cited report of Division 17 of the American Psychological Association says

> When we consider these discussions and look at the contribution counseling psychologists are making and can make to society, we can summarize what is important about the specialty by saying that it focuses on *plans* individuals must make to play productive *roles* in their social environments. Whether the person being helped with such planning is sick or well, abnormal or normal, is really irrelevant. The focus is on assets, skills, strengths, possibilities for further development. Personality difficulties are dealt with only when they constitute obstacles to the individual's forward progress (1961, p. 6).

Another suggested distinction regarding goals has been made by Hahn and MacLean (1955), who indicate that the counselor would give heavy emphasis to prevention of disruptive deviations, whereas the psychotherapist might give primary emphasis to present deviations with secondary attention to prevention. They make another distinction with regard to reality testing and indicate that a goal of counseling is to permit reality testing in a somewhat sheltered situation, whereas in psychotherapy testing is permitted in an almost completely sheltered situation. Finally, they say that counseling has as a goal long-range educational and vocational planning. Their total emphasis seems to involve distinguishing counseling as being concerned with preventive mental health and psychotherapy with remediation.

Another distinction is sometimes made with regard to the goal of these two activities in that counseling is more concerned with narrowly situational matters, while psychotherapy is more concerned with changing the organisms so that the client can handle not only the present but future problems. In other words, counseling sometimes is defined as being more peripheral and psychotherapy more central.

Shaw (1957, p. 357) indicates that counseling should be more concerned with creative help, while psychotherapy is more concerned with mental illness. That is, counseling is not so much involved with curing or treating as with pointing out new vistas of opportunity. Mowrer (1953) has indicated the possibility of distinguishing the goals of counseling and psychotherapy on the basis of two kinds of anxiety. Normal anxiety is the proper business of counseling, whereas psychotherapy might more appropriately deal with neurotic anxiety.

Tyler (1961, p. 58) suggests that counseling is the process of helping the client to attain a clear sense of identity but that psychotherapy attempts to make changes in the basic developmental structure. Again Tyler (1961, p. 12) indicates that psychotherapy deals with personality change, while counseling deals with the utilization of resources; psychotherapy with intrapersonal conflict, counseling with role problems.

Vance and Volsky (1962, pp. 565–570) suggest that a common goal in much psychotherapy and counseling is the reduction of psychological discordance. When this discordance is accompanied by considerable psychopathology, it falls more appropriately into the domain of the psychotherapist, but when it is reality-based as, for example, with a client whose goals call for abilities he lacks, it calls for counseling skills. However, these authors contend that the dimensions of discordance and psychopathology are correlated, and they therefore believe that all psychologists who offer personalized treatment services will do both psychotherapy and psychological discordance reduction.

The most ambitious attempt to distinguish counseling from psychotherapy has been made by Wolberg (1954). Wolberg distinguishes three kinds of approaches to problems in this area: supportive, insight-reeducative, and insight-reconstructive. Supportive psychotherapy has as its object emotional equilibrium with a minimization of symptoms so that the individual can function near his norm. Examples of treatment in this area would be directive guidance, environmental manipulation, externalization of interest, and persuasion. These and other supportive treatments might appropriately be given by a counselor. In passing, he suggests that indications for the appropriateness of this goal would include (1) a strong ego beset by temporary problems or (2) an ego so weak that even psychotherapy would not be useful. Contraindicators would include great authority problems and therefore a tendency to resist persuasion or to succumb to it.

Insight psychotherapy with reeducated goals, according to Wolberg, attempts to modify attitudes of behavior to more adaptive life integration. The goal of such psychotherapy would be to further insight into conscious processes so that behavior might be changed or goals might be changed. Wolberg would include in this area counseling as well as social casework. By implication this treatment is indicated for those relatively slight problems or problems in a circumscribed area.

Finally, Wolberg writes of insight psychotherapy with reconstructive goals. In this kind of psychotherapy the practitioner works toward an awareness of unconscious conflicts and hopes to make extensive alterations of the character structure of the client. He points out that although supportive therapy and reeducative psychotherapy may lead to reconstructive psychotherapy, it is important to make distinctions among these three approaches in terms of their goals. Reconstructive therapy, particularly in the form of psychoanalysis, is indicated for those who have neuroses sufficiently severe to justify the considerable expenditure of time and money and who are, at the same time, bright and neither too young to be "reasonable" nor too old to be "flexible." Contraindicators include severe symptoms which demand rapid attention, psychosis, irremediable life situations provoking neurotic defenses, and great scondary gains which accrue to the neurosis. If we accept Wolberg's distinction, the psychotherapist would be concerned with reconstructive goals and the counselor with reeducative and supportive goals. Obviously, however, there might be occasions when a psychotherapist would properly work toward supportive or reeducative goals, and there also would be times when the counselor might find himself doing reconstructive psychotherapy.

In summary, the goals of psychotherapy usually involve quite a complete change of basic character structure. The goals of counseling are apt to be more limited, more concerned with aiding growth, more concerned with the immediate situation, more concerned with helping the individual function adequately in appropriate roles.

Clients.   Some attempts have been made to distinguish counseling from psychotherapy on the basis of the clients they serve. Traditionally it has been said that the counselor deals with normal people, and the psychotherapist with the neurotic or psychotic. The most systematic delineation of this kind has been made by Hahn and MacLean (1955) who indicate that the normal is a major type of client for the counselor and a secondary type for the psychotherapist. The neurotic would be seen by the counselor only on an emergency basis or as a consultant to other specialists, whereas the neurotic would be the usual type of client for the psychotherapist. Finally, a psychotic would be seen by a counselor only in an emergency or on a consultative basis, whereas he might be treated by a psychotherapist working in collaboration with a medical doctor.

These distinctions while once widely accepted now seem to be under some attack. Tyler (1961, p. 13) specifically rejects a distinction between counseling and psychotherapy which is based on clients or settings. Others, too, have complained that while the distinction between normal and neurotic is easy to make clear, it may be difficult to make practical. Still many would say that one useful distinction between counseling and psychotherapy is that the counselor is primarily trained to deal with normal people and that the psychotherapist is primarily trained to deal with disturbed people.

Practitioners.   Distinctions between counseling and psychotherapy necessarily involve some consideration of the practitioner himself. Black says "that a major share of therapy done today is performed by people who are not even called therapists" (1952, p. 302). The previously discussed report—Current Status of Counseling Psychology (1961)—points out that there is considerable overlap in membership in Division 17 (Counseling Psychology) and Division 12 (Clinical Psychology) in the American Psychological Association. In 1957 25 percent of the members of Division 17 also belonged to Division 12. There is indication, however, that this overlap is less among new members.

It should be remembered that although this report indicates that psychological therapists and counseling psychologists are very similar in their training and professional identification, we are speaking here only of the more highly trained counselors. It is estimated that there are about ten thousand full-time counselors operating in the American schools and perhaps another ten thousand part-time counselors. The average training for these people would probably be less than that represented by a master's degree in guidance in a college of education. Most counseling is done by people with considerably less training than that held by psychotherapists, even if we should agree that some psychotherapy is done by those with training at this low level.

Perhaps it could be said that the better-trained counselors are scarcely distinguishable from the better-trained psychotherapist. Both will have basic training in personality theory, interviewing and research methods, considerable background in biological and physical sciences, in sociology, in mathematics, and in community organization. Both will have a formal internship of two or more years and will be apt to hold a doctor's degree. The relatively untrained psychotherapist, however, would be most apt to have either a master's degree in social work or in clinical psychology, whereas the relatively untrained counselor might have almost any kind of a background but generally a teaching credential plus a few guidance courses. Some will have a master's degree in counseling, but most will have not even this much preparation. The difference, then, in the practitioners may be great or minimal. It may be true on occasion, but certainly not always, that one can tell whether counseling or psychotherapy is going on by looking at who is doing it. Thompson and Super (1964) report the conclusions of a recent important conference on the training of counseling psychologists and point out that degrees may be granted by departments of either psychology or education.

Settings. Some attempt has been made to distinguish between counseling and psychotherapy in terms of where it is happening. It is observed that psychotherapists are more apt to work in hospital settings or in private practice; counselors are more apt to be working in educational settings. While this is true, to some extent, it is less a distinguishing feature than it once was. The Veterans Administration, for example, is hiring counselors to work in hospitals to do vocational counseling with disabled veterans. On the other hand, school systems and colleges are now hiring clinical psychologists and other therapeutically oriented practitioners. Still, as a generalization, it could be said that although counseling may more often occur in educational institutions and psychotherapy more in medical settings, we cannot always determine which activity is going on by noting where it is happening.

Methods. In distinguishing counseling from psychotherapy on the basis of difference of methods, we should run counter to the advice of Patterson (1959, p. 10), who sees no differences between them. This, of course, would be the general position of most client-centered counselors. Certainly commonality in method is great. Where universals or essentials of method have been listed for psychotherapy and for counseling, they have much overlap. Black (1952, p. 305) believes that all psychotherapists would have in common the building of rapport between patient and therapist, the acceptance and appreciation of the basic human worth of the individual (although not necessarily the complete negation of any possibility of evaluation as in the Rogerian theory), the supportive relationship of the psychotherapist to the patient, the status implicit or explicit of the psychotherapist, and the provision of controls and limits in the relationship. These universals of psychotherapy would be equally applicable to counseling. Counseling, too, involves rapport, acceptance, support, status, control, and limits.

Tyler lists what she feels are the essentials of any counseling relationship, and again they would seem to apply to psychotherapy (1961, p. 14): interest by the counselor in the client, confidence in the counselor by the client, limits on their relationship, the use of information as a resource when appropriate, and a relationship which has as a goal the facilitating of the development of the client. Black and Tyler seem to say that the methods of psychotherapy are varied and the methods of counseling are varied and that sometimes there would be more differences within the several approaches in therapy than between therapy and counseling and more differences within the several approaches in counseling than between counseling and psychotherapy.

Wolberg (1954) believes that concern with the conscious level is more characteristic of counselors and that concern with the unconscious level is more characteristic of therapists. Other distinctions between counseling (reeducative psychotherapy) and therapy (reconstructive psychotherapy) are these: (1) Counseling is usually of less duration than therapy; (2) the sessions are apt to occur less frequently; (3) less case history taking and more psychological examination is typical and characteristic of counseling; (4) more advice giving and less transference is characteristic of counseling. Whereas a therapist is more apt to make his individual assessment or diagnosis chiefly through a clinical interview, the counselor may frequently make use of psychometric tools.

Method has been discussed by Bordin who feels that the distinction should be primarily quantitative rather than qualitative. (He believes that both counseling and psychotherapy should be preceded by a medical examination.) Counseling would deal with less emotionally intense matters and be more generally positive than would therapy (1955, p. 160). Counseling more than therapy would deal with cognition and therapy more than counseling would deal with conative aspects. A major contribution of Bordin to the problem of definition is made when he deals with the concept of ambiguity (1955, p. 138). Statements can be ambiguous with regard to the topic to be discussed, the relationship between the counselor and the clients, or the goals of counseling. To the extent that the counselor moves toward a more ambiguous structure in his counseling, he is moving toward therapy. Ambiguity leads to anxiety, and the forcing of anxiety leads to a more therapeutic relationship. The method of counseling then would be to limit the ambiguity, and the method of therapy to maximize it.

To summarize some differences in method between counseling and psychotherapy, we can say that counseling is characterized by shorter duration of treatment, less frequent visits, more use of psychological examination, more concern with the client's present daily problems, more focus on his conscious activities, more advice giving, less concern with transference, more emphasis on the reality situation, more cognition and less emotional intensity, more clarity and less ambiguity.

Summary. The distinction between counseling and psychotherapy cannot be made with complete clarity and satisfaction. At the same time an attempt must be made to at least distinguish the master's level school counselor and the psychoanalyst as well as many intermediate positions. The total length of training for school counselors is presently averaging about one year of graduate work, and of that probably less than half is psychological in nature. Can we not make it clear to these counselors that they are not trained as therapists? The position of this chapter is that at least the extremes of differences between counseling and psychotherapy can be identified. While it is true that "tall" cannot be distinguished from "short" when men are roughly five-foot-nine, it is equally clear that five-foot-two is different from six-foot-five. An attempt to distinguish between these two activities—counseling and psychotherapy—is made particularly difficult by the prestige structure in American academic circles. In general, education is less valued than psychology as a discipline. Since education departments train most counselors, counseling does not have the prestige of psychotherapy. As a consequence master's level school counselors like to think of themselves as counseling psychologists, counseling psychologists sometimes like to think of themselves as clinical psychologists, and clinical psychologists like to muddy the distinction with psychiatry. Although snobbery—and professional psychopathy—makes these distinctions difficult, the distinctions themselves are not without value.

In attempting to point to some differences between counseling and psychotherapy, we can now look at the several elements we have considered and compare the two activities with regard to their position on various continua. (1) Counseling tends to be concerned with instrumental behavior, with role problems, with situations, with choices which must be made, and with actions which must be taken. Goals of counseling are more limited than those of psychotherapy, but this does not mean that these limited goals are unimportant or that changes in immediate behavior may not have lasting global effects. (2) Counselors deal primarily with normal individuals. (The distinction between "normal" and "neurotic" is as fraught with difficulties, of course, as the distinction between counseling and psychotherapy.) (3) The practitioner of counseling may be trained at the doctoral level with a two-year internship as would be his counterpart in clinical psychology. Many counselors, however, are trained at less than a doctoral level or at the doctoral level but with relatively little psychology and little or no formal supervised internship. These people because of the prestige rank of psychology and because of their own confused role concepts may quickly come to think of themselves as psychotherapists. Although they have difficulty making the distinction, there is no reason why more objective observers should. (4) The setting in which counseling takes place is most apt to be an educational setting or a community agency, although counselors may work in a medical setting or in private practice. (5) The methods used will indicate that counseling shows more concern than psychotherapy with present events than with those of the past, more concern with cognition than with affect, more concern with clarity than with ambiguity.

There seems to be no litmus paper which will distinguish counseling from psychotherapy as it changes from blue to red. Combinations of clues, however, may be helpful in distinguishing the two activities. If we see an interview relationship in which the professional person is trained at less than a doctoral level (or at the doctoral level without a formal two-year internship), if he is dealing with a normal client, if he is dealing with him in an educational setting, if he is primarily concerned with conscious processes, and if his goals are to help the client play one of his life roles more effectively by making better choices, we can say that counseling is going on. On the other hand, if the practitioner has been trained primarily in clinical psychology, if his client seems quite disturbed, if they are working in a medical setting, if the goals are to reconstruct the personality of the client, and if the methods are characterized by ambiguity, intense emotion, and concern for unconscious processes, we may more appropriately label the activity as psychotherapy.

Counseling Distinguished from Instruction

If to a counseling practitioner the thunder on the left is representative of psychotherapy, the thunder on the right is representative of instruction. There are educational theorists who see little distinction between counseling and teaching. Certainly in a broad sense their goals may be much the same since both are concerned with helping an individual develop to the point where he can assume responsibilities for himself and live a satisfying life. More narrowly, however, the goals of counseling are more determined by the needs of the individual as he sees them, whereas the goals of instruction are more apt to be societally determined. The most permissive and student-centered teacher of an algebra class has some views as to what should be covered in an instructional situation because society has, to some extent, defined those goals, but in the counseling situation the counselor has less preconception about what will be needed to help the individual.

With regard to the client (or student), instruction is thought to be for all. With regard to counseling, there are those who think counseling should be given to everyone, but frequently it happens that counseling is only given to those who voluntarily request it or perhaps to those seen as "needing" it.

The practitioner of teaching has been trained in specific instructional techniques and subject matter, while hopefully the counselor has had additional training in interviewing, psychometrics, occupational information, and other competencies required by his specialized role. It would seem to be true, however, that often teachers do counseling and sometimes counselors do teaching. The wisdom of having the same person play both roles can be questioned because the teacher is required to be judgmental and to operate as a representative of an educational institution with certain responsibilities determined by the function of that institution, whereas the counselor has primary responsibility to the individual and so can be less judgmental. Part of this confusion stems from the fact that educational institutions in America have two purposes—the developmental and the screening. They have the job of helping a student grow, but they also have the job of acting as gatekeeper to certain occupations and roles. This screening function, which is now being performed by the educational institution, would seem to inhibit the kind of relationship which is thought to be most helpful in counseling. The counseling, then, particularly if it concerns individual educational problems, may be difficult to distinguish from instruction.

The methods of teaching are more apt to be group methods, and the methods of counseling are more apt to be individual methods. However, teachers may teach one student at a time, and this tutoring function has long been recognized and valued, while more and more counselors are experimenting with group procedures.

If we see an individual in a group being dealt with by a teacher with some societally determined preconception as to the goals of the interaction, we are apt to call this activity instruction rather than counseling.

Substantive Elements
in Theories of Counseling

Having considered the activity of counseling, let us now return to our discussion of theory.

We have previously considered the nature of theory and the formal attributes of a theory. Since we are concerned with a special kind of theory—one dealing with counseling—we need now to look at the substantive elements which would characterize such a theory. Substantive elements are determined by what the theory is about, what it deals with. Substantive elements in learning theory might involve such matters as environmentalism versus nativism and historical versus contemporary causation, while in administrative theory such matters as direction, staffing, and planning might be included. The substantive elements of a counseling theory would include (1) assumptions regarding the nature of man, (2) beliefs regarding learning theory and changes in behavior, (3) a commitment to certain goals of counseling, (4) a definition of the role of the counselor, and (5) research evidence supporting the theory.

While we have previously noted that counseling theory may not necessarily derive from a specific philosophy, some assumptions must be made about what kind of a creature man is in order to construct a theory about counseling him. As we examine specific theories, we shall note whether the theorist is assuming the innate goodness or evil of man, the problems attendant upon the human condition, and the pliability of man, that is, whether he is sufficiently plastic in nature that he can be shaped in one way or another by the interaction of genetic elements and environment.

Counseling theories also include beliefs about how people change or learn. There is some agreement that counseling constitutes a learning process, but theorists may disagree on how this learning takes place. Is it furthered by a general atmosphere or by specific stimulus-response situations? Change would seem to be a goal of counseling, but there may be great differences among theorists regarding how change comes about.

The goals of counseling will differ for different theories. We have indicated previously that even if we assume that mental health is the goal we are aiming at, there are various definitions as to what constitutes mental health. For example, the usual high school counseling seems to assume that mental health can be equated with a mastery of environment, particularly as exemplified by grades in school or the ability to get along in an educational institution and meet the expectations of the teachers. Glad (1959) at least by inference suggests that the goals of various therapeutic approaches are so different that one person could be considered to have been successfully treated by advocates of one theory and at the same time be seen as in need of therapy by advocates of another theory. A good counseling theory will be explicit and clear regarding its goals.

The role of the counselor will be different in different theories. This role will differ with regard to the place and importance of diagnosis, for example, and some may make much use of tests, case histories, and screening interviews, while others will not. Other elements on which there would be differences would be the extent to which interpretation, advice, and persuasion are thought to be proper behavior for the counselor. We may find differences in the extent to which theories permit and support the intrusion of counselors' values into the counseling situation. There may be differences with regard to what actually is done in the initial contact and to what attitude the therapist has toward group procedures. Above all, the basic counseling style and its clarification regarding such matters as acceptance as opposed to interpretation, advice as opposed to clarification, use of authority as opposed to denial of authority, and encouragement of transference versus denial of transference will typify a theory. Finally, there may be differences with regard to such special problems as dependency of the client, the communication problem, and other elements which may appear to help define the role of the counselor.

The different theories may lend themselves to illustrative case material which will tell us in more specific terms how the theory functions in a given case. It is only by examining such typescripts that we can see the relationship between logical constructs and the events of the counseling interview. Since a theory deals not only with logical structure but with specific data, we shall want to look for research evidence and support with regard to the theories which we are considering. A theory which is completely abstract is a poor theory not because it is wrong, but because it does not help us to understand the facts which are already available. In summary, a theory of counseling must meet not only certain formal ciriteria but must make explicit its position regarding certain substantive elements which have been isolated above and which are those that seem appropriate to the judgment of a theory in this field.

BIBLIOGRAPHY

Black, John D. Common factors in patient-therapist relationship in diverse psychotherapies. *J. clin. Psychol.*, 1952, **8**, 302–306.

Bone, Harry. Personality theory. In *American handbook of psychiatry*. New York: Basic Books, 1959. Pp. 88–113.

Bordin, Edward S. *Psychological counseling*. New York: Appleton-Century-Crofts, 1955.

Brammer, Lawrence M., & Shostrom, Everett L. *Therapeutic psychology*. Englewood Cliffs, N.J.: Prentice-Hall, 1960.

Campbell, Norman R. The structure of theories. In *Readings in the philosophy of science*. New York: Appleton-Century-Crofts, 1953. Pp. 288–308.

The current status of counseling psychology—A report of a special committee of the Division 17 of Counseling Psychology of the American Psychological Association, 1961.

English, Horace B., & English, Ava Champney. *A comprehensive dictionary of psychological and psychiatric terms*. New York: McKay, 1958.

Eysenck, H. J., The effects of psychotherapy. In *Handbook of abnormal psychology*. New York: Basic Books, 1961. Pp. 697–725.

Frank, Phillip. *Modern science and its philosophy*. Cambridge, Mass.: Harvard, 1949.

Glad, Donald D. *Operational values in psychotherapy*. Fair Lawn, N.J.: Oxford University Press, 1959.

Goldman, Leo. Another log. *Amer. Psychologist*, 1964, **19**, 418–419.

Good, Carter V. (Ed.) *Dictionary of education*. New York: McGraw-Hill, 1945.

Gustad, J. W. In R. F. Berdie (Ed.), *Roles and relationships in counseling*. Minneapolis: University of Minnesota Press, 1953.

Hahn, M. E. Conceptual trends in counseling. *Personnel Guid. J.*, 1953, **31**, 231–235.

Hahn, Milton E., & MacLean, Malcom S. *Counseling psychology*. (2nd ed.) New York: McGraw-Hill, 1955.

Hall, Calvin S., & Lindzey, Gardner. *Theories of personality*. New York: Wiley, 1957.

Hall, Edward T. *The silent language*. Garden City, N.Y.: Doubleday & Company, Inc.; and Greenwich, Conn.: Fawcett, 1961.

Jahoda, Marie. *Current concepts of positive mental health*. New York: Basic Books, 1958.

McCabe, George E. When is a good theory practical? *Personnel Guid. J.*, 1958, **37** (1), 47–52.

McDaniel, H. B., Lallas, John E., Saum, James A., & Gilmore, James L. *Readings in guidance*. New York: Holt, 1959.

Moore, Gilbert D. A negative view toward therapeutic counseling in the public schools. *Counselor Educ. Suprv.*, 1961, **1** (2), 60–68.

Mowrer, O. H. *Psychotherapy—Theory and research*. New York: Ronald, 1953.

Patterson, C. H. *Counseling and psychotherapy: Theory and practice*. New York: Harper & Row, 1959.

Pepinsky, Harold B., & Pepinsky, Pauline. *Couseling—Theory and practice*. New York: Ronald, 1954.

Pepper, Stephen C. *World hypotheses*. Berkeley, Calif.: University of California Press, 1961.

Phillips, E. Lakin. *Psychotherapy—A modern theory and practice.* Englewood Cliffs, N.J.: Prentice-Hall, 1956.

Shaw, Franklin J. Counseling. In *Annual review of psychology.* Palo Alto, Calif. Annual Reviews, 1957.

Shoben, Edward Joseph, Jr. The counselor's theory as a personal trait. *Personnel Guid. J.,* 1962, 40, 617–621.

Shostrom, Everett L., & Brammer, Lawrence M. *The dynamics of the counseling process.* New York: McGraw-Hill, 1952.

Theobald, Robert. *The challenge of abundance.* New York: Mentor Books, New American Library of World Literature, Inc., 1961.

Thompson, Albert S., & Super, Donald E. *The professional preparation of counseling psychologists.* Report of the 1964 Greystone Conference. New York: Bureau of Publications, Teachers College, Columbia University, 1964.

Traube, M. R. Pupil personnel work. V. Counseling services. In *Encyclopedia of educational research.* New York: Macmillan, 1950. Pp. 930–938.

Tyler, Leona E. Theoretical principles underlying the counseling process. *J. counsel. Psychol.* 1958, 5 (1), 3–8.

Tyler, Leona E. *The work of the counselor.* New York: Appleton-Century-Crofts, 1961.

Vance, Forrest L. & Volsky, Theodore C., Jr. Counseling and psychotherapy: Split personalities or siamese twins. *Amer. Psychologist,* 1962, 17, 565–570.

Wolberg, Lewis R. *The technique of psychotherapy.* New York: Grune & Stratton, 1954.

Wrenn, C. Gilbert. *Student personnel work in college.* New York: Ronald, 1951.

Wrenn, C. Gilbert. Philosophical and psychological bases of personnel services in education. *Personnel Services in Education.* 1958 Yearb. nat. Soc. Stud. Educ., Part II. Chicago: The University of Chicago Press, 1959.

chapter 2

DONALD L. GRUMMON |

Client-centered Theory

Client-centered theory or nondirective theory, as it is sometimes called, derives from the work of Carl R. Rogers, his students and colleagues. As it has developed over the years, it has come to encompass many areas such as personality development, group leadership, education and learning, creativity, interpersonal relations, and the nature of the fully functioning person. But the theory began with Rogers's attempts to make sense of the events occurring in his psychotherapeutic and counseling interviews, and psychotherapy has remained the core of the theory to the present time.

Rogers has become widely recognized as a distinguished teacher, researcher, and writer, but he began his professional career as a practicing clinician in a community child guidance clinic, and even in his mature professional years he has continued to engage extensively in the professional practice of counseling and psychotherapy. While one of his primary interests is theory development and validation, he believes that for himself the best avenue for reaching this objective is to remain close to the actual experience of interacting with clients. The firsthand experience of the interview—the interviewer's experience as well as the client's—becomes the breeding ground for the insights and hypotheses about the nature of the helping relationship. He believes that the methods of science—rigorous thinking and research validation—are needed to avoid self-deception, but it can hardly be overemphasized that for Rogers the *subjective* nature of the client-counselor interaction is one of the fundamental characteristics of the interview and that no scientific theory can fully capture its meaning:

> I let myself go into the immediacy of the relationship where it is my total organism which takes over and is sensitive to the relationship, not simply my consciousness. I am not consciously responding in a planful or analytic way, but simply react in an unreflective way to the other individual, my reaction being based (but not consciously) on my total organismic sensitivity to this other person. I live the relationship on this basis.
>
> The essence of some of the deepest parts of therapy seems to be a unity of experiencing.... In these moments there is, to borrow Buber's phrase, a

real and 'I-thou' relationship, a timeless living in the experience which is *between* the client and me. It is the opposite pole from seeing the client, or myself, as an object. It is the height of personal subjectivity (Rogers, 1955, pp. 267–268).

In this chapter client-centered theory will be presented on the intellectual or conceptual level, an approach which of necessity largely ignores the subjective nature of the counseling interview. While the theory can be understood on this conceptual level, it is impossible to learn to use it effectively in the counseling situation without attending to one's own subjective experience. The very nature of the theory prohibits learning a set of rules and procedures and then applying these mechanically and objectively in the counseling interview.

Learning to use client-centered theory, or any counseling theory for that matter, involves discovering for oneself what the theory builder originally discovered for himself. The theory can serve as a map along the route to discovery, but it cannot by itself teach one to become an effective counselor. Thus, the application of counseling theory is quite different from the application of theory in the physical sciences. Physical theories can be applied with little regard for the subjective element of human interaction; but counseling theory, being applied in the give and take between two persons, must be integrated into the counselor's personality. To apply it as we customarily apply theory in physics or chemistry would thereby be to view oneself and the client as objects and would result in the loss of the subjective element that Rogers and many others see as essential. It is in this sense, perhaps, that counseling and psychotherapy will always remain an art, no matter how refined and sophisticated our theories become.

For reasons of clarity and ease in presentation, Rogers's theory will be presented in declarative style. This will tend to give the reader the impression that Rogers considers his theory to be established fact. Nothing could be further from the truth. Rogers has repeatedly emphasized that his theory cannot be taken as dogma, but that it can best be used as an impetus to spur new discovery. His theorizing has changed in the past, and he fully expects it to change in the future as new clinical insights are discovered and as new research evidence becomes available. Rogers (1959a) notes that even mature theories contain an unknown amount of error and mistaken inference, and this is apt to be especially true of counseling theory which has advanced only a little beyond the stage of hypothesis development and crude discovery.

Rogers (1959a) also points out that a theory is a more dependable guide when it is applied to the realm of events out of which the theory grew; here less inference is needed in the application of the theory, and unknown errors are apt to be of less consequence. The theory becomes a less dependable guide as it is used to explain more remote events, that is, more inference is required, and slight errors may be magnified.

The significance of this point to the present discussion is that client-centered theory was developed from interviews somewhat different in emphasis and aim from the interviews which are the primary concern of this book. In terms of the continuum running from guidance through counseling to psychotherapy suggested in Chapter 1, client-centered theory was developed in a context falling somewhere between counseling and psychotherapy. It has concerned itself very little with the guidance type of interview—the interview roughly characterized by the imparting of information.

However, the theory is so closely related to many counseling situations that it will be presented as originally formulated by Rogers. The presentation will draw heavily on his most recent theoretical statement published in 1959, although earlier and later writings will also be considered. After the presentation of the theory, its application to a number of special counseling problems will be examined. Because of space limitations, the theory will be abbreviated and at times quite tersely stated. For a fuller view the reader is referred to Rogers's three main books in the area (1942; 1951; 1961b) and to the formal theory as stated in 1959 (Rogers, 1959a).

CONCEPTION OF MAN

As stated in Chapter 1, all theory development is influenced by the underlying beliefs and assumptions of the theory builder, and we shall briefly outline Rogers's conception of man before presenting the formal theory.

1. Belief in the democratic ideal.   Rogers is strongly committed to both the practical utility and the moral value of the democratic ideal. Although the democratic ideal can be described in many ways, one of its central ideas is a belief in the dignity and worth of each individual. Other core features are the belief that each man should have the right to his own opinions and thoughts and that each man should be in control of his own destiny with the right to pursue his own interests in his own way as long as he does not trample upon the rights of others. A corollary belief is that the democratic society's needs are served best by social processes and institutions which encourage the individual to be an independent, self-directing person.[1]

[1] Rogers has frequently spoken and written about the need to examine counseling, educational, student personnel, and other procedures in the light of democratic val-

2. *Fundamental predominance of the subjective.* The significance of the subjective elements in client-counselor interaction has already been mentioned, but Rogers's belief in the fundamental predominance of the subjective extends beyond the practice of counseling to most of man's functioning. "Man lives essentially in his own personal and subjective world, and even his most objective functioning, in science, mathematics, and the like, is the result of subjective purpose and subjective choice" (Rogers, 1959a, p. 191). Rogers would note that the reader's very act of reading this chapter can ultimately be traced to a subjective choice.

Rogers believes that developments in the behavioral sciences will someday enable us to understand man's behavior objectively and in lawful terms, much as we now understand events in the physical world. However, he also holds

. . . a very different view, a paradox which does not deny the objective view, but which exists as co-equal with it.

No matter how completely man comes to understand himself as a determined phenomenon, the products of past elements and forces, and the determined cause of future events and behaviors, he can never *live* as an object. He can only *live* subjectively. . . .

The person who is developing his full potential is able to accept the subjective aspect of himself, and to *live* subjectively. When he is angry he is *angry*, not merely an exhibition of the effects of adrenalin. When he loves he is loving, not merely "cathected towards a love object." He moves in self-selected directions, he chooses responsibly, he is a person who thinks and feels and experiences; he is not merely an object in whom these events occur. He plays a part in a universe which may be determined, but he lives himself subjectively, thus fulfilling his own need to be a person (1961e, pp. 20–21).

3. *Tendency toward actualization.* Rogers's early writings emphasized that the client's natural capacity for growth and development is

---

ues. He fears that unknowingly we often act on contrary assumptions. He is suspicious of the "approach of the expert" in which one individual sets himself up, so to speak, as the person who best can select the goals and decide on the most appropriate behavior of another individual. Rogers thinks that too frequently counselors and educators proceed on the assumption that they know best what are the *real* needs of clients and students, and in so doing, they reduce the opportunity for the client or student to develop into a mature, self-directing individual. He becomes particularly concerned by the prevalent tendency for counselors and educators to urge the democratic ideal, while at the same time, apparently unaware of any contradiction, they are developing more effective and more subtle ways of controlling students and clients. See Rogers (1948).

an important human characteristic on which counseling and psychotherapeutic procedures should rely. Over the years, his conviction has
grown stronger that the *inherent* tendency of man is to move in
directions which can be described roughly as growth, health, adjustment, socialization, self-realization, independence, and autonomy. This
directional tendency is now labeled the *actualizing tendency* which
Rogers defines as " . . . the inherent tendency of the organism to develop
all its capacities in ways which serve to maintain or enhance the organism" (1959a, p. 196).

This conception is simple and all encompassing. In fact, it is the
fundamental characteristic of all life itself which applies not only to
man but to a one-celled protozoan, a starfish, a daisy, or a lion. The
essential nature of life is that it is an active process, not a passive one,
in which the organism interacts with its environment in ways designed
to maintain, to enhance, and to reproduce itself.

The actualizing tendency is expressed differently in different species.
An acorn develops into an oak tree, tall and sturdy in favorable soil
and climatic conditions, scrubby and gnarled under less favorable conditions, but a live oak tree nonetheless maintaining, enhancing, and
reproducing itself as conditions allow.

In man the actualizing tendency expresses itself in more varied
ways. One illustration is provided by the infant learning to walk. The
infant need not be taught to walk. Because of the forward direction of
growth and development inherent in the child's nature, he learns to
walk if only the proper conditions are present. This directional process
is not, of course, smooth and unfaltering. The child takes a few steps,
falls, and experiences pain. For a time he may revert to crawling. But
in spite of the bumps and the pain and in spite of walking at first
being a less efficient means of locomotion than crawling, the child tries
again and again. The process is a painful struggle, but because of his
nature, the child continues with his efforts until he learns to walk and
eventually to run and to skip and to jump.

This life-force can be observed in many areas. At the physiological
level the organism's tendency to maintain itself can be seen in the
assimilation of food, the maintenance of body heat, and the regulation
of body chemistry. At another level the child strives to feed himself
rather than to be fed, to dress himself rather than to be dressed, and to
read to himself rather than to be read to. Studies show that man shares
with other animals the spontaneous tendency to curiosity, to explora-
tory behavior, and to producing changes in the stimulus field. Man
tends to actualize himself by learning to use tools and verbal concepts
and to maintain himself by building shelter against sun and cold. Man
builds theories to improve his understanding and control of his world.

Man also exhibits the tendency to strive for meaningful interpersonal contacts and toward socialization, broadly defined.

Rogers's thinking has been influenced by many theorists who have observed and emphasized different aspects of this forward moving characteristic of the organism. Maslow (1954) speaks of a hierarchy of motives and needs. As the organism satisfies the needs lower in the hierarchy such as the need for food, water, and safety, it then is motivated by higher needs such as those for belongingness and love and the need for self-actualization. Goldstein (1940) also uses the term self-actualization for this basic striving. Mowrer and Kluckhohn speak of the "... the basic propensity of living things to preserve and increase integration" (1944, p. 74). Rogers has been particularly influenced by Angyal, who stresses that a fundamental characteristic of life is to move in the direction of increasing independence, self-regulation, and autonomy, and away from control by external forces. Angyal says, "Life is an autonomous dynamic event which takes place between the organism and the environment. Life processes do not merely tend to preserve life but transcend the momentary status-quo of the organism, expanding itself continually and imposing its autonomous determination upon an ever increasing realm of events" (1941, p. 48).

Rogers wishes to emphasize several ideas by his stress upon the actualizing tendency:

1. The actualizing tendency is the primary motivating force of the human organism.
2. It is a function of the whole organism rather than of some part of it. Needs and motives can be, and characteristically have been, thought of as more specific. While men do seek such specific things as food, sex, and self-esteem, Rogers has some doubts about whether these more specific conceptions of motivation may not have obscured more truth than they have encouraged. In any event, he wishes to emphasize that the organism responds as a whole. Even though at one moment in time the organism may seek food or sex, it characteristically seeks these in ways which enhance rather than diminish self-esteem and the other strivings of the organism. Maslow's hierarchy of needs is similar, although not identical to Rogers's conception.
3. It is a broad conception of motivation which includes the usual needs and motives such as physiological needs for food and water, those aspects of motivation often termed *tension reduction* or *need reduction,* curiosity, and the seeking of pleasurable activity. However, more than some theories of motivation, Rogers emphasizes man's tendency to physical growth, maturation as illustrated by the infant learning to walk, the need for close interpersonal relationships ("man is incurably social"), and the tendency of man to impose himself on his environment—to move in directions of autonomy and away from external control.

4. Life is an active and not a passive process. Rogers sees the organism as an "active, directional initiator," and he rejects the "empty organism" conception of life in which nothing intervenes between stimulus and response. He rejects Freud's thinking that the nervous system would, if it could, maintain itself in an altogether unstimulated condition.

5. Man has the capacity required to actualize himself as well as the tendency or motivation. These capacities, often more latent than evident, are released under the proper conditions. Counseling is not aimed at doing something *to* or *for* the individual; it is aimed at freeing the individual's capacities for normal growth and development. Counseling theory attempts to specify the conditions which allow this to occur.

4. Man is trustworthy.   Closely related to the above is Rogers's confident view of man as basically good and trustworthy. Such words as "trustworthy," "reliable," "constructive," or "good" describe characteristics which seem inherent in man.

Let it be said immediately that Rogers is fully aware that man frequently behaves in ways which are untrustworthy and "evil." Man is certainly capable of deceit, hate, cruelty, and stupidity. But Rogers views these unsavory characteristics as arising out of a defensiveness which alienates man from his inherent nature. As defensiveness diminishes and man is more sensitively open to all his experience, he tends to move in ways we think of as socialized and trustworthy. He strives for meaningful and constructive relationships with his fellow man in ways which make for his own development and also for the development of the species.

Rogers's conception contrasts sharply with the view of many (not all) psychoanalysts who see man as innately destructive and antisocial: Man is born with instinctual urges which must be controlled for healthy personality development to occur. To this Rogers says,

I have little sympathy with the rather prevalent concept that man is basically irrational, and that his impulses, if not controlled, will lead to destruction of others and self. Man's behavior is exquisitely rational, moving with subtle and ordered complexity toward the goals his organism is endeavoring to achieve. The tragedy for most of us is that our defenses keep us from being aware of this rationality, so that consciously we are moving in one direction, while organismically we are moving in another. But in the person who is living the process of the good life, there would be a decreasing number of such barriers, and he would be increasingly a participant in the rationality of his organism. The only control of impulses which would exist, or which would prove necessary, is the natural and internal balancing of one need against another, and the discovery of behaviors which follow the vector most closely approximating the satisfaction of all needs. The experience of extreme satisfaction of one need (for aggression, or sex, etc.) in such a way as to do violence to the satisfaction of other needs (for companionship, tender relationships, etc.)—an experience very common in the defensively organized person—would be greatly decreased. He would participate in the vastly complex self-regulatory activities of his organism—the psychological as well as physiological thermostatic controls—in such a fashion as to live in increasing harmony with himself and with others (1961f, pp. 299–300).

5. Man is wiser than his intellect. Closely related to the foregoing is Rogers's belief that man is wiser than his intellect, wiser than his conscious thought. When man is functioning nondefensively and well, he trusts his total organismic reaction, and this often results in better although more intuitive judgment than conscious thinking alone.

In recent years Rogers (1963) has puzzled about the function of consciousness or awareness in the life of man. He sees awareness as one of the latest evolutionary developments, as a "... tiny peak of awareness, of symbolizing capacity, based upon a vast pyramid of nonconscious organismic functioning" (1963, p. 17). When the organism functions freely and effectively, awareness is only a small part of the total activity and "... tends to be reflexive rather than the sharp spotlight of focused attention" (1963, p. 17). Awareness is sharpened and focused when the organism encounters some difficulty in functioning. Rogers is challenged by Whyte who says, "The main purpose of conscious thought, its neobiological function, may be first to identify, and then to eliminate, the factors which evoke it" (1960, p. 37).

If Rogers's and Whyte's views are correct about how man functions best, then the question arises as to why man's conscious thinking and functioning is so often at odds with his organismic functioning. This problem is considered in the next section on personality theory.

PERSONALITY THEORY

The theory presentation will cover Rogers's theory of personality and his theory of therapy. Of these two, the theory of therapy was developed first and has seen more refinements as the result of research investigations. However, the therapy theory is essentially descriptive and contains little explanation of why the client should change with successful counseling. The explanatory concepts are contained in the assumptions and in the personality theory, and to this we now turn before presenting Rogers's more important contribution in the area of therapeutic theory.

Although still tentative and mainly a skeletal outline, client-centered personality theory has been elaborated into a series of interlocking, formal propositions (Rogers, 1951; Rogers, 1959a). For a part of the theory Rogers has drawn heavily on Standal (1954). The present account will be considerably abbreviated, and the above sources should be consulted by the reader wishing to examine the theory for inconsistencies and major omissions.

1. Every individual exists in a continually changing world of experience of which he is the center (Rogers, 1951, p. 483)

This is the private world of each individual's experience which is sometimes called the *phenomenal field* or the *experiential field*. It includes all that goes on within the organism that might reach consciousness, although only a small part of the organism's experiences are ever conscious at any given time.[2] For example, I can be deeply engrossed in a game or a conversation and not be consciously aware of the physiological accompaniments of hunger which are being experienced by my organism.

An important fact which Rogers wishes to emphasize in this proposition is that this world of experience can be known in any genuine and complete sense only by the individual himself. We can never know the full experience of another as he fails an examination or rises to give a report in his history class. We can observe another individual, measure his reactions to various stimuli, have him record his thoughts and reactions on psychometric tests, etc., but we can never know in full and vivid detail how any given situation is experienced and perceived by him.

Of course, in his ordinary functioning many of the individual's experiences are not readily available to his awareness and thus are not a part of his phenomenal field. If he is to become aware of them, it will only be under certain conditions which are discussed more fully in other parts of the theory.

2. The organism reacts to the field as it is experienced and perceived. This perceptual field is, for the individual, "reality" (Rogers, 1951, p. 484)

[2] Awareness and consciousness are used synonymously in client-centered theory. Consciousness is the symbolization, although not necessarily the verbal symbolization, of experience. This symbolic representation of experience may have varying degrees of vividness and clarity and, in the figure-ground terminology of Gestalt psychology, may be in the central focus of awareness as figure or in the background of awareness as ground.

3. Behavior is basically the goal-directed attempt of the organism to satisfy its need as experienced, in the field as perceived (Rogers, 1951, p. 484)

These two propositions emphasize that we do not react to some absolute reality but to our perceptions of that reality. Rogers has observed that a man dying of thirst in a desert will struggle as hard to reach a mirage as he will to reach a real body of water. Snygg and Combs (1949) cite a personal example to emphasize this point. One of the authors was riding as a passenger in a friend's automobile down a lonely Western highway at night. Suddenly a large object loomed in the headlights in the middle of the road. The driver appeared unconcerned, but the passenger feared a serious accident. At the last moment he grasped the steering wheel and guided the car around the object. The driver, a native of the West, had seen the object as a harmless tumbleweed, whereas the passenger, who lived in a landslide area of the East, had seen the object as a boulder. Each reacted in terms of his own perceptual reality. Knowing the "perceptual reality" of each, we can understand and even predict the behavior of both persons without knowing the objective reality of whether the object was actually a rock or tumbleweed.

Rogers notes that man is continually checking his perceptions against one another in order to make them a more reliable guide to reality. Each perception is in the nature of an hypothesis to be checked against further perceptions: A material first seen as salt is found to taste sweet, and the perception changes to sugar. Man's perceptions tend to become accurate representations of reality as he interacts with his environment in attempts to satisfy his needs. Yet many of man's perceptions remain unconfirmed or only partially confirmed. The important psychological fact to remember is that reality for any given individual is that person's perceptions of reality, regardless of whether or not those perceptions have been tested and confirmed.

4. The best vantage point for understanding behavior is from the internal frame of reference of the individual himself [3] *(Rogers, 1951, p. 494)*

Rogers defines the *internal frame of reference* as "all of the realm of experience which is available to the awareness of the individual at a

[3] See Snygg and Combs (1949) for a discussion of an assumption which seems to be inherent in this and the preceding propositions, namely, that a meaningful and complete psychological theory of behavior can be based on an examination of behavior from the internal frame of reference.

given moment. It includes the full range of sensations, perceptions, meanings, and memories, which are available to consciousness" (1959a, p. 210). Understanding another individual from the internal frame of reference is to concentrate on the *subjective reality* which exists in the experience of that individual at any given time. Empathy is needed to achieve this understanding. By contrast, understanding another individual from the *external frame of reference* is to view him, without empathy, as an object, usually with the intent of emphasizing *objective reality*. Objects such as a stone or an electron have no experience with which we can emphasize. Persons become objects in this sense when we make no emphatic inferences about their subjective experiences.

Rogers sees these as two different ways of knowing, each of which has its usefulness. His theory of therapy is built on understanding the internal frame of reference of the client, but hypotheses of that theory can be verified only by adopting the external frame of reference.

It is worth noting that understanding another person from the external frame of reference is to view him from our own internal frame of reference. The counselor's internal frame of reference may more closely approximate objective reality than the client's, but it is still only the counselor's *perception* of objective reality; and it tends to ignore the client's subjective experience of reality.

5. Most of the ways of behaving which are adopted by the organism are those which are consistent with the concept of self (Rogers, 1951, p. 507)

The *self-concept* or *self-structure* is an important construct in the client-centered theoretical system. For Rogers it is an organized conceptual gestalt consisting of the individual's perception of himself alone and of himself in relation to other persons and objects in his environment together with the values attached to these perceptions. The self-concept is not always in awareness, but it is always available to awareness. That is, the self-concept by definition excludes unconscious self-attitudes which are not available to consciousness. The self-concept is considered to be fluid and changing, a process rather than an entity, but at any given moment it is a fixed entity.

Stated more informally, the self-concept is the picture an individual has of himself along with his evaluation of this picture. For example, the client may perceive of himself as above average in intelligence, as a good student except in mathematics, as unattractive to members of the opposite sex, as liking to work with his hands, as loving his parents, as afraid of the future, etc. And he may value many of these character-istics either positively or negatively.

The importance of the self as a regulator of behavior was one of the earliest ideas emphasized by the client-centered group, and it assumed considerable importance in their counseling long before most other parts of the personality theory were developed. Of course, many theo-rists have been interested in the self, but attention was first drawn to the importance of the self in client-centered counseling because clients continually talked about their "selves" once they became deeply in-volved in counseling. Expressions like the following were common: "I just cannot see myself as capable of directing a bunch of unruly kids in a classroom." "I am good at jokes and making small talk, but I am really a very shy person underneath." "I have always been a loving and dutiful son, and I owe it to my father to consider carefully his wishes about my schooling." "I am capable of doing the work when I study, but I am really more the socializing type." "I try to hide the real me." "I'm just no good underneath this false front."

Over the years clinical observation and considerable research made it apparent that attitudes toward the self were an important deter-miner of behavior. Changes in the client's behavior and attitudes toward others seemed to follow changes in attitudes about himself. As the evidence accumulated, the self-concept evolved into the central construct of client-centered theory.

Needs, of course, are also important determiners of behavior. But needs can usually be satisfied in a wide variety of ways, and the partic-ular behavior selected to meet a need is chosen to be consistent with the self-concept. For example, the need for food or physical activity is satisfied by behaviors consistent with the person's view of himself: "I need food, but I also consider myself an honest person and therefore do not steal from the local supermarket." Similarly, a person who does not view himself as possessing aggressive tendencies in his makeup, does not react with anger and violence when some need is frustrated by another person. Instead, he may cajole or flatter or withdraw in an attempt to meet his need elsewhere in ways more consistent with his self-picture.

The reader should note that this part of client-centered theory states that most of the behavior adopted by a person is consistent with his self-concept. However, maintaining this consistency often encounters difficulties. This happens, for example, if the satisfaction of a strong need necessitates behavior which objectively would be contrary to the individual's self-structure. In such situations the individual can employ various defensive maneuvers in an attempt to keep his perception of his behavior consistent with his self-picture. This kind of situation forms the basis for Rogers's view of maladjustment and will be considered in the next sections presenting the client-centered theory of childhood development and the theory of threat and defense.

6. Early childhood development and the basic estrangement of man. This part of the theory attempts to explain how it happens that man is so often at war with himself. Rogers calls this the problem of incongruence or dissociation which is repeatedly encountered by those who study the dynamics of human behavior. A clarifying example would be the student who consciously wishes to succeed in school but who repeatedly engages in behavior which diverts him from his studies and ensures his failure.

In general terms Rogers's answer is that an incongruence or rift develops between the individual's self-concept and his organismic experience. This happens because love from his parents and significant others is made conditional upon his introjecting certain constructs and values as if they were his own. These become incorporated into his self-concept. These constructs and values are often rigid and static and are contrary to the child's normal process of evaluating his experience. Because of this, the child develops and attempts to actualize a self which is contradictory or incongruent with organismic processes based on the actualizing tendency.

a. The organismic valuing process. As the human infant begins life, he evaluates his experiences against the criterion of his basic *actualizing tendency,* which as noted earlier is the only motive postulated by the theoretical system. The infant values and seeks those activities which are experienced as furthering the aim of the actualizing tendency and those negating this aim he values negatively and avoids. This is known as the *organismic valuing process.* It involves a kind of regulatory or feedback mechanism which ensures that the infant's behavior will meet his motivational needs.

b. The development of the self-concept. Some of the infant's experiences are differentiated and crudely symbolized as an awareness of being. These are termed *self-experiences* and eventually become elaborated into the *self-concept.* A part of the actualizing tendency becomes differentiated as a tendency toward self-actualization.

c. The development of the need for positive regard. As his awareness of self is emerging, the infant is also developing a *need for positive regard* which can be roughly thought of as the need for warmth and love from his mother. According to Rogers and Standal, this is a persistent and pervasive need which is universally present in all human beings.[4]

[4] It seems to the writer that this comes close to postulating a second motive in the

The infant must infer from his mother's tone of voice, gestures, and other ambiguous stimuli whether or not he is receiving positive regard. Partly because of this ambiguity, the child develops a total gestalt about how his mother regards him, and each new experience of approval or disapproval tends to generalize to his total experience of being loved or unloved. Because of this and because of the strength of the need for love, the infant can at times become more responsive to his mother's approval than to experiences which actualize the organism.

d. The development of the need for positive self-regard. The experiences of being loved or not loved become attached to self-experiences and thus to the developing self-concept. For theoretical reasons that we cannot elaborate on here, this results in the development of a learned need for *positive self-regard.*

e. The development of the conditions of worth. Development of the need for positive regard sets the stage for the child to seek experiences, not because they satisfy his actualizing tendency, but because they satisfy his need for his mother's love. When these sought after experiences are self-experiences, they also satisfy his learned need for positive self-regard. In this way the need for positive self-regard also becomes selective.

We now come to an important characteristic of the need for positive self-regard, namely, that it can be satisfied or frustrated in the absence of interaction with the mother or other significant persons in the child's life. In time, therefore, the child comes to seek (or avoid) self-experiences solely because they satisfy (or frustrate) the need for positive self-regard. In other words, the child learns to discriminate the conditions under which his need for his mother's love and his own self-esteem are more apt to be satisfied. When the infant seeks or avoids self-experiences on this basis, he is, in Rogers's terminology, living by the *conditions of worth* or, in Rogers's older terminology, is living by values introjected from others. Thus, a second regulatory system of behavior comes into existence which can be in conflict with the organismic valuing process where the actualizing tendency is the criterion.[5]

---

theoretical system, especially since the need for positive regard is seen as universally present in infancy and since it sometimes acts in opposition to the actualizing tendency. However, Standal (1954), who developed this portion of the theory, presents a rationale for this being a learned need arising out of the infant's developmental situation.

[5] The reader will probably observe in the foregoing some similarity between the Freudian conception of opposition between the id and the superego. However, closer examination will show many differences. Rogers's actualizing tendency, for example, is quite different from Freud's id.

f. The development of incongruence between self and experience.
Incongruence, or inconsistency, between the self-concept and experience is a key concept in client-centered theory. A state of *incongruence*
exists when an individual's self-concept is different from the actual
experience of his organism. A child is incongruent if he thinks of
himself as loving and wishing to take care of his younger sister when
he is organismically experiencing anger and jealousy over having to
share his mother's love and attention with his sister.

We can now return to our account of childhood development and
explain how incongruence between self and experience is brought
about. As noted earlier, self-experiences are the raw material out of
which the self-concept develops. Self-experiences which are consistent
with both the organismic valuing process and the conditions of worth
present no problems of course. These are accurately perceived and
symbolized in awareness and become incorporated into the self-concept. However, self-experiences which contradict the conditions of
worth would, if accurately perceived and assimilated, frustrate the
child's need for positive self-regard. Thus, these tend to be selectively
perceived and distorted in awareness, or even completely denied to
awareness, in an attempt to make them consistent with the conditions
of worth. This maneuver makes it possible for the child to act in terms
of his actualizing tendency and still meet his need for self-esteem. These
denied or distortedly perceived self-experiences cannot, however, be
accurately integrated into the developing self-concept. It is in this manner that the self-concept becomes partially incongruent with organismic experiences based on the actualizing tendency.

g. Summary and the basic estrangement of man. This highly abstract presentation can perhaps be brought to life by an informal
recapitulation and an illustration.

The child learns to need love and to avoid behavior which he anticipates might bring disapproval. Soon he learns to view himself and his
behavior as he thinks his mother views him, even though his mother is
absent. This results in seeking some behaviors which are not organismically satisfying, and when these are also self-experiences, they may
become incorporated into the developing self-concept. Other behaviors
which are organismically satisfying are distortedly perceived in awareness in an attempt to maintain his mother's love and his own self-
esteem. Nor can these experiences be satisfactorily integrated into the
developing self-concept. The end result is an incongruence between self
and experience.

The basic tendency of the organism is to fulfill itself according to
the actualizing tendency; however, as the self-concept develops, this
same inherent characteristic is also expressed as a tendency to actualize

the self. As long as the self-concept and organismic experience are congruent, man remains whole and integrated. But when incongruence develops between self and experience, man is at cross purposes, torn between the basic actualizing tendency and the actualization of self. He is now vulnerable to psychological maladjustment. He can no longer live as a whole, integrated person. He becomes a person divided against himself, with one part of him true to the actualizing tendency and one part of him true to the inaccurate self-structure and its incorporated conditions of worth.

Rogers sees this situation as the basic estrangement in man. Because of the natural but tragic developments in early life resulting in specific types of social learning, man has become untrue to himself.

Consider the young child who has just discovered his mother's good tea cups. Young children are naturally interested in the world around them, and the child will use all his senses to examine the tea cups. He notices their shape and color; he feels them to see if they are rough or smooth; he puts them in his mouth to see how they taste; he swings them in the air to experience their weight; and he bangs them against something to hear how they sound. It is the very unusual mother who is not emotionally upset to discover her child among the almost inevitable wreckage. She roughly grabs the remaining cups away, plunks the child (not too gently or lovingly) into his playpen, and berates him as a naughty, bad child. In short, an experience which was organismically satisfying is now associated with loss of love and diminished self-esteem.

It should not be difficult for the reader to imagine the child experiencing an almost endless repetition of this general situation. The child experiences loss of love if he touches this or that, if he asks too persistently for help when his parents are engaged in other activities, if he fights with his brother over a toy, if he hits his sister when he is jealous and angry with her, if he wanders away from home and frightens his mother about his safety, if he shows too much interest in his sexual organs, if he urinates out-of-doors, and so on ad infinitum. It is small wonder that the child develops a self-concept which is incongruent with many organismic experiences based on his actualizing tendency.[6]

7. Threat and the process of defense. "The essential nature of threat is that if the experience (which is incongruent with the self-

---

[6] In theory, the incongruence between self and experience would not develop if the child were unable to discriminate any of his self-experiences as being more or less worthy of love than any other self-experience. In practice, this never happens. However, less incongruence will develop as more of his self-experiences are met with love and acceptance.

concept) were accurately symbolized in awareness, the self-concept would no longer be a consistent gestalt, the conditions of worth (incorporated within the self) would be violated, and the need for self-regard would be frustrated. A state of anxiety would exist" (Rogers, 1959a, p. 227).

When an individual is incongruent, he is also *vulnerable:* An accurate perception of his organismic experience would threaten a disruption of his self-concept. If, in addition, he is aware, even dimly aware, of this threat, a state of tension or *anxiety* exists. The threat need not be clearly perceived. It is sufficient that it be *subceived,* a term Rogers borrows from experimental studies of perception. To be subceived means to be discriminated just below the level of conscious awareness. *Anxiety* is thus the response of the organism when a discrepancy between the self-concept and experience threatens to enter awareness, thus forcing a possible disruption of the self-concept.

The individual defends himself against threat and the accompanying anxiety by denying the experience, or more frequently by misperceiving the experience to make it more consistent with the self-concept. By this maneuver, the individual maintains the consistency of his self-structure and reduces both the awareness of threat and the anxiety. The actual threat, of course, remains (he is still vulnerable), but the person has defended himself against it. He pays the price for this gain, however, in a rigidity of perception and a distortion of reality.

In response to strong and unsatisfied needs of the organism, behavior sometimes occurs which is inconsistent with the self-concept in a context where it cannot be easily denied or distorted. In such instances the person typically disowns the behavior with reactions like "I didn't know what I was doing"; "I was very upset and not myself"; or "If the evidence wasn't right in front of me, I wouldn't believe it. It's just not like me at all."

The probability of this kind of reaction increases with the severity of emotional disturbance. Neurotic behavior is often incomprehensible to the individual himself, since "it is at variance with what he consciously 'wants' to do, which is to actualize a self no longer congruent with experience" (Rogers, 1959a, p. 203). Statements like the following are frequent in the counseling interviews of neurotic clients: "I didn't want to do it, but I did. I just can't understand why." Or, "I just have no control over this feeling. It doesn't even seem a part of me but is like some intruder."

The usual defensive behaviors so frequently discussed in the literature (such as projection, rationalization, wish-fulfilling fantasy, and the like) can, according to Rogers, be fitted into the client-centered scheme of threat and defense, but we shall not take the time to illustrate this here.[7]

8. *The process of change.* To change the process of threat and defense, the self-concept must become more congruent with the individual's actual organismic experiences. But changes in the self-structure are resisted because these tend to violate the conditions of worth and the learned need for positive self-regard. The avenue to change, therefore, involves creating the conditions where there is less threat and less need to resist. According to the theory, what is basically involved in this is a corrective relationship with another person which decreases the necessity to act upon the conditions of worth and increases the individual's positive self-regard. That is, there must be a reversal of the conditions described in the section on infant development. The theory of therapy, to be presented shortly, describes the conditions which make this possible. The aim is to relax, little by little, the boundaries of the client's self-concept so that it may assimilate denied and distorted experiences. In this way, the self becomes more congruent with experience.

9. *Optimal adjustment or the fully functioning person.* The ideally adjusted person is completely open to all his experiences. His experiences are not, of course, always in awareness, but they are always available to awareness in accurately symbolized form. That is, he exhibits no defensiveness. There are no conditions of worth, and the individual experiences unconditional positive self-regard. His self-concept is congruent with his experience, and he acts in terms of his basic actualizing tendency which also actualizes the self. Since his experiences change as he meets different life situations, his self-structure becomes a fluid gestalt, always in the process of assimilating new experiences. The individual experiences himself, not as a static being, but as a process of becoming.

This hypothetical, fully functioning person would be

> fully open to his experience [and] would have access to all of the available data in the situation, on which to base his behavior; the social demands; his own complex and possibly conflicting needs; his memories of similar situations; his perception of the uniqueness of this situation. The data would be very complex indeed. But he could permit his total organism, his

---

[7] Psychotic behavior is accounted for by a different part of the theory and results when a failure of the defenses is accompanied by a serious disorganization and a breaking down of the self-structure.

consciousness participating, to consider each stimulus, need and demand, its relative intensity and importance, and out of this complex weighing and balancing, discover that course of action which would come closest to satisfying all his needs in the situation. An analogy which might come close to a description would be to compare this person to a giant electronic computing machine. Since he is open to his experience, all of the data from his sense impressions, from his memory, from previous learning, from his visceral and internal states, are fed into the machine. The machine takes all of these multitudinous pulls and forces which are fed in as data, and quickly computes the course of action which would be the most economical vector of need satisfaction in this existential situation. This is the behavior of our hypothetical person.

The defects which in most of us make this process untrustworthy are the inclusion of information which does *not* belong to this present situation, or the exclusion of information which *does*. It is when memories and previous learning are fed into the computations as if they were *this* reality, and not memories and learning, that erroneous behavioral answers arise. Or when certain threatening experiences are inhibited from awareness, and hence are withheld from the computation or fed into it in distorted form, this too produces error. But our hypothetical person would find his organism thoroughly trustworthy, because all of the available data would be used, and it would be present in accurate rather than distorted form. Hence his behavior would come as close as possible to satisfying all his needs—for enhancement, for affiliation with others, and the like.

In this weighing, balancing and computation, his organism would not by any means be infallible. It would always give the best possible answer for the available data, but sometimes data would be missing. Because of the element of openness to experience, however, any errors, any following of behavior which was not satisfying, would be quickly corrected. The computations, as it were, would always be in process of being corrected, because they would be continually checked against their consequences [8] (Rogers, 1962c, pp. 27–28).

THEORY OF THERAPY AND PERSONALITY CHANGE

Rogers's theory of therapy and personality changes follows an "if-then" model and consists of three main parts: condition, process, and outcomes. If certain *conditions* exist, then a definable *process* is set in motion which leads to certain *outcomes* or changes in the client's personality and behavior.

---

[8] Rogers's theory of creativity is closely related to his theory of the fully functioning person.

A. Conditions of Therapy

Rogers attempts to be precise about the conditions which are both *necessary and sufficient* for setting the process of therapy in motion, that is, the process will commence only if the stated conditions are present and will not commence unless they are present. Other conditions which might be helpful in getting the process under way are not included in the formal theory.

Rogers points out that one weakness of the theory is that the conditions are stated in all-or-none terms, whereas they should be understood as existing on continua. As more research is done, Rogers hopes it will become possible to specify the degree to which the various conditions must be met. With present knowledge he can only say that the greater the degree to which the conditions are present, (1) the more likely it is that the process will get under way and (2) the greater is the amount of personality reorganization which will occur.

It should also be noted that in formulating this part of the theory, Rogers had all forms of psychotherapy in mind, not just client-centered psychotherapy. In fact, he even proposes extending the theory to any interpersonal relationship which results in personality change such as a relationship between friends. He hopes that the theory will stimulate research which can test these extensions of his theory.

As paraphrased from Rogers (1957; 1959a) the theory states that the therapeutic process will occur to the extent that:

1. The client and therapist are in *contact* with one another.
2. The client is in a state of *incongruence,* being *vulnerable* or *anxious.*
3. The therapist is *congruent* in the relationship.
4. The therapist experiences *unconditional positive regard* toward the client.
5. The therapist experiences *empathic understanding* of the client's *internal frame of reference.*
6. The client perceives, at least to a minimal degree, the therapist's *unconditional positive regard* for him and the therapist's *empathic understanding* of his *internal frame of reference.*

The first proposition merely calls attention to the logical necessity that there must be at least a minimal relationship between the client and the counselor. Two persons are in *contact* if each makes a difference in the experience of the other. This condition will most certainly be met in most counseling situations, although Rogers points out that it often appears necessary for the contact to be of some duration before the therapeutic process begins. The condition might be very difficult to meet in working with extremely withdrawn psychotics.

The reader will recall from the section on personality theory that the client is *incongruent* and therefore *vulnerable* when his self-concept is different from the actual experience of his organism. While Rogers theorizes that the process can get under way if the client is merely vulnerable, he believes the process is more likely to begin if the client is also *anxious,* that is, if he also has an awareness of the threat to his self-concept.

Propositions 3, 4, and 5 all refer to the behavior and attitudes of the counselor as he relates to the client. They are intended to result in what Rogers has sometimes referred to as the client's experience of being fully accepted or fully received.

The early formulations of the client-centered point of view stressed the importance of the counselor's basic acceptance of the client and respect for his integrity as an independent, autonomous individual. The relationship was to be free of any type of pressure or subtle coercion. Not only was the counselor to refrain from intruding his own values and biases into the counseling relationship, but he was to forego such commonly used procedures as setting goals, giving advice, persuading, making interpretations, and delineating topics for discussion. The counselor did not play a passive role as has sometimes erroneously been stated. Great emphasis was placed on an active warmth and responsiveness to the client, a sensitivity to his feelings, and a genuine acceptance of the client as a person. The counselor's aim was an active and sensitive understanding of the client as he experienced and revealed himself during the interviews. The counselor concentrated on creating a permissive atmosphere, free of threat to the client's self, so that he felt free to express the doubts, the unspoken attitudes, and the unwanted impulses which complicated his life. It was this atmosphere which released the growth potential of the client and enabled him to effect constructive changes in his personality and way of living.

The foregoing still generally describes the attitudes and functions of the counselor. However, the current formulation speaks much less than did earlier writings about what the counselor should refrain from doing, e.g., not making interpretations, expressing his own feelings, and the like. Though to some extent the theory implicitly frowns on disruptive activities, the current emphasis is on creating the conditions whereby the client feels fully received—no matter how this may be achieved by a particular counselor.

Neither does the current theory speak of the nondirective techniques which were frequently discussed in the earliest literature. In finding ways to implement the counselor's basic orientation to the client, the early writings stressed such techniques as structuring the interview, silence, simple acceptance, and reflection of feelings versus responding to intellectual content. Counselor techniques have gradually been deemphasized because it became evident that the so-called "nondirective" techniques could be used to implement quite different attitudes from those advocated by the theory. For example, it is quite possible to make a reflection of feeling in a cold and even accusing manner. Moreover, too much concern with techniques sometimes distracted the counselor from his basic aim of empathic understanding of the client as he experiences himself. Still another reason for deemphasizing techniques was the realization that some psychotherapists using directive techniques created with their clients the therapeutic conditions described by Rogers.

The client-centered counselor does, of course, still use many of the nondirective "techniques" (particularly reflection of underlying feeling), but he does not feel bound by them or employ them as planfully and deliberately as he once did.

The early concepts of acceptance and warmth have been replaced in the current theory by the more technical term *unconditional positive regard.* The counselor experiences unconditional positive regard for his client to the extent that he finds himself feeling a genuine acceptance for all aspects of the client's self-experiences. The counselor experiences none of the client's self-experiences as being more or less worthy of positive regard. The new term also appears to place more emphasis on the counselor's liking the client which clinical and some research evidence indicates is an important accompaniment of successful counseling. Rogers speaks about "caring" for the client, although he would carefully point out that this is not a possessive caring arising out of the counselor's own needs.

Standal (1954) developed the term *unconditional positive regard* to emphasize that there are no conditions attached to the acceptance of the other person. None of the client's self-experiences are discriminated as being more or less worthy of positive regard. It is the opposite of placing conditions on the acceptance of another, as when we say in effect, "I like you when you do this and that and fail to like you, or even dislike you, when you do that." Butler (1952) has resurrected Dewey's terms *prizing* and *appraising* to help define this concept. To "prize" another person means to value or to esteem him. "Appraising," on the other hand, implies an ongoing discriminating, comparing, and selecting process in which different values are assigned to the various aspects of the person thus discriminated.

Thus, the concept of unconditional positive regard implies that the counselor is not appraising the client but rather is prizing him no matter what feelings and motivations the client experiences during the interview. The client is prized as much when he experiences "bad" feelings such as hate, selfish desire, confusion, or self-pity as when he experiences "good" feelings such as friendliness, accomplishment, mature self-confidence, or tender affection.

Some persons become disturbed and think that this concept implies approval of all the client's behavior. It does not. None of the client's behaviors are judged as making the client more or less worthy of being prized as a person.

The term unconditional positive regard is an unfortunate choice, as Rogers has pointed out, in that it implies an absolute, all-or-none characteristic, whereas it should be thought of as a matter of degree. The counselor can experience more or less unconditional positive regard for the client, but the complete experience of this, as the term seems to make mandatory, is not a practical possibility (although Rogers does think there are brief periods in counseling when the counselor experiences a complete and unconditional positive regard for his client).

It should be noted that the theory states that the counselor must *experience* unconditional positive regard for the client. The word "experience" means that the counselor actually *feels* a prizing for the client. It is not enough that the counselor hold abstract attitudes of respect and acceptance of the dignity and worth of other persons. This abstract or intellectual attitude may help the counselor to develop feelings of unconditional positive regard for his client, but the crucial condition is that the counselor experience such feelings as he relates to his client. Obivously this experience cannot exist until there is a basis for it in the client-counselor interaction. In this sense there is always an element of uncertainty and risk in each new counseling case.

Although client-centered counselors have written much about unconditional positive regard and the related concepts of acceptance, respect for the client's separateness, prizing, and even love for the client, it is difficult to convey the precise meaning of the concept. It is a deep and pervasive experience on the part of the counselor; yet it is not blind, maudlin, intense, or possessive. Perhaps it involves basically a deep feeling and respect for life, for what *is,* and for being and a willingness to experience this fully, without reservation, as it is revealed through the client.

Most counseling theories have concepts similar to the client-centered concept of positive regard for the client, and many non-Rogerians feel angered if there is an implication that they do not accept and respect their clients. They are right, of course, because who is to say from their writings just what their experience is as they relate to their clients. Yet it also seems true that the client-centered position places greater emphasis on acceptance or unconditional positive regard as a crucial condition necessary to successful counseling. Also, client-centered counselors think that other theoretical orientations employ additional concepts which contradict at least to a degree the full meaning of unconditional positive regard. For example, counseling approaches which call for considerable diagnostic activity on the part of the counselor must introduce situations in which the client will experience that some of his self-experiences are being more or less prized by the counselor.

Another condition for getting the counseling process under way is that the counselor is experiencing an *empathic* understanding of the client's *internal frame of reference*.

Rogers defines the state of being empathic as perceiving

> ... the internal frame of reference of another with accuracy, and with the emotional components and meanings which pertain thereto, as if one were the other person, but without ever losing the "as if" condition. Thus it means to sense the hurt or pleasure of another as he senses it, and to perceive the causes thereof as he perceives them, but without ever losing the recognition that it is *as if* I were hurt or pleased, etc. If this "as if" quality is lost, then the state is one of identification (1959a, pp. 210–211).

From the section on personality theory, the reader will recall that to concentrate on the client's internal frame of reference is to concentrate on the client's *experience* of reality as contrasted with objective reality. One of the difficulties in mastering the client-centered approach to counseling is that in the main we are not accustomed to concentrating on the internal frame of reference of another individual but instead view that individual and his situation from our own internal frame of reference, that is, from our own view of what objective reality is for the individual and his situation. The client-centered approach thus requires that the counselor unlearn familiar ways of relating to others.

The most recent development in this part of the theory is proposition 3, which states that the counselor needs to be congruent in the relationship with his client. This means that all aspects of the counselor's organismic experience during the interview are freely admissible to his awareness and that his self-concept is congruent with these experiences.[9] In more familiar language, the counselor is a genuine, integrated person within the counseling relationship. He is fully and freely himself with no front or facade, even unknowingly.

Since counselors are human beings and cannot be expected to achieve the ideal of perfect adjustment, let us note immediately that the theory does not say that the counselor must be a completely con-

---

[9] This can and in fact often does mean that the counselor's self-concept changes as he interacts with his client.

gruent person. It states that if the counselor is congruent *in this relationship with his client,* then the process of therapy will get under
way. It is sufficient that the counselor be accurately himself during the
counseling hour. In addition, this proposition, like the others, should
be understood as existing on a continuum rather than on an all-or-none
basis.

If the counselor is to be congruent in the relationship, a question
arises as to how much he should overtly communicate himself and his
experience to the client. The aim of counseling is not, of course, for the
counselor to discuss his own feelings with the client. At one level, this
part of the theory is intended to stress the therapeutic value which
results from the client interacting with a counselor who is genuinely
himself in the relationship. At another level the theory stresses that
counseling will be inhibited if the counselor feels one way about the
interview and the client but attempts to act in a different way.

On occasion the counselor's genuineness will result in feelings which
run contrary to propositions 4 and 5 dealing with unconditional positive regard and empathic understanding. If I am bored or irritated
with what my client is saying to me, I cannot be congruent with this
feeling and at the same time be experiencing unconditional positive
regard for my client and an empathic understanding of his internal
frame of reference.

How best to handle conflicts of this nature poses a theoretical and
practical problem for the client-centered counselor which has been
receiving increasing attention in recent years. The trend in current
thinking is to give priority to the need for the counselor to be genuine
or congruent in the relationship. Although it is fraught with difficulties
and unknowns, there is an increasing tendency for counselors to bring
their feelings openly into the interview when these are persisting feelings which interfere with the counselor's experiencing an empathic
understanding of the client's internal frame of reference. This helps to
keep the counselor genuine in the relationship, and even where the
counselor's feelings pose a problem for the client, the difficulty is now
at least out in the open where the client has the opportunity to deal
with it.

Sometimes considerable therapeutic movement follows the genuine
expression of the counselor's feeling. The writer recalls a case in which
he was becoming more and more tense in the relationship and finally
expressed his feeling by saying, "I just feel very manipulated in this
relationship." Not only did this clear the air for the counselor, but it
proved to be an insightful experience for the client and a turning point
in the counseling. The value in this instance seemed to be that it

allowed the client to experience in a relatively nonthreatening atmosphere the genuine reaction of another to his own behavior.

From that part of the personality theory dealing with childhood development, it can be inferred that when the counselor does communicate his feelings, it is important that he both recognize and express the feeling as his own and not as something for which the client is to blame. It is after all the counselor's and not the client's feeling. To be sure, the feeling arose in the client-counselor interaction, but another counselor might react quite differently. In the case just cited, the counselor did not say, "You are a manipulating and dominating person, and your behavior is blocking our efforts here." This may appear to be a subtle difference of little consequence, but it seems to have a quite different impact upon the client—probably because the recommended approach does less to thwart the client's experience of being prized as a person.

The theory about the necessary conditions of therapeutic change is still very much alive and growing (Butler, 1958; Gendlin, 1961b; Gendlin, 1962a; Hart, 1961; Rogers, 1962b; Seeman, 1956). Although still not being presented as formal theory, the trend is to emphasize more and more the genuine person-to-person relationship as crucial to therapeutic movement. Client-centered therapists talk and write about the intimacy of the relationship, therapist spontaneity, the therapist attending to much of his own immediate experience in the relationship and sharing this with his client, etc. There is an increasing focus on helping the client get closer to the flow of his own immediate experiences, and client-centered therapists engage in varying activities to further this aim. There is a recognition that perhaps some therapists create a meaningful and genuine relationship in which this aim can be realized by a directive, no-nonsense approach similar to Rosen's work with schizophrenics. Some therapists are talking about the importance of empathically feeling the client's immediate unconscious experiences, not with the intent of intellectualizing these and pointing out how the unconscious attitudes influence the client's behavior, but with the intent of sharing all the client's experience and helping him get closer to the totality of his being.

The final condition listed by Rogers in the formal theory is that the client himself must perceive the counselor's genuineness, his experience of unconditional positive regard, and his empathic understanding. Obviously the client will not unless the counselor successfully communicates his experiences to the client. The counselor, therefore, strives to relate to the client in such a way that his basic attitudes are implicit in everything he says and does. Bodily posture, facial expression, tone of voice, comments made, comments not made, etc., are all important. When these arise naturally and spontaneously out of the counselor's experience of unconditional positive regard and empathic understanding of the client's internal frame of reference, much of the problem of communication is solved.

During the past five years a number of well-designed studies have provided research support for that part of the theory dealing with the counselor-determined conditions deemed necessary to getting the process of counseling under way, that is, the counselor's genuineness or congruence, his unconditional positive regard, and his empathic understanding of the client's internal frame of reference.

One method of researching the theory has been to employ a relationship inventory in which both the client and the counselor can make after-interview ratings of the counselor's congruence, empathy, and unconditional positive regard. Findings with this method support the theory (Barrett-Lennard, 1962).

Another method has been to have judges rate sections of interviews on reliable rating scales which were built to measure the three therapeutic conditions. Halkides (1958), as reported by Rogers (1961c), compared "most successful" with "least successful" counseling center cases and found that high levels on each of the three conditions were associated with successful outcomes at the .001 level of confidence.

In a large project conducted by Rogers, Gendlin, and Truax, Truax (1962) summarizes an elaborate series of studies to test the client-centered theory of therapeutic change in schizophrenics. The methods were generally the same as those employed by Halkides, except that Truax employed a wide variety of outcome measures and included within-therapy process measures. Truax reports on a fourth condition variable which is hypothesized as necessary to getting the therapeutic process under way. This variable, called *therapist intensity* and *intimacy of interpersonal contact*, distinguishes between the therapist who might be described as formal, aloof, or reserved and the therapist who relates to his clients in an intimate, personal, and feeling way.

Truax's voluminous findings lend support to the theoretical model with surprising consistency. Many of the correlations between the therapeutic conditions and both the process and outcomes measures are of the same order of magnitude as the correlations found between our better tests and college grades. An unexpected finding, which Truax believes needs confirmation with other research populations, was that clients actually got worse when their therapeutic hours provided a low degree of the conditions.

This group of studies is of special importance because it is the first attempt to study empirical cause and effect in psychotherapy. The studies represent a successful, although initial and primitive, attempt to isolate and measure the fundamental change-producing influences in psychotherapy. Research of this kind promises to be very useful in sharpening and modifying our theoretical thinking about the nature of counseling.

B. *The Process of Therapy*

Client-centered counselors have been especially interested in discovering the underlying order in the process of counseling and psychotherapy. Does a characteristic sequence of events occur during a series of successful counseling interviews? And what is it in the process which brings about changes in the personality and behavior of the client? These questions, particularly the latter, are difficult but crucial to the understanding of counseling and psychotherapy. Over the years they have been approached in a number of different ways, and a considerable body of reliable knowledge about process has been developed. However, there is no *one* client-centered position about process, and the search for deeper understanding still continues.

1. Early formulation. In the earliest formulation Rogers (1942) described the process as proceeding through successive but overlapping stages of release and exploration of feeling, through seeing relationships and the achievement of insight, followed by decision making and positive action. This description was confirmed when Snyder (1945) and later Seeman (1949) studied case protocols and found that the release of negative feelings was followed by the expression of positive feelings and that successful counseling tended to move from statements of problems, to insight, to discussing and planning of activity.

2. Characteristic changes in the self. Another approach has been to describe the process in terms of changes in the self-concept and attitudes toward the self. Many studies examining electrically recorded and transcribed cases have shown that there is a movement from negative to positive feelings about the self over successful client-centered counseling and that this movement fails to occur or is much less pronounced in unsuccessful cases (Raimy, 1948; Seeman, 1949; Sheerer, 1949; Stock, 1949). It should not be supposed, however, that there is an even progression over the series of counseling interviews. Frequently negative feelings increase during the counseling before the trend to positive feelings is seen. Wide swings between positive and negative feelings are fairly common.

These shifts in self-attitudes are seen as an important part of the process which account for other kinds of changes taking place in the client. For example, Sheerer (1949) has shown that increased acceptance of self is accompanied by an increased acceptance of other persons.

Raskin (1952) investigated the hypothesis that a significant part of the counseling process is that the reference point for valuations shifts from others to the self during the course of successful counseling. He found that there was a significant tendency over counseling for the client to place greater emphasis on himself as the evaluator of experience.

3. The formal theory of process. In 1959 Rogers (1959a) published a formal theory about the process of therapy which is based on the accumulated evidence from research and clinical experience. This theory is spelled out in a series of propositions which are abbreviated and summarized below. Following the "if-then" model, the theory states that if the conditions of therapy presented earlier are established and maintained over a period of time, then the following process is set in motion:

1. The client gradually becomes freer in expressing his feelings in verbal and motor channels, and these feelings increasingly have references to the self rather than to the nonself.
2. "He increasingly differentiates and discriminates the objects of his feelings and perceptions, including his environment, other persons, his self, his experiences, and the interrelationships of these" (Rogers, 1959a, p. 216). In so doing, the client's experiences become more accurately symbolized in his awareness, and he gradually becomes aware of experiences which he has previously denied or distorted.
3. "His expressed feelings increasingly have reference to the incongruity between certain of his experiences and his concept of self" (Rogers, 1959a, p. 216). Because of this the client experiences threat and anxiety. The defensive process presented in the theory of personality would prevent this overt experience of threat were it not for the ". . . continued unconditional positive regard of the therapist which is extended to incongruence as much as to congruence, to anxiety as much as to the absence of anxiety" (Rogers, 1959a, p. 216).
4. The self-concept gradually becomes reorganized to include experiences which were previously denied or distorted in awareness. Thus there is an increasing congruence between self and experience with less need for defensiveness.
5. The client increasingly feels positive self-regard and reacts to his experiences less in terms of the conditions of worth based on the values intro-

jected from others and more in terms of the organismic valuing process based on the actualizing tendency.

It should be noted that this formal theory does not attempt to explain why this process should lead to constructive changes in the client. The theory restricts itself to describing the fundamental nature of the process which occurs once the appropriate conditions are established and maintained. The explanation of why this leads to successful outcomes is contained in the basic assumptions and in the theory of personality.

4. The role of immediate experience in psychotherapy. Although the formal theory just presented has been helpful in understanding the therapeutic process, Rogers is still not satisfied that he has captured the significant events of the interviews which are responsible for personality changes in the client.

Insight was long assumed to be the crucial event in counseling which accounted for change, but this view is now questioned. Not only is insight seen as resulting from other events, an end-product so to speak, but it also appears that sometimes change occurs without insight (see Hobbs, 1962).

In early papers Gendlin and Zimiring (1955) and Gendlin (1961a) focused on the character of the client's experiences during the therapeutic hours as the crucial ingredient of change. Later in an important book Gendlin (1962b) treated the concept of experiencing systematically and attempted to show its underlying explanatory power for many other concepts in psychotherapy.

The concept of experiencing, while not entirely new, is difficult to convey in words. It is similar to what is often thought of as emotional insight versus intellectual insight, as working through, feeling through, and being completely involved, as experiencing affect versus talking about affect, as experiencing oneself versus talking about oneself as an object, etc. It may help to understand this conception if the reader considers the difference between thinking about playing some competitive sport versus the intense absorption of actually engaging in the sport. For example, when I am effectively involved in a game, perceptions, emotions, ideas and bodily functions are smoothly blended into one whole, and I am completely absorbed in the immediate experience at hand.

"Experiencing" in a special sense is seen as the essence of therapeutic change. It is an immediately felt process which is perceived, sometimes only dimly, by the individual at a given moment in time. It is viewed as an elemental unit of life which forms the basis for under-standing and learning about oneself.

The kind of experience which Gendlin (1962b) sees as crucial to therapeutic change occurs in the immediate present and "can be *directly* referred to by an individual as a felt datum in his own phenomenal fields." However, Gendlin defines experience as a preconceptual process. It is implicitly meaningful, and it guides conceptualization, but it is something different from the conceptualization of the experience. He cites the rather common occurrence of clients referring to their experience during the interview without being able to label it or even to describe it very adequately. Instead, they point to their experience with phrases like, "this all tied-up feeling," or "This thing I sense . . . I don't know, but it is really something."

Not infrequently client and counselor will communicate meaning-fully about the experience for some considerable time, and yet each has only the vaguest idea what the experience actually is. It is implicitly meaningful but still preconceptual.

Oversimplifying, the essence of therapy for Gendlin, is the having of such experiences with both client and therapist groping to conceptualize their implicit meanings without at the same time intellectualizing and diverting the experience. He sees both the reflection of feelings of the client-centered approach and *properly timed* interpretations of other approaches as capable of accomplishing this objective.

Rogers cites the following example as illustrating what he calls a "molecule of change."

In the thirty-first interview she is trying to discover what it is that she is experiencing. It is a strong emotion. She thinks it is not guilt. She weeps for a time. Then:

Client: *It's just being terribly hurt!* . . . and then of course I've come to see and to feel that over this . . . see, I've covered it up.

A moment later she puts it slightly differently.

Client: You know, it's almost a physical thing. It's . . . It's sort of as though I were looking at myself at all kinds of . . . nerve endings and-and bits of . . . things that have been sort of mashed. (Weeping)

Therapist: As though some of the most delicate aspects of you—physically almost—have been crushed or hurt.

Client: Yes. And you know, I do get the feeling, Oh, you poor thing. (Pause)

Therapist: You just can't help but feel very deeply sorry for the person that is you (Rogers, 1959b, p. 52).

Rogers thinks that repeated experiences such as these are the essence of psychotherapy and have the following characteristics:

1. It occurs in the existential moment. It is not "thinking about" but "an experience of something in this instant."
2. There are no barriers to the experiencing, no holding back.
3. The experience is complete in that all elements are freely present in awareness. Often the experience is not really new; it may have been experienced before but not experienced completely. It has a new intensity.
4. It has a quality of being acceptable to the client. The feeling *is,* it exists, and it is found acceptable on this basis. The client in the example above "*is* the self-pity she feels—entering fully and acceptingly into it—and this is integration at that moment" (Rogers, 1959b).

Working along these general lines, Rogers (1961a; 1961d) has attempted another conception of the process of client-centered therapy. He defines seven stages of a continuum along which an individual may move in therapy from rigidity and fixity of perceptions, feeling, and experience to "flowingness" and "changingness." By rating samples of the client's behavior throughout a series of interviews, it is possible to see how much he has moved along the continuum during his therapy and to relate this movement to independent measures of outcome.

Rogers (1961d) reports that two initial studies show that movement on the scale distinguishes sharply between successful and unsuccessful cases. Several dimensions are involved in the ratings, and there is not space to describe these here, but a summary of one part of the scale may give the reader an idea of how Rogers is currently attempting to conceptualize and study the essential ingredient of personality change:

> The process involves a change in the manner of experiencing. The continuum begins with a fixity in which the individual is very remote from his experiencing and unable to draw upon or symbolize its implicit meaning. Experiencing must be safely in the past before a meaning can be drawn from it and the present is interpreted in terms of these past meanings. From this remoteness in relation to his experiencing, the individual moves toward the recognition of experiencing as a troubling process going on within him. Experiencing gradually becomes a more accepted inner referent to which he can turn for increasingly accurate meanings. Finally he becomes able to live freely and acceptingly in a fluid process of experiencing, using it comfortably as a major reference for his behavior (1961d, pp. 156–157).

Many readers may think this discussion of experiencing has relevance for psychotherapy but little significance for counseling as these two are differentiated by Stefflre in Chapter 1, and it is true that both Gendlin and Rogers are working more in the psychotherapeutic tradition. However, the writer believes that there is considerable relevance for counseling. Personality change can involve sizable reorganization of the personality, or the personality change can be limited to such small areas as, for example, the immediate considerations involved in the choice of a college major. Many students become quite involved in trying to verbalize the private meanings the various alternatives have for them, and this can easily become a process of personal exploration and change in the limited area under consideration. The more the student becomes involved in the process, the less likely it is that he can neatly verbalize and describe his thoughts and feelings. At this point many counselors rush to the student's assistance with a conceptual scheme to help the student organize his thoughts. Or when the client becomes vague and uncertain, the counselor may urge him to be more specific. The counselor thinks this will help the student clarify the situation. But all too frequently these actions have the effect of cutting off the experiencing process for the client. The counseling becomes intellectual and not experiential. The student thus learns less about himself in relation to the possible choices, and to the extent that there is merit to the theorizing presented above, the student is denied an opportunity for change.

C. Outcomes of Counseling and Psychotherapy

It is difficult to distinguish clearly between process and outcomes.[10] When we study outcomes directly, we examine the differences between two sets of observations made at the beginning and end of the interview series. Many process studies make successive observations over a series of counseling interviews and, in a sense, are miniature outcome measures which establish a trend line for the case. Most of the process studies referred to in the previous section are in one sense as much outcome studies as they are process studies. Consider, for example, the studies showing an increased acceptance of self and others between the beginning and end of counseling.[11]

Nor does the formal theory make a clear distinction between process and outcomes. The main proposition in Rogers's theoretical statement about outcome is, "The client is more congruent, more open to his experience, less defensive" (1959a, p. 218), but we note that the process theory has already stated that these same conditions are gradually developing throughout the interviews. The outcome theory does go on to spell out some of the theoretical implications of this main outcome, but these could be considered logical deductions within the framework

[10] For a detailed discussion about the relationship between process and outcomes see Cartwright (1956) and Gendlin (1956).
[11] Process studies which attempt to isolate the actual events which produce change are in a somewhat different category.

of the personality theory rather than main propositions in their own right. For example, the theory states that the client's psychological adjustment improves, that he experiences more acceptance of others, that he becomes more realistic and objective, that his self-ideal becomes more realistic, that his behavior is seen by others as more socialized and mature, etc.

More readers will probably be interested in the concomitants in everyday behavior than in the more general outcomes just presented. As the result of client-centered counseling, does the client earn better grades, make more intelligent vocational choices, maintain better relations with his peer group, improve his leadership capacities, show greater originality, less frequently drop out of school, etc?

In a moment we shall list a number of areas in which research studies have shown change to take place, but before doing this, we wish to interject a note of caution.

There are almost an unlimited number of specific behaviors which might be investigated in outcome studies. Which ones of these should be investigated?

One approach is to select for study those behaviors that we especially value. Most educational communities, for example, value good grades, and many school counselors may wish to establish that their work helps students achieve this desired result. We can study the effect of counseling on school dropouts. Or some might wish to determine whether counseling results in better school citizenship. And sometimes college professors want to know whether counseling results in more students' choosing to major in their particular field of study.

We immediately see a problem in this approach to outcome studies, namely, that different people value different things. That more good students elect to study journalism as the result of counseling may be valued by the journalism faculty and be devalued by the liberal arts faculty. This problem appears to be circumvented when there is more general agreement about the value, as in the case of good grades in the educational community, but even this can present problems. On occasion, poorer grades could be the concomitant of successful counseling. We might argue for this (although some would not) in the case of an "overachieving" student who, before counseling, spent all his time anxiously striving for academic perfection to the exclusion of all social life, school activities, and even friendly relations with his fellow students.

There is still another problem when the value orientation is used to select the criterion to be studied. If we are going to rest our case about the effectiveness of counseling on whether or not it promotes this or that desirable behavior, we must also consider whether some other procedure might not produce the result more economically and to an even greater degree. We might grant that improved grades are a desirable result but find that counseling is far less effective in promoting this than, for example, better audio-visual aids or a study methods course.

The value problem cannot, of course, be avoided in considering the outcomes of counseling. What can be avoided is letting the value orientation deter us from learning more about what specific events in counseling lead to what specific kinds and amounts of behavior changes. We need much more of this kind of information before we can make intelligent value judgments about the usefulness of particular kinds of counseling.

Another possible answer is to avoid the specifics of behavior and investigate more general characteristics which, on theoretical or research grounds, are thought to bear a relationship to quite a number of specifics. This at least simplifies the task, although not as much as one might think. For example, we can determine through personality tests whether adjustment improves, on the assumption that general adjustment changes will have far-reaching effects. Or we can study perceptual rigidity in problem solving and infer that any changes noted would also operate in a wide variety of everyday life situations. The difficulty with this approach is that personality and behavior theory is still filled with uncertainties. In one sense the investigations are as much personality research as they are counseling outcomes research.

If one is willy-nilly going to become involved in personality research, it seems only logical that the outcomes to be studied should be relevant to the personality theory on which the counseling is based. The outcome study results can then be fed back into the main theory, and in so doing, we not only improve the theory, but we also promote insights into why particular outcomes occur or fail to occur. This approach to outcome studies has frequently, but not always, been used by the client-centered group. There is more frequent study of constructs, such as the self, which are more important to client-centered theory than to trait-and-factor or psychoanalytic behavior theory. This is as it should be if the investigator is to get the most explanatory mileage from his efforts.

The strategy of outcome research is complicated and full of pitfalls, but we cannot dwell further on these here, except to say that results must be interpreted with caution. We shall move on to listing some of the outcomes not mentioned in the previous section on process which, on the evidence available, seem to be associated with successful client-centered counseling.

1. There is an improvement in psychological adjustment as shown on the Rorschach, the Thematic Apperception Test, and personality inventories of the self-report type (Dymond, 1954a; Dymond, 1954b; Grummon and John, 1954; Haimowitz & Haimowitz, 1952; Mosak, 1950; Muench, 1947; etc.).

2. There is less physiological tension and greater adaptive capacity in response to frustration as evidenced by autonomic nervous system reactivity (Thetford, 1952).

3. There is a decrease in psychological tension (or an increase in personal comfort) as measured by the Discomfort-Relief Quotient (Assum and Levy, 1948; Cofer and Chance, 1950; N. Rogers, 1948).

4. There is a decrease in defensiveness (Grummon and John, 1954).

5. There is a greater degree of correspondence between the client's description of his self-picture and his description of his wanted or ideal self. Among other things, this is sometimes viewed as an index of self-esteem (Butler and Haigh, 1954; Hartley, 1951).

6. Friends tend to rate the client's behavior as more emotionally mature (Rogers, 1954b).

7. There is an improvement in overall adjustment in the vocational training setting (Bartlett, 1949, in Seeman and Raskin, 1953). This study is perhaps of special interest to the general counselor since the outcome measure was training officers' observations over a six-month period of such things as interpersonal factors, academic achievement, efficiency in study and work habits, tendency to worry, and commitment to goals.

8. Axline's (1947) research suggests that client-centered play methods with elementary school children may result in accelerated reading improvement even though no special reading instruction has been given.

APPLICATION OF THE THEORY TO GENERAL COUNSELING

As noted earlier, Rogers states that his theory, like all theories, is a more reliable guide when it is applied to the events which the theory was developed to explain. Since client-centered theory was developed primarily from interviews aimed at personality change, we shall now examine some of the issues which arise when the theory is applied to general counseling where attention is frequently focused on such problems as educational and vocational choice.

Before doing this, however, it should be noted that general counseling has changed much in the last twenty-five to thirty years so that today it includes dealing with many personal and emotional problems that were formerly considered outside the province of counseling. As late as 1947 Hahn and Kendall (1947) divided student problems into two broad groups of educational-vocational problems and personal-social-emotional problems and considered the latter group to belong to the province of psychotherapy. In 1955 (Hahn & MacLean, 1955), however, Hahn spoke of counseling as dealing with educational-vocational-personal problems and noted that many of the activities formerly thought of as guidance have become more administrative than counseling functions. This same shift in emphasis is seen in much of the counseling literature, and today there is a general recognition that feelings and emotions influence the everyday behavior of normal as well as disturbed individuals. Today counselors are expected to deal with such problems as homesickness, family conflicts, disturbing love affairs, anxiety over examinations or classroom participation, conflict with authority, lack of self-confidence, and frequent loss of emotional control.

Such personal problems are the very type of counseling situation out of which client-centered theory developed, and for this part of the general counselor's work there is no need to discuss the theory further. The counselor may prefer to operate from some other theory, but there is no question about the direct relevance of the client-centered approach. For many, the client-centered theory will offer distinct advantages over competing theories. Its major concepts do not arise primarily from the study of psychopathology; its major aim is not the "cure" of "sick" people but is to help people live more satisfying and creative lives regardless of the level at which they enter counseling; and one of its major tenets is that the counselee has the capacity to direct his own life. The theory is perhaps more broadly applicable than many theories because the client does not have to view himself as sick or disturbed in order to seek help with personal problems.

In spite of this broader definition of the counselor's function, the general counselor still deals with many client problems in which cognitive and more or less objective considerations have long been viewed as important to their proper resolution. The so-called educational and vocational problems are the most important of these. The modern viewpoint does not, of course, hold that educational and vocational problems are uncomplicated by or unrelated to other problems. On the contrary, it is generally agreed that attitudes, values, and other aspects of the self are usually important. That is, personality change often is needed for the effective resolution of educational and vocational problems. So to at least this extent, client-centered theory is relevant for educational and vocational counseling. However, there is considerable ambiguity in client-centered theory when it comes to considering the cognitive and informational elements in general counseling, and it is to this and closely related problems that we now turn our attention.

Problems associated with the goals of counseling. A significant difference between counseling theories is that the client-centered counselor does not set specific goals for the counseling whereas many other counseling approaches do. The client-centered counselor typically does not ask how he can cure the client, solve a particular problem, or promote this or that specfic change. He asks how he can provide a relationship which the client can use for his own personal growth, in ways pertinent to his own situation. Within this emphasis there is, of course, the expectation that the client will discover better ways of meeting life problems and that his behavior will change in ways which are more mature, more socialized, and more self-enhancing; but the counselor does not set forth specific problem solutions or specific behavior changes as the goal of counseling. Specific problems may be solved and specific goals reached, but these are the problems and goals set by the client rather than the counselor.

Specific goals for counseling are not set because the counselor's primary objective is to create the conditions (unconditional positive regard, empathic understanding, etc.) which Rogers theorizes are necessary to promote meaningful change. Emphasis on determining and then promoting specific goals tends to interfere with creating the desired conditions.

In much of his work, the general counselor finds it difficult not to focus the counseling on specific goals, for example, to assist the student in making wise educational decisions or to spot and improve weaknesses in study habits and skills. Although it is not explicitly covered by the theory, the writer believes the general counselor can set more definite goals than Rogers advocates and still retain much of the client-centered approach. More will be said about this further on, but the conditions deemed necessary for change exist on continua rather than on an all-or-none basis. Focusing the counseling on specific goals does interfere with establishing the conditions to the maximal extent possible, but they can still be achieved to a substantial degree if the counselor focuses on creating the conditions as well as on specific goals of the counseling.

Closely related to the above view of goals is the fact that client-centered theory is concerned primarily with personality and personality changes. The goal of counseling as implied by the theory is to dissolve the conditions of worth and thereby increase the degree of congruence between the self-concept and experience. In this way the client becomes a more fully functioning person.

But what if the successful resolution of the client's problem does not require personality change? Under these conditions is client-centered theory relevant?

Before dealing with this, consider the question whether personality change is helpful to the resolution of educational, vocational, and related problems which constitute much of the general counselor's work. A firm answer is not available and must await further research. However, the best available evidence indicates that the answer is a matter of degree, that is, resolving an educational or vocational problem sometimes necessitates considerable personality change and sometimes very little, with all degrees in between these extremes. Rogers thinks that incongruence between self and experience is more frequently an issue in these problems than is often supposed, but he would probably agree that a continuum is involved.

From this perspective it might be concluded that client-centered theory with its central focus on the self and personality change is sometimes relevant and sometimes almost irrelevant to the work of the general counselor. However, such a deduction is only partially correct for two reasons: (1) Rogers's theory of therapy and personality change is itself stated in terms of a continuum, and (2) his theory also deals with the interpersonal relationship in which all counseling of whatever sort must take place.

Although Rogers's writings have usually stressed the maximal degree of his therapeutic conditions with the aim of promoting maximal personality change, the theory permits lesser degrees of both; also counseling practice and research confirm that lesser degrees are useful. It follows that there is room within the theory for the counselor to have other goals in addition to a concern with personality change, even though having such additional goals may result in a lesser degree of the therapeutic conditions being established.

Rogers does state as one of his necessary conditions for counseling that the client must be incongruent and preferably anxious as well. In applying the theory to general counseling, the writer thinks that this part of the theory should be amended to say that the client must be incongruent in areas of his personality that are significantly related to the problem bringing him to counseling. Otherwise, that part of client-centered theory encompassing the conditions of worth and increasing the congruence between the self-concept and experience would not be relevant to the presenting problem with which the counseling must often deal. To illustrate, at Michigan State University first- and second-year students wishing to change their majors are expected to come to the Counseling Center for assistance. That such students may have marked incongruence in the sexual areas of their lives or in their relationships with their parents may be essentially irrelevant to the resolution of the immediate problem. If we assume no incongruence of consequence in areas related to their choice of majors (an assumption which seems justified in many instances), then counseling as conceived of by Rogers would not get under way with the immediate problem at hand. Of course, counseling might get under way in the other areas where the client is incongruent, but desirable as this might be, it still leaves both client and counselor with the issue of selecting an appropriate major.

This kind of situation would pose no particular problem in the settings where client-centered theory was primarily developed, because in these settings it would have been perfectly appropriate to ignore the choice of major and deal instead with the sexual problem or the conflict with the parents. But very frequently counselors work in institutional settings which require that the presenting problem be resolved, and if a reorganization of self need not be a significant part of this resolution, the counselor must make modifications in the client-centered approach.

As noted earlier, portions of client-centered theory are relevant to the interpersonal relationship in counseling even though personality change in the client is not being sought. The counselor's genuineness, his empathic understanding of the client and his situation, and his liking and respect for the client as a person help to create an effective working relationship between client and counselor which is beneficial for many counseling objectives. Thus this part of the theory can be relevant to general counseling even though the counselor must sometimes adapt parts of client-centered theory (and perhaps draw on other theories as well) for portions of his work.

The practical problems surrounding goals are less troublesome than the theoretical issues considered in the foregoing. Clearly, we have to get to know the student before we can determine whether incongruence is or is not an important part of his problem. To do this the client-centered counselor follows his usual approach of concentrating on the internal frame of reference of the client, and he can modify his approach when this seems indicated. Perhaps some time would be lost, but this is far less serious than too quickly proceeding on the assumption that no significant self-issues are involved. The writer believes that at least some self-issues are often involved and that all too frequently the approach of the cognitively oriented general counselor does not allow these to emerge. Discussing tests, posing questions about past educational history, and focusing on what the client does or does not know about alternative majors he has considered will hardly encourage the student to feel that he can discuss some of the more personal elements which he vaguely perceives are involved in his choice.

A concern often expressed by others about the client-centered view of goals deserves consideration. It is asserted that the counselor cannot, as a responsible member of society, accept all goals that the client might conceivably set for himself. Suppose, it is argued, that the client elects to settle his financial problem by stealing, or his conflict with a roommate by physical violence. And what about suicide? Do not examples of this nature prove, it is argued, that the counselor must set at least some goals for the client?

The specific setting in which many counselors work impose similar, although not always such obvious questions. The teacher who refers a student because of persistent disruptive behavior in the classroom expects some improvement in this behavior, and by accepting the student for counseling, does not the counselor commit himself to a particular goal? If we work with students experiencing academic failure, may not the nature of the counselor's job require setting the goal of academic improvement or alternatively, dropping school for some more appropriate objective?

The client-centered counselor has many answers for these and related questions which space does not allow us to consider here; however, the fundamental basis of these answers lies in the truth or falsity of the theory itself. If the theory is correct, allowing the client to set goals will not result in the socially unacceptable consequences which the questions are intended to imply. A paradox in client-centered theory is that more constructive personality and behavioral changes occur when the counselor refrains from setting goals (no matter how desirable these goals may be) and concentrates instead on creating the proper conditions for change. Rogers would add that even though the theory is not proved, it rests on considerable research support, and that research in other areas supports conclusions similar to the client-centered view (for an account of some of these, see Rogers, 1951, pp. 56–64).

There are, however, practical problems in leaving the goals of counseling to the client. Whether it is desirable or not, the counselor in accepting his job frequently does commit himself to certain goals for his clients. High school counselors may have administrative responsibility for determining the student's course of study. We have previously mentioned that at the writer's institution students in the first two years of college are required to confer with a counselor before changing their major area of study. For many of their cases, Veterans Administration counselors are required by law to certify the feasibility of the client's training objective.

An important characteristic of these and similar situations is that the goal is imposed on both client and counselor. In the case of the Veterans Administration counseling, for example, the goal is imposed on the counselor because of terms of his employment and on the veteran because he wishes to qualify for training benefits which are offered by the government only under certain conditions. Such externally imposed goals are not uncommon in counseling. They create a special case for client-centered counseling, but they need not seriously interfere with the establishment of an effective counseling relationship so long as the nature of the situation is understood and accepted by both client and counselor. Sometimes the client does not accept the externally imposed conditions, and the counselor must be alert to this possibility. The counselor deals with this as he would with any other issue arising in counseling: He attempts to understand and clarify the meaning which the situation has for the client.

An externally imposed goal often means that counseling is not voluntary with the client; it is a hurdle to be got over. This can cause severe complications which are best avoided whenever possible. Sometimes the counselor can work with and change the client's feelings about undergoing counseling, but unless he can, counseling is usually unsuccessful.

Most counselors of whatever persuasion agree that the desirable outcome of counseling is self-realization and self-direction. However, in many settings the limits imposed on the counselor's time with any one counselee will prevent the full realization of this objective. All theories, not just the client-centered theory, have difficulty coping with this reality limitation. The most frequent answer when a case threatens to be long is to circumscribe the problem area to be dealt with, that is, to set a more limited goal. Client-centered counselors, perhaps more than most counselors, are reluctant to do this because of their emphasis on letting the client set goals and because of their great concern with self-actualization. However, short-term counseling can be done. Useful assistance in limited areas of the client's life is not infrequently reported even in one-interview cases. Bartlett's (1949) research (see section on *Outcomes*) reporting on the postcounseling adjustment of veterans in training situations was done on cases with only a limited number of interviews.

The problem of time is most acute with clients presenting frankly emotional problems, and usually these clients require quite a number of interviews before we see significant change. When practical considerations do not allow a lengthy series of interviews, it is possible as suggested above to set limited goals for the counseling; however, an alternative approach more congenial to the client-centered counselor is to set limits on time and still leave the client free to use the allowed time as he wishes (Lewis, Rogers, & Shlein, 1959; Shlein, 1957). The writer with some success has told clients that because of the waiting list, they could have only a limited number of appointments. The client may be disappointed, and less change can be expected; but usually the client can use the remaining time constructively.

Is the client-centered approach effective with all clients? In the previous section we considered whether the aim or goal of client-centered counseling (resolving incongruence) is appropriate for all clients coming to the general counselor. In this section we shall assume that the goal is suitable and talk about the effectiveness of client-centered counseling with various kinds of clients.

Until recently client-centered counselors have believed that their approach is suitable for all clients, and this position is still held in the current formal theory (see the section Conditions of Therapy, pages 49 to 57). The fundamental problem of all clients coming for counseling is seen as an incongruence between the self-concept and organismic experience, and the counselor attempts to create the counseling conditions which make it possible for the self and experience to become more congruent. Rogers does not set up one set of conditions for one type of client and another set of conditions for another type of client. Here he departs sharply from other theoretical approaches which usually are much concerned with varying counseling and therapeutic conditions to fit particular clients.

There is considerable support for the client-centered claim: Clinical observation and numerous research studies have shown that client-centered counselors, particularly highly skilled counselors, obtain good results with many different kinds of clients and that the pattern of successes and failures does not coincide with the usual diagnostic categories of clients. Of course, not all cases are successful, but research tends to confirm that if the conditions outlined by Rogers are in fact established, then the counseling will be successful. Furthermore, there is some research which indicates that counselor variability contributes more to establishing the necessary therapeutic conditions than does client variability. That is, the counselor's ability to use the client-centered approach is the crucial factor.[12]

[12] Rogers's insistence over the years that the counselor's effectiveness is not dependent on extensive knowledge of personality theory, psychopathology, and the like has given many persons the idea that it requires very little skill and training to become a successful client-centered counselor. Even if one agrees with Rogers about not needing to master psychological concepts and theory, there is still the problem of the experiential training of the counselor. Being genuine in the counseling relationship and empathically sensitive to one's client is a complex skill, and the writer's experience is that for all except a very few persons the successful training of client-centered counselors involves intensive training in a clinical setting.

A number of persons trained in the client-centered approach, including the writer, believe that knowledge of personality theory and extensive firsthand experience

Although the evidence supporting the client-centered view is impressive, there is little systematic investigation which has been aimed at determining the value of the client-centered approach over other approaches. This would require studies in which the counselor approach and the initial state of the client are used as the independent variables and in which outcome measures are used as the dependent variables. The vast amount of research from the client-centered group includes little research in which the counselor's approach is systematically varied and examined in relation to client types and outcomes. Of particular importance to the general counselor is the absence of such research with clients presenting educational and vocational problems.[13]

Some recent research findings have caused Rogers to question whether client-centered counseling, at least as now practiced, can be successful with all clients. Kirtner & Cartwright (1958) found a lower incidence of success in client-centered counseling among clients who accept little self-responsibility for their problems and who see the source of their problems as residing outside of themselves. In a recent paper formulating a slightly different view of the therapeutic process, Rogers (1961d) speculates that all psychotherapists, not just client-centered therapists, have not yet learned much about how to create effective therapeutic conditions for clients showing such characteristics as the following:

Communicates only about externals and is unwilling or unable to communicate self

---

with psychopathology are very useful to the counselor who works with clients having severe emotional problems. Although there is considerable evidence that the client-centered approach can be helpful with psychotics and extremely neurotic individuals, the writer thinks that it is unwise for the general counselor to attempt counseling with such persons unless his training and experience have prepared him to relate effectively with these persons. Without this background too many counselors will feel uncomfortable in the relationship and be unable to create the conditions Rogers sees as necessary for personality change. Incidentally, the counselor's difficulty in relating effectively to the more disturbed client often comes after an initial relationship is established, and the client feels freer to express openly his psychopathology and to make more demands of the counselor.

The writer agrees with Rogers that academic training in the behavioral sciences frequently teaches a diagnostic point of view which can interfere with establishing effective counseling relationships. But the danger is not substantive knowledge of personality dynamics and behavior theory; rather it is the diagnostic point of view which so often results in the counselor treating his clients as objects.

[13] A systematic investigation of the suitability of various counseling approaches for different types of clients is a very complex undertaking which has not yet been seriously attempted by any school of thought. Many of the problems are quite similar to those discussed in the Outcome section of the theory presentation in this chapter.

Neither recognizes nor owns feelings and personal meanings
Has rigid personal constructs and thinks of them as fact rather than as constructs
Avoids close and personally communicative relationships which are constructed as dangerous
Either does not recognize problems or perceives them as external to the self

Persons like this are characteristically shut off from their own internal experience. They are incongruent, but they have so little awareness of this that they experience little anxiety.

Rogers comments that clients like these seldom present themselves voluntarily for therapy. However, many clients of this general type do come to counseling centers which are recognized in their communities as dealing with problems of educational and vocational choice. This happens, perhaps, because it is so easy to externalize these problems as having little to do with self and to believe that the counseling will deal exclusively with externals—with objective reality rather than the personal and subjective elements involved in choice. These clients apparently do not want the counselor to interact with them in a close and interpersonal way, and they are frequently disappointed—even irritated and threatened—if the counselor attempts this. They want the interpersonal relationship with the counselor, if it can be called that, to be carefully circumscribed and depersonalized.

Knowing how to work effectively with such clients is a difficult problem for any theoretical orientation, but it is especially difficult for the client-centered counselor with his predominant emphasis on subjective experience, the reorganization of the self, and the deeply communicative and personal relationship between client and counselor. Too often the counselor's approach does not result, as it is intended, in the client's experiencing acceptance and understanding in the counseling relationship. Instead, he is apt to feel misunderstood and threatened, and the basic conditions postulated by Rogers as necessary to getting the process under way are defeated.

This problem deserves further study. The solution may lie in client-centered counselors' developing more effective ways of relating to clients of this general type, that is, finding new ways of creating the therapeutic conditions. Or it may be that the process fails to get under way with some clients even when the necessary and sufficient conditions as stated by Rogers are in fact fulfilled. Still another possibility is that the conditions cannot be fulfilled for some clients and that other conditions and another process must be substituted.[14]

[14] Other approaches putting more emphasis on objective reality and cognitive considerations may appear to be more effective with the externally motivated client. Cognitively oriented counseling may be less threatening to the client because he can

Giving information.   A serious weakness of the theory for general counseling is that it says little about the role of information in assisting clients, or, if we confine ourselves to the terminology of the theory, the role of information in self-actualization.[15] The theory does, of course, assume that the individual is continually interacting with his environment and is differentiating new aspects of the environment in an attempt to meet his needs. The theory's deficiency is that it says little about the influence of the stimulus situation in this interaction between person and environment. Instead, the theory stresses that it is the individual's perception of the environment (or of the information, if you wish) which determines his behavior.

There is much value in Rogers's reminding us that reality for the individual is his perception of that reality. In psychology generally and in counseling in particular, we often slide over this truth too quickly. Just giving the client information about an occupation or a course of study does not mean that he perceives this as we intended. It is also valid and useful to call attention to the role of the self and the defensive process in determining what is actually perceived. However, it is equally valid and useful to recognize how perception is influenced by information and the stimulus situation generally. The theory's failure to elaborate how the environment influences perception and behavior is for the writer a significant omission which has special relevance for many counseling situations.[16]

---

more easily avoid confrontation with the subjective elements of his problem. The counseling may proceed at the intellectual level to clarify many of the objective considerations relevant to the educational or vocational choice. Sometimes it is even possible to deal with self-characteristics such as interests and abilities, although often the externally motivated client deals with these considerations impersonally and without really owning them as a part of himself. Such intellectual problem solving may result in decisions which are not integrated with significant aspects of the client's personality, and in all likelihood at some later date the client will again have difficulty with the same problems that he considered resolved at the conclusion of the counseling. Most experienced counselors have encountered numerous clients with prior counseling who have very distorted ideas of what took place in that counseling. Inaccurate memories about test results and their implications are particularly common. The writer suspects that the cause of these distortions is that the counseling failed to deal in any meaningful way with the subjective elements of the choice process.

[15] Actually Rogers has written about the use of information in educational and vocational counseling in a little book jointly authored with Wallen (1946). The book is rather practical in its approach and was written before the present theory was fully developed, but it is still of considerable interest to the general counselor.

[16] In one sense this is an unfair criticism. The essential point underlying the writer's criticism is that counseling practice needs to be based on a complete theory of behavior, and Rogers makes no pretense that his personality theory and therapeutic

Information can alter perception and behavior, and it is appropriate that educational and occupational information is a time-honored tool of the counselor. Consider the preengineering student who has his heart set on engineering but is having difficulty with mathematics. Counseling reveals that his perception of "an engineer" more accurately fits the role of a technician in a mechanical field. When presented with a realistic job description of the two occupations, he cheerfully makes plans to enter a technical school where he can get training to do what he wanted to do all along.

Since client-centered counselors do in fact give information to their clients, the question arises as to how information giving can be integrated into the theory as it is currently formulated.

To be maximally useful, information must be accurately assimilated and used by the client in an integrative manner. We can infer from client-centered theory that if the information is threatening to the self, it will be distorted and resisted in some way. Under these circumstances the counselor can profitably play down the need for information and concentrate instead on creating the conditions which reduce the threat and allow the self to change. On the other hand, if the information is not threatening but can be perceived by the client as providing ways to maintain and enhance the self, then the information should be provided. In other words, appropriate information can be assimilated when it helps the client to meet his perceived needs and to achieve or to formulate his goals. Sometimes it is also given to change a perceived goal to a more suitable goal, but this is apt to be effective only when the information is perceived as nonthreatening to the self and when it points to a new goal which is perceived as self-enhancing.[17]

---

theory constitutes a complete theory of behavior. Behavior is a function of the interaction between the individual and his environment ($B = f: I \leftrightarrow E$), and a complete behavior theory must deal explicitly with both sides of this interaction. Personality, therapeutic, and counseling theories invariably fail to meet this test, and the writer knows of no single, internally consistent theory which is complete enough to guide all the counselor's actions with his clients. Learning theory approaches are a possible exception to this statement in that they place considerable emphasis on interaction between the organism and its environment, but to date they have given such superficial treatment to many of the important problems encountered by the counselor that they have only limited value to counseling practice.

[17] An alternative and more elaborate theoretical formulation might be developed along the following lines. Instead of thinking about threat to the self in all-or-none terms (which most certainly is too simple a view), we should think about degrees of threat. Similarly, the nature of the stimulus situation to force a given perception would be thought of as a matter of degree. Whether the information is actually assimilated and used would depend on the balance between the degree of threat to

In the illustration of the preengineering student cited above, the information given was nonthreatening and pointed to a new but self-enhancing goal. It was assimilated and used in integrative fashion. Slightly altering our example might produce a quite different result. Suppose that the student were under considerable pressure from his parents to enter the university and qualify in engineering, and further suppose that the student's need for self-esteem was perceived by him to be dependent on meeting the expectations of his parents. The information supplies by the counselor would be threatening and would tend not to be accurately assimilated and appropriately used. While we might all agree that the information is of great potential value to the client, the counselor is still faced with the problem of how the client can assimilate and use the information.

This suggested modification of the theory provides a guide to the use of information in general counseling, but on logical grounds the theory is still vulnerable since in practice the counselor cannot always know in advance whether relevant information will threaten the client's self-concept. Thus the counselor in providing information will sometimes violate the conditions of reduced threat which client-centered theory postulates as necessary for therapeutic change. Fortunately, most clients are not as delicate as we sometimes think. Even when the counselor supplies information which proves threatening to the client's self-concept, little damage is done if the conditions for the therapeutic relationship have been established and are being generally maintained and if the information is communicated with warmth, understanding, and a readiness to receive fully the responses of the client. The counselor must, of course, be alert to any threat created by the information and attempt to deal with this constructively. He should not force the issue and attempt to convince the client that the

---

the self and the degree to which the stimulus situation forces a particular perception of the situation. For example, flunking out of school is usually threatening to the self-concept of a student, but the balance between the degree of threat and the compelling nature of the evidence before him often results in the student's accepting that he is going to be dropped from school, and he proceeds to make plans accordingly. This model would need to be even more complicated. The perception of the stimulus situation would be dependent on prior experience and a "self-commitment" to a particular view of the stimulus situation. For example, the individual "knows" the meaning of the grading system, "believes" that universities should maintain certain standards, and is "certain" that the dean will act in terms of his announced intentions. On the other side of the equation we have to deal with the possibility that while the individual assimilates the information that he is going to be dropped from school, he distorts the meaning of this (in ways the stimulus situation allows) to preserve certain aspects of his self-picture. It is possible that many counselors work implicitly from some such model as this.

information provided is both correct and relevant. If even subtle resistance is met, the counselor can profitably concentrate on trying to
understand the personal meaning that the new information has for the
client. If the client has a different perception of the information from
what the counselor intended, the client's perception must be recognized and explored. Denying the validity of the client's perception and
attempting to prove it unfounded will not change the fact of the
client's feelings about the matter. Too frequently counselors become
ego-involved and defensive once they have committed themselves to a
particular view of the situation.

This discussion would not be complete without mentioning some
additional factors which the client-centered counselor considers before
too quickly supplying information to his client. First, the presenting
problem frequently is not the real problem that the client wishes to
bring to counseling. He may be "testing the situation out" with a
superficial problem which appears to lend itself to a cognitive-informa-
tion approach. Empathic listening and getting to know the client often
allows the real problem to emerge.

Second, most problems the client brings to the counselor are not
basically problems of lack of information. Students have ample opportunities to pick up information about courses of study, financial aids,
occupations, employment opportunities, and the like. If they do not
have the information, it is usually readily available. Therefore, there is
presumptive evidence that the essential nature of the problem is not
lack of information but blocks to the effective gathering and use of the
information. Information will not be particularly helpful until these
blocks have been explored and resolved.

Third, too much emphasis on information and external reality can
divert the client from significant self-problems. Too often the client
gets the impression that his subjective feelings and attitudes about the
problem are not appropriate to the counseling situation. He feels that
he is expected to be rational and objective about the matter. In any
case, these subjective self-elements are at least mildly threatening and
often only dimly perceived by the client. The client can readily be
diverted, and the counselor's approach therefore needs to make it easy
for the client to bring self-elements into the interview.

In brief, the attitude of nonevaluative listening and empathic understanding can help avoid many pitfalls surrounding the use of information in counseling. It allows the more personal and threatening self-
elements to emerge, and it helps the counselor to know what, if any,
information may be pertinent and how it can best be communicated.

Because beginning client-centered counselors are sometimes overly cautious about providing information, it need also be said that the counselor's failure to give information under some circumstances can be perceived by the client as rejecting, while the giving of information can be experienced as a sign of caring and acceptance. For example, the repeated parrying and avoiding the client's questions can defeat the central aim of the client-centered approach.

Using tests. Although Rogers (1946) has written one article about the use of tests in counseling, the current theory makes no mention of their use, and for many counselors this will be a significant omission.

Tests are used by counselors in two ways: (1) to provide the counselor with diagnostic information and (2) to provide the client with information of value to self-understanding and decision making. We shall reserve the problem of diagnosis for a separate section and concentrate here on the second use of tests.

It is immediately apparent that using tests as a source of information for the client is essentially the problem of information giving discussed in the preceding section. The chief difference is that tests, by their very nature, provide information of great relevance to the self, and because of this, test information is more likely to instigate the process of threat and perceptual defense. The client is seldom indifferent or neutral to what tests may reveal about him.

Many client-centered counselors find it easiest to use tests infrequently. They see educational and vocational problems, where tests are traditionally used, as just another variety of personal problem. And as in other kinds of counseling, the counselor is interested in the person, not merely in the initial problem which he presents. This does not mean that the presenting problem is ignored. On the contrary, as with other presenting problems, the counselor is interested in how the client views his problem and himself in relation to it, and the counseling relationship develops on this basis. It is perfectly possible for the client to clarify, reformulate, and reach decisions about an educational or vocational problem by considering himself in relation to any number of issues, e.g., to work and school experiences, to family relationships, or to social values. Test information is not essential and at times may even divert the client from more significant issues.

The client-centered counselor preferring this approach will not automatically exclude the use of tests. "The client may, in exploring his situation, reach the point where, facing his situation squarely and realistically, he wishes to compare his aptitudes and abilities with those of others for a specific purpose. When tests come as a real desire from the client, they may enter into the situation" (Rogers, 1946, p.

142). According to this principle, however, tests will be used infrequently, and when they are used, it is likely to be in the later stages of counseling.

One of the special problems about tests arises because so many clients come to counseling expecting them. Often this seems to reflect the client's interest in having someone else make a decision for him. He, of course, wants the decision to be made in his own interests, and this requires that he be known and understood. Tests, he thinks, will provide this understanding. No doubt tests can be used, and too often are used to make the client's decisions for him; however, for the writer this is not a function of counseling. It is far better, as Meehl suggests, to put the tests and other information into a computer and grind out a result. The writer understands that some matrimonial services are, in fact, using this system to introduce potential marriage partners to one another. If counseling is to justify itself, it must offer something more than this. This "something more" for the client-centered approach is that counseling is a learning experience involving the functioning and organization of the self. Tests can be useful in this process, provided that the information they supply is integrated into the self-concept.

This does not, of course, entirely dismiss the problem of the dependent client who seeks magical answers in test information. Not infrequently, withholding tests from these clients is experienced as rejection, and they merely go elsewhere for help. Although this issue has not been studied extensively by the client-centered group, some suggestions can be made.

Giving tests to dependent clients may help them to discover that tests do not provide the satisfying answers they had anticipated, and at this point it may be possible for client and counselor to embark on a more fruitful counseling experience. But this will not happen if the counselor uses the test information to make the client's decision for him.

The problem of dependence, at least mild dependence, is extremely common, and most counselors would agree that counseling should help the client move in the direction of independence and self-direction. Rogers (1946), Bordin and Bixler (1946) and others have pointed out that the traditional use of tests in educational and vocational counseling does little to foster independence. Bordin and Bixler note that students coming to the Counseling and Testing Bureau at the University of Minnesota typically project responsibility for their problem onto the counselor or the referring agent. The counselor reinforces this when he asks the many questions needed for an appraisal, when he selects and assigns tests, etc. Rogers states, "If the counselor suggests the taking of tests, he is both directing the conversation and is implying, 'I know what to do about this.' To administer tests routinely or to have them administered at the beginning of the contacts is to proclaim in the strongest possible terms, 'I can measure you, find out all about you,' and this implies to the client that the counselor can also tell him what to do" (1946, p. 141).

To help meet this problem and also to facilitate the client's assimilation and use of test information, Bordin and Bixler (1946) developed a procedure for client self-selection of tests.[18] Although this procedure involves using tests more frequently than Rogers appears to advocate, it does retain much of the client-centered approach to counseling. The counselor states in nontechnical language the type of judgment the test can make, and it is then left to the client to decide whether the information would be useful in considering his particular problem. The authors report that this is often a struggle for the client. He usually explores his feelings and doubts about the self-relevance of the appraisal under consideration and often brings forth a wealth of significant material. This helps the client develop a deeper understanding of his problem which sometimes results in a radical restatement of the problem. The approach also encourages active participation by the client and a coming to terms with self-responsibility. The authors think a further advantage of this approach is that the client is better motivated to take a long test battery and that in taking the tests he is keenly aware of the significance of his own performance.

Seeman (1948) investigated the effectiveness of client self-selection of tests and reports evidence that the client's selections are relevant to their situations. He also reports that the self-selection situation is unstructured enough to allow the client to explore many areas unique to his situation.

How the process works can be illustrated by a recorded interview excerpt from Seeman's research.

C: This math test would give you an indication of your background in math and also help predict how a person is likely to do in our College of Engineering.
S: I'm a little scared of math. But (pause) that would give me an idea of where I stand now in my math background. Right?
C: That's right.
S: Well, I think I've got an idea of where I stand now in my math background; it's one of my weaker points. But I've always been told that if I work at it, I could do well in it. But I don't know.

---

[18] Shostrom and Brammer (1952) report a similar procedure using a printed test selection guide. Bordin (1955) also discusses this approach in his more recent work entitled *Psychological Counseling*.

C: It's hard for you to know about what others say concerning your potentialities.

S: That's right. At times in math, I've done very well when I applied myself a little more. But then at other times I didn't do so well and it
just seemed like I hated it. And as a result, well, I got mighty low marks.

C: You really had some ups and downs in math.

S: Yes, that's sure. Well, it seemed to make a lot of difference as to the instructor I had. Some would tell me that I—well, in junior high school I
was told that I was quite hopeless with it, and that sort of discouraged
me. So I let it go for a year and then went to summer school to—well, to
do what I'm doing now, to find if I could do it or not. Well, I got a B in
it. So my math background now, I don't think, I know just about where
I stand in that, I think.

C: You feel that the test wouldn't be necessary because you can size it up for
yourself.

S: I can size it up pretty well for myself, that I'm not very high in math.

C: Umhum.

S: Well, on the other hand, maybe it wouldn't be a bad idea to take it.

C: You're a little undecided on that one, aren't you?

S: Yes . . . so I'd know actually just how bad off I am.

C: So even though you don't think you're going to do well on it, you'd like
to take it.

S: Even though I don't think I'll do well on it at all (1948, p. 340).

The interpretation of test results in educational and vocational counseling often introduces a crucial phase of the counseling in which the
client either integrates test predictions into his thinking and planning
or distorts and rejects them. Bixler and Bixler (1946) describe a client-
centered approach which encourages the client to participate in test
interpretation and to relate test results to other relevant material. They
recommend that test results be reported factually with a minimum of
the counselor's opinion as to their implications for the client. The
counselor does not say, "This result indicates you will not do well in
college." Instead he says, "Ten out of one hundred students with scores
like yours will succeed in college," and leaves the interpretation of this
fact for the client to decide for himself. "When the counselor allows
the client to make his own interpretation, he is free to express these
attitudes which so frequently interfere with his use of test data. As he
expresses them to an accepting counselor, there is a greater opportunity for them to dissipate and the client will gain a better insight into
his motivation. It is only as the client can understand and accept
himself that he can make actual use of tests" (Bixler & Bixler, 1946, p.
154).

The following excerpt illustrates the Bixlers' approach to test interpretation. The counselor has just pointed out that fifteen to twenty students of each one hundred with scores like hers succeed in college:

S: (looks stunned, then confused)
C: This is awfully disappointing.
S: Yes, it is. I had hoped I'd find something I could succeed in.
C: It seems to leave you without anything to go into.
S: Yes, but I can do the work. I have trouble concentrating, my study habits are poor, I never studied in high school and I don't know how.
C: You feel the reason for your trouble is your poor study habits, not a lack of ability.
S: Yes, I didn't get good grades in high school, but I didn't study either. Now when I want to study I worry and get tense. My mind goes blank when I take tests.
C: You're pretty worried about your school work and that seems to make it harder to succeed. (Pause).
S: It's my last hope. (Head sinks on chest, lips quiver.)
C: You're so upset about this you feel like crying.
S: (Does) I feel so silly. (C recognizes her embarrassment, and she continues to cry and discuss various elements of her anxiety about school.) I've got to make good. I'm not as smart as most kids, that's true. There are some subjects that go over me, but I think I can make it. I don't know what to do.
C: You have to make good and yet you're afraid you can't. It leaves you pretty badly mixed up.
S: Decides to continue seeing C. until she can work out a solution (1946, p. 153).

This excerpt illustrates the main features of how the client-centered counselor handles the introduction of test or other kinds of information into the counseling interview. The information is presented as factually and objectively as possible. The client is not urged to accept any particular implication the information has for his situation. Instead the counselor concentrates on empathically understanding what the information means to the client and by this assists the client to explore further and to assimilate and use the information.

Diagnosis and appraisal. Unlike other approaches, client-centered theory does not find diagnosis by tests or other means to be useful in counseling. Diagnosis or appraisal, being in the external frame of reference, serves no function since, regardless of the findings, the client-centered counselor concentrates his attention only on the client's *internal frame of reference.* Diagnosis is thus a waste of time. Moreover, diagnosis may interfere with counseling for the following reasons: (1) by treating the client as an object, diagnosis tends to violate the conditions seen as necessary for change; (2) diagnosis tends to place the locus of responsibility for doing something about the problem in the counselor rather than in the client; (3) the gathering of diagnostic information (which by itself produces no change in the client) can sometimes dominate the interviews; and (4) the counselor may become so committed to a diagnostic formulation that he fails to appreciate and understand significant new attitudes which emerge in later interviews.

Calling attention to the implications and dangers in diagnostic thinking is a worthwhile contribution, but it does not completely resolve the problem. In the immediately preceding sections, we have implied that the general counselor will have to decide whether or not tests should be offered, whether or not relevant information would be threatening to the client's self-concept; whether or not some change of approach is indicated for the rigid client who externalizes his problems, etc. We have also suggested that the general counselor without first-hand experience with disturbed individuals should not attempt counseling with psychotics and extreme neurotics. In other words, the application of client-centered theory to the general counseling situation, while not requiring extensive diagnostic workups, may, on occasion, call for diagnostic or appraisal activity on the part of the counselor. Since appraisal activity tends to distract the counselor from concentrating his full attention on the client's internal frame of reference, to this extent it violates the logic of the theory.

This need not be a serious problem, however. Diagnostic activities tend to lead to, but do not inevitably lead to, the adverse effects mentioned above. Diagnosis is less likely to have adverse effects if diagnostic thinking is kept to a minimum, if it arises naturally out of the interaction between the client and the counselor, and if the general tone of the relationship conforms to the conditions postulated by Rogers as necessary for setting the process of change in motion. One bit of confirming evidence for this viewpoint is that client-centered counselors have repeatedly employed diagnosis for research purposes without this interfering with the counseling process.

As it is commonly used, diagnosis views the client as an object and attempts to classify him according to some system of external reality. Information is collected from many sources, the information is analyzed, and inferences are made about the proper categories to which the client belongs. However, diagnosis can proceed by concentrating largely on the client's internal frame of reference. This kind of diagnosis is more congenial to the client-centered approach, and is often more revealing and more useful in counseling than the traditional approach to diagnosis.

SUMMING UP

Client-centered theory focuses on the nature of personality and the process of personality change. It was developed in counseling and psychotherapeutic settings where attitudinal and emotional problems (although not necessarily frank psychopathology) were the central concern, and the client-centered approach concentrates on changing the functioning and organization of the self as the best avenue for helping clients live more constructive and meaningful lives.

Twenty to forty years ago client-centered theory would have had only marginal relevance to the field of general counseling because at that time the guidance counselor tended to confine his counseling to client problems which lent themselves to a cognitive-informational approach. However, today client-centered theory is directly relevant because of two changes which have occurred in the conception of general counseling: (1) Motivations, attitudes, and emotions are now seen as important in such life tasks as choosing educational and vocational objectives, and (2) the general counselor is now expected to work with many frankly personal and emotional problems which have been the central concern of client-centered theory.

In spite of the theory's relevance, there are several considerations which are important to the general counselor but which are not dealt with satisfactorily in client-centered theory. The two most important of these are: (1) The functioning and organization of the self may not be a crucial aspect of all the problems brought to the general counselor, and (2) the cognitive-informational approach is a useful counseling procedure with many clients.

A fundamental weakness of client-centered theory is that it fails to take sufficient note of how behavior is influenced by the stimulus situation and the nature of the environment generally, and perhaps this omission is far more important to the general counselor than to the therapeutic counselor. In the final analysis, general counseling needs to be based on a complete theory of behavior. However, the present state of knowledge in the behavioral sciences offers no complete theory of behavior which can guide all the counselor's activities, and in practice all counselors, knowingly or unknowingly, tend to draw upon several theories. If the counselor uses tests or other information which allow for predictions about the client's future performance in an academic program or a vocation, he is drawing upon a body of knowledge often called trait-and-factor theory. Similarly, if the counselor agrees that test or other information may sometimes be resisted by the client, he is drawing upon self-theory, some other dynamic theory, or perhaps learning theory.

Many of the counseling situations not covered adequately by client-centered theory can be handled quite successfully in actual practice, although some originality and adaptability is called for from the counselor. This chapter has suggested some possible adaptations which are consistent with the client-centered approach.

As a final point, it should be emphasized that all counseling takes place in an interpersonal relationship, and that client-centered theory deals more than anything else with the *nature of the interpersonal relationship* in which constructive personality growth and change can take place (see Rogers, 1962a). In this sense client-centered theory is directly relevant to any helping relationship. Even though the practice of the general counselor may call for adaptations of the formal theory and departures from some of the usual procedures employed in client-centered therapeutic counseling, the counselor will be maintaining the essence of the client-centered approach if he succeeds in creating a counseling relationship in which his client has the experience of being fully received.

BIBLIOGRAPHY

Angyal, A. *Foundations for a science of personality.* New York: Commonwealth Fund, 1941.

Assum, A. L., & Levy, S. J. Analysis of a non-directive case with followup interview. *J. abnorm. soc. Psychol.,* 1948, 43, 78–89.

Axline, Virginia M. Nondirective therapy for poor readers. *J. consult. Psychol.,* 1947, 11, 61–69.

Barrett-Lennard, G. T. Dimensions of therapist response as causal factors in therapeutic change. *Psychol. Monogr.,* 1962, 76, No. 43 (Whole No. 562).

Bartlett, M. R., & staff. Data on the personal adjustment counseling program for veterans. Personal Adjustment Counseling Division. Advisement and Guidance Service. Office of Vocational Rehabilitation and Education. Washington, D.C., 1949.

Bixler, R. H., & Bixler, Virginia M. Test interpretation in vocational counseling. *Educ. psychol. Measmt.,* 1946, 6, 145–155.

Bordin, E. S. *Psychological counseling.* New York: Appleton-Century-Crofts, 1955.

Bordin, E. S., & Bixler, R. H. Test selection: A process of counseling. *Educ. psychol. Measmt.,* 1946, 6, 361–374.

Butler, J. M. The evaluative attitude of the client-centered counselor: A linguistic-behavioral formulation. Dittoed paper, Counseling Center, University of Chicago, about 1952.

Butler, J. M. Client-centered counseling and psychotherapy. In D. Brower & L. E. Abt (Eds.) *Progress in clinical psychology.* Vol. 3. *Changing conceptions in psychotherapy.* New York: Grune & Stratton, 1958.

Butler, J. M., & Haigh, G. V. Changes in the relation between self-concepts and ideal concepts consequent upon client-centered counseling. In C. R. Rogers & Rosalind F. Dymond (Eds.), *Psychotherapy and personality change.* Chicago: University of Chicago Press, 1954. Chap. 4.

Cartwright, D. S. A synthesis of process and outcome research. *Discussion papers,* Counseling Center, University of Chicago, Vol. 2, No. 19, 1956.

Cofer, C. N., & Chance, J. The discomfort-relief quotient in published cases of counseling and psychotherapy. *J. Psychol.,* 1950, **29,** 219–224.

Dymond, Rosalind F. Adjustment changes over therapy from Thematic Apperception Test ratings. In C. R. Rogers & Rosalind F. Dymond (Eds.), *Psychotherapy and Personality Change.* Chicago: University of Chicago Press, 1954. Chap. 8. (a)

Dymond, Rosalind F. Adjustment changes over therapy from self sorts. In C. R. Rogers & Rosalind F. Dymond (Eds.), *Psychotherapy and personality change.* Chicago: University of Chicago Press, 1954. Chap. 5. (b)

Gendlin, E. T. Outcome and process. *Discussion papers,* Counseling Center, University of Chicago, Vol. 2, No. 21, 1956.

Gendlin, E. T. Experiencing: a variable in the process of therapeutic change. *Amer. J. Psychotherapy.* 1961, **15,** 233–245. (a)

Gendlin, E. T. Sub-verbal communication and therapist expressivity: Trends in client-centered psychotherapy with schizophrenics. *Discussion papers,* Wisconsin Psychiatric Institute, University of Wisconsin, No. 17, 1961. (b)

Gendlin, E. T. Client-centered developments and work with schizophrenics. *J. counsel. Psychol.,* 1962, **9,** 205–212. (a)

Gendlin, E. T. *Experiencing and the creation of meaning.* New York: Free Press, 1962. (b)

Gendlin, E., & Zimiring, F. The qualities or dimensions of experiencing and their change. *Discussion papers.* Counseling Center, University of Chicago, Vol. 1, No. 3, 1955.

Goldstein, Kurt. *Human nature in the light of psychopathology.* Cambridge, Mass.: Harvard, 1940.

Grummon, D. L., & John, Eve S. Changes over client-centered therapy evaluated on psychoanalytically based Thematic Apperception Test scales. In C. R. Rogers & Rosalind F. Dymond (Eds.), *Psychotherapy and personality change.* Chicago: University of Chicago Press, 1954. Chap. 11.

Hahn, M. E., & Kendall, W. E. Some comments in defense of non-nondirective counseling. *J. consult. Psychol.,* 1947, **11,** 74–81.

Hahn, M. E. & MacLean, M. S. *Counseling psychology.* (2nd ed.) New York: McGraw-Hill, 1955.

Haimowitz, Natalie Reader, & Haimowitz, M. L. Personality changes in client-centered therapy. In W. Wolff (Ed.) *Success in psychotherapy.* New York: Grune & Stratton, 1952, Chap. 3.

Halkides, Galatia. An investigation of therapeutic success as a function of four variables. Unpublished doctoral dissertation, University of Chicago, 1958.

Hart, J. T. The evolution of client-centered psychotherapy. *Psychiatric Institute Bulletin,* Vol. 1, No. 2, University of Wisconsin, 1961.

Hartley, Margaret. Changes in the self-concept during psychotherapy. Unpublished doctoral dissertation, University of Chicago, 1951.

Hobbs, N. Sources of gain in psychotherapy. *Amer. Psychologist*, 1962, **17**, 741–747.

Kirtner, W. L., & Cartwright, D. S. Success and failure in client-centered therapy as a function of initial in-therapy behavior. *J. consult. Psychol.*, 1958, **22**, 329–333.

Lewis, Madge, Rogers, C. R. & Shlein, J. M. Time-limited, client-centered psychotherapy: Two cases. In A. Burton (Ed.) *Case Studies in Counseling and Psychotherapy*. Prentice-Hall, 1959. Chap. 12.

Maslow, A. H. *Motivation and Personality*. New York: Harper & Row, 1954.

Mosak, H. Evaluation in psychotherapy: A study of some current measures. Unpublished doctoral dissertation, University of Chicago, 1950.

Mowrer, O. H., & Kluckhohn, C. A dynamic theory of personality. In J. McV. Hunt, *Personality and the Behavior Disorders*. New York: Ronald, 1944.

Muench, G. A. An evaluation of non-directive psychotherapy by means of the Rorschach and other tests. *Psychol. Monogr.*, 1947, No. 13, 1–163.

Raimy, V. C. Self references in counseling interviews. *J. appl. Psychol.*, 1948, **12**, 153–163.

Raskin, N. J. An objective study of the locus of evaluation factor in psychotherapy. In W. Wolff (Ed.), *Success in psychotherapy*, New York: Grune & Stratton, 1952. Chap. 6.

Rogers, C. R. *Counseling and psychotherapy*. Boston: Houghton Mifflin, 1942.

Rogers, C. R. Psychometric tests and client-centered counseling. *Educ. psychol. Measmt.*, 1946, **6**, 139–144.

Rogers, C. R. Some implications of client-centered counseling for college personnel work. *Educ. psychol. Measmt.*, 1948, **8**, 540–549.

Rogers, C. R. *Client-centered therapy: Its current practice, implications, and theory*. Boston: Houghton Mifflin, 1951.

Rogers, C. R. Changes in the maturity of behavior as related to therapy. In C. R. Rogers & Rosalind F. Dymond (Eds.), *Psychotherapy and personality change*. Chicago: University of Chicago Press, 1954. Chap. 13.

Rogers, C. R. Persons or science? A philosophical question. *Amer. Psychologist*, 1955, **10**, 267–278.

Rogers, C. R. The necessary and sufficient conditions of therapeutic personality change. *J. consult. Psychol.*, **21**, 1957, 95–103.

Rogers, C. R. A theory of therapy, personality, and interpersonal relationships, as developed in the client-centered framework. In S. Koch (Ed.) *Psychology: A study of a science*. Vol. III. *Formulations of the person and the social context*. New York: McGraw-Hill, 1959. Pp. 184–258. (a)

Rogers, C. R. The essence of psychotherapy: A client-centered view. *Annals of Psychotherapy*, 1959, **1**, 51–57. (b)

Rogers, C. R. The process equation of psychotherapy. *Amer. J. Psychotherapy*, 1961, **15**, 27–45. (a)

Rogers, C. R. *On becoming a person*. Boston: Houghton Mifflin, 1961. (b)

Rogers, C. R. The characteristics of a helping relationship. In C. R. Rogers, *On becoming a person*. Boston: Houghton Mifflin, 1961. Chap. 3. (c)

Rogers, C. R. A process conception of psychotherapy. In C. R. Rogers, *On becoming a person*. Boston: Houghton Mifflin, 1961. Chap. 7. (d)

Rogers, C. R. The potential of the human individual: The capacity for becoming fully functioning. Mimeographed paper, University of Wisconsin, 1961. (e)

Rogers, C. R. A therapist's view of the good life: The fully functioning person. In C. R. Rogers (Ed.), *On becoming a person*. Boston: Houghton Mifflin, 1961. Chap. 9. (f)

Rogers, C. R. The interpersonal relationship: The core of guidance. *Harvard Educ. Rev.*, 1962, **32**, 416–429. (a)

Rogers, C. R. Some learnings from a study of psychotherapy with schizophrenics. *Discussion papers, Wisconsin Psychiatric Institute*, No. 27, University of Wisconsin, 1962. (b)

Rogers, C. R. Toward becoming a fully functioning person. In *Perceiving, behaving, becoming*. 1962 Yearbook Association for Supervision and Curriculum Development, National Education Association. (c)

Rogers, C. R. The actualizing tendency in relation to "motives" and to consciousness. *Nebraska symposium on motivation*. Lincoln: University of Nebraska Press, 1963.

Rogers, C. R., & Dymond, Rosalind F. (Eds.) *Psychotherapy and personality change*. Chicago: University of Chicago Press, 1954.

Rogers, C. R., & Wallen, J. L. *Counseling with returned servicemen*. New York: McGraw-Hill, 1946.

Rogers, Natalie. Measuring psychological tension in nondirective counseling. *Personal Counselor*, 1948, **3**, 237–264.

Seeman, J. A study of client self-selection of tests in vocational counseling. *Educ. psychol. Measmt.*, 1948, **8**, 327–346.

Seeman, J. A study of the process of nondirective therapy. *J. consult. Psychol.*, 1949, **13**, 157–168.

Seeman, J., & Raskin, N. J. Research perspective in client-centered therapy. In O. H. Mowrer (Ed.), *Psychotherapy theory and research*. New York: Ronald, 1953. Chap. 9.

Seeman, J. Client-centered therapy. In D. Brower & L. E. Abt (Eds.), *Progress in clinical psychology*, Vol. V. New York: Grune & Stratton, 1956.

Sheerer, Elizabeth T. The relationship between acceptance of self and acceptance of others. *J. consult. Psychol.*, 1949, **13**, 169–175.

Shlein, J. M. Time-limited psychotherapy: An experimental investigation of practical values and theoretical implications. *J. counsel. Psychol.*, 1957, **4**, 318–322.

Shostrom, E. L., & Brammer, L. M. *The dynamics of the counseling process*. New York: McGraw-Hill, 1952.

Snyder, W. U. An investigation of the nature of nondirective psychotherapy. *J. gen. Psychol.*, 1945, **33**, 193–223.

Snygg, D., & Combs, A. W. *Individual behavior: A new frame of reference for psychology*. New York: Harper & Row, 1949.

Standal, S. The need for positive regard: A contribution to client-centered theory. Unpublished doctoral dissertation, University of Chicago, 1954.

Stock, Dorothy. The self-concept and feelings toward others. *J. consult. Psychol.*, 1949, 13, 176–180.

Thetford, W. N. An objective measure of frustration tolerance in evaluating psychotherapy. In W. Wolff (Ed.), *Success in psychotherapy.* New York: Grune & Stratton, 1952. Chap. 2.

Truax, C. B. Elements of psychotherapy. *Discussion papers.* Wisconsin Psychiatric Institute, No. 38, University of Wisconsin, 1962.

Whyte, L. L. *The unconscious before Freud.* London: Tavistock Publications, 1960.

chapter 3

PAUL T. KING | *Psychoanalytic*

Adaptations

Assumptions Regarding the Nature of Man

It is difficult for the layman to regard Freud's theories without being appalled at the basic content and apparent seaminess of his fundamental concepts. Perhaps an early distinction should be made between the psychoanalytically formulated nature of man as perceived by the layman and what was intended by the psychoanalysts in their tentative formulations. The layman's view of psychoanalysis often seems to be that of a system bent on discovering man's basest self and confronting him and society with his rascality and depravity. Often the dominating aura of psychoanalysis eventuates in a perception of man as a fragile, logical, and moralistic organism easily overthrown by an archaic and mysterious unconscious. People find it hard to be dispassionate about such a theory.

Freud and his followers were aware of the impact that his discoveries were having on his contemporaries in Europe, and specifically on the medical students who attended his Vienna lectures during the winter semesters of 1915–1917. Sensing the resistance with which some of his ideas about unconscious motivation were being received, he admonished the interns that by repudiating that which was unfamiliar and distasteful to them, they were repeating the mechanism of the dream structure and were denying his hypotheses a rational and considerate treatment.

Freud and present-day analysts have been subjected to criticism for using this particular type of admonition. The implication that resistance to psychoanalytic theories stems from one's own personal resistance to unconscious motivation rather than to empirical resistance to Freud's idea has been a sore spot to scientifically trained psychologists for a long time. While it is true that many psychoanalytic theories are either presently experimentally unverified or are unverifiable by their nature, much resistance to the acceptance of analytic theory appears to stem from the repulsiveness of the content with which it is concerned. The analytic viewpoint of the nature of man, as it is perceived by the

91

layman, seems more closely linked with the latter type of resistance (resistance to content) than to the former (resistance because of empirical nonverification).

What is the nature of man as seen from a psychoanalytic framework? Semantically oriented analysts point out that there is no nature of man but "natures of men." To the analyst the unique and individual development of each person transcends in importance the common elements that can be ascribed to human beings in general or in a particular culture. His therapy is based on this uniqueness. Also, different schools of analytic thought would regard man's nature from different perspectives with somewhat different "natures" resulting. The classically Freudian school, which gives central importance to the sexual drives, the instinct of aggression, and the significance of biological needs, emerges with a different nature of man than do the nonlibido schools, which emphasize the primary needs of the human self and place the instincts in a secondary position.

Still, certain common denominators about what sort of a being man is do arise from the theoretical fabric of psychoanalysis, and these are capable of being delineated.

Man is born with certain structural limitations that are imposed by the genetic union of his parents. There are certain limits—intellectual, physical, maturational—beyond which it is unreasonable to think any individual organism might go. Such structural restrictions preclude the average man from becoming a theoretical physicist or from pole-vaulting 16 feet. Within these restrictions, however, there is great latitude for personalistic, idiosyncratic development. The ability to discriminate cues afforded by the environment and to base adjustive actions on these discriminations, the severity or munificence of the milieu, and the good fortune one has had in escaping trauma or disease give each person his individuality, but within the structural limits of the organism. Dissension arises between psychoanalytic schools concerning the importance of this environmental molding. The more stringent Freudian position would give preeminence to the biological needs and instincts of the organism.

While man decidedly has been shaped by his environment, man has also modified his environment extensively to meet his demands. Ruth Munroe points out,

> Man proposes to master his environment rather than adapt his body to it, to create a human world in which temperature is regulated by a thermostat instead of a furry skin, in which food comes so regularly and so neatly packaged that he is scarcely aware that the terms of his body require the unsportsmanlike killing of fellow animals on a grand scale. In general, man's needs as an organism, the terms he presents for tenancy on this planet,

have become so confused with the terms he has imposed on his environment that it has become difficult to say where one set of terms leaves off and the other begins (1955, p. 6).

All psychoanalytic schools encompass both concepts of heredity and environment, but differ in the relative importance they attach to each.

Man is seen as being both animalistic and human simultaneously. Man shares with animals his activations of behaviors that serve homeostatic ends—the need for nutritional restoration, elimination, etc. —and his need to reproduce the species and propagate his kind. In addition, man has developed communicative techniques that have liberated him from a more instinctual, animallike existence. As a result of this liberation and the consequent elaboration of the communicative process, man has developed distinctly human qualities cherished by himself and endearing to society. Courage, honor, devotion, and loyalty are essentially human qualities that will vary in form from culture to culture but are almost universally positively regarded. This approaches the lower boundaries of man's spiritual or religious self. These latter qualities man shares minimally, if at all, with animals. So, then, psychoanalytically, man is animalistic, but with something added. To accept man's human self does not deny his animalistic being.

American and European cultures have had difficulty in seeing psychoanalysis in constructive terms in spite of the increasing publicity it has had over the last several decades as a potent and useful therapeutic tool. The layman often fears that the nobility and sublimity of man will be seriously threatened by an acceptance of the tenets of psychoanalysis. Analysts, on the other hand, feel that an acceptance of man's more primitive self in no way attenuates his good qualities but that a lack of acceptance of the more primitive self does not tend to ennoble life but instead makes it incomprehensible.

Freud had this to say about the suppression of unpleasurable psychic content in his ninth lecture which was concerned with dream censorship. The audience was protesting that psychoanalysis was attributing so much of man's behavior to a fundamental, evil predisposition. Freud confronted his audience with their blindness to the egotistical baseness in human nature and man's more or less unreliability in all that concerns sexual life. He further pointed to the war then devastating Europe, hinting that so much destruction could not have been loosed by a few unprincipled, ambitious men if these destructive tendencies were not also present in most of us. Freud says: "It is no part of our intention to deny the nobility in human nature, nor have we done anything to disparage its value. On the contrary, I show you not only the evil wishes that are censored but also the censorship which suppresses them and makes them unrecognizable" (Riviere, 1958, p. 154).

Man's behavior is seen as being determined and capable of being understood in terms of the individual's dynamics, character structure, unconscious motivation, and social learning. There is some overlap in the referents to which these terms apply. Man, only to a limited extent, is master of his fate. He is shaped, goaded, and bent to follow lines of conduct that gratify his basic biological needs, instincts, and instinct derivatives. Behavior, regardless of its significance, cannot be considered accidental or as being too ephemeral or transient to be determined. If we knew enough, it could all be explained, even the most minute parts, although it might not be practicable to do so.

Man's behavior is partly determined by unconscious processes that are motivational and goal-directed in nature. He wishes, wants, fears, and abhors things of which he is consciously unaware. These forces strive for expression, but must be disguised because of their nature and content, which results in man's occasional inexplicable behavior even to himself and leads to the formation of distorted and censoring operations of the ego. One never has access to his unconscious; one can only see its operation and insistence in terms of symbolism and transference manifestations.

Every act is considered to have a double meaning. One meaning is its commonplace, realistic meaning that would characteristically be ascribed to the act by a nonpsychological observer. The other meaning, its symbolic meaning, stems from unconscious and repressed urges and can best be understood in terms of analysis and insight.

Persons are most clearly revealed by examining their past and focusing on their specific lines of genetic development. A longitudinal and historical perspective makes for the most accurate prediction of how an individual might act in the future and gives the most enriched and comprehensive explanation of his present behavior.

> Psychoanalysts differ as to just how early experiences structure later personality trends and as to the specific role of the infantile unconscious. Adler and Horney tend to think of the problem mainly through a more careful interpretation of the old saw: as the twig is bent so the branch inclines. In their view, early experiences set the pattern for later expectations and later techniques of adaptations. Freudians, however, tend to think of a relatively separate history for the various aspects of development, of the actual freezing of some aims at the infantile level by the mechanism of repression, while other aims develop more or less in accordance with the requirements of the social milieu and are only influenced by the persistence of the repressed aims (Munroe, 1955, p. 33).

Whatever the school, all psychoanalysts make use of and respect the genetic approach to understanding human behavior.

The importance of understanding childhood comes from several directions. Childhood is a time when behavior is the most open, flexible, and tractable. It is also a time when emotional experiences tend to be the strongest, and consequently traumas and early learning experiences tend to be overlearned and are instrumental in shaping the character structure of the child.

Assumptions Regarding Changes in Behavior

One of the most frequent questions asked by persons who are in the initial stages of psychological counseling is "How is just talking about my problem going to help?" Often this is followed by the explanation that the person has discussed it before, perhaps with friends or relatives, and has experienced little relief. The prospective client sees little that can be accomplished by talking and is frequently suspicious that the sessions will be an inconvenient waste of time. This attitude is often typical of persons who have sought therapy of their own volition as well as of those who have been urged by friends and relatives who are concerned for the client.

This question needs to be resolved by the beginning client before he is able to make any sort of substantial commitment to psychotherapy or counseling. Many therapists will try to answer this question in a supportive and nontechnical way. This has the effect of reassuring the client that he has come for a definite purpose, and that he can expect a sincere and conscientious effort on the part of the therapist. The therapist may interpret the initial resistance the client has to the commencement of working on his problems which is implied by the question. Frequently the analytically oriented therapist will choose to minimize such support and reassurance by immediately responding to the person's obvious ambivalence and uncertainty about initiating therapy. Such a position would depend on the therapist's estimate of the client's ego strength, the maladjustment with which he is suffering, and assessments of his anxiety and maturity. In general, reassurance would seem more appropriate with narcissistically regressed clients or those who would defect in therapy without early indications of authoritative help on the part of the therapist.

Brenner (1955), in speaking of research, mentions several psychoanalytic principles which he feels must be accepted as valid from the outset. These principles seem to be equally applicable to analytically oriented counseling. On the basis of these assumptions, the counselor will apply his therapeutic vigor with the expectation that the client will be improved by this process. Let us take a look at these assumptions.

The therapist will assume the existence of unconscious mental processes, such as urges, wishes, and fears, of which the client is unaware. He will also accept as valid certain characteristics of the operation of the primary process, including symbolism. He will regard the primary process as placing continuous demands on the ego to find outlets for gratification, and he will regard the content of the primary process as timeless, that is, repressed material which, when discharged, appears as fresh and as real as at the time of the original repression.

He would also accept as valid the separation of the *functions* of the mind into ego, superego, and id. He would tend to concentrate particularly on the concept of conflict between impulses of the id and the defenses of the ego and on the relation of such conflicts to anxiety and pain.

The attitude toward anxiety is of central importance in psychoanalytic thinking, although the explanations of how it emerges and what functions it performs for the organism are varied and contested. Whatever anxiety is, it seems to be something to which the organism is extremely sensitive and when it occurs in large doses, can find intolerable.

Because of anxiety's central position in psychoanalytic theory, it seems necessary to avoid an oversimplification of the concept and to give the reader some feeling for its complexity. The following discussion of anxiety has this as its purpose.

Freud, while not overlooking the importance of environmental influences, related anxiety to instinctual sources in keeping with his consistent biological position. Culturally oriented analysts (Fromm, Horney, Sullivan) feel inner impulses arise through the mediation of cultural pressures, which, if repressed, are perceived as a frustration of the person's potentialities with consequent hostility, renewed repression, and anxiety. Baura (1955, p. 95) reports in summarizing Horney's position on anxiety, "The development of anxiety would not be seen as the expression of the ego's fear of being overwhelmed by instincts or by being punished by the superego but as a failure of specific safety devices erected against external dangers."

Zetzel (1955) points out two sets of variables in connection with anxiety: (1) anxiety as an exaggerated response to minimal external danger and (2) anxiety as identical with normal fear but arising in response to an internal subjective threat.

She also says that unrelieved external dangers from which flight is impossible produces reactions indistinguishable from pathological anxiety.

Zetzel (1955) and Rangell (1955) both differentiate between primary anxiety and secondary, or signal, anxiety.

Anxiety seems likely to occur when the ego is confronted by threat from within which it can neither bind nor discharge. This primary anxiety is a reaction to danger, the danger being a continuance or worsening of the helpless state in which the ego is threatened with overthrow or extinction. It is traumatic in nature.

Signal anxiety operates in a different manner. It, too, is a response to danger, but the anxiety, being less intense, is welcomed by the organism as a warning of impending trouble that can now be avoided. The person is able to make some constructive use of the warning message. Under conditions in which the ego is weakened or regressed, the discharge of anxiety becomes more diffuse and explosive, the use of anxiety as a signal degenerates, with a consequent loss of effective action. Rangell sees anxiety, signal or traumatic, as a physiological reaction to danger perceived by the person and suffered, not produced, by the ego.

There is some speculation that the early mother-child relationship determines the ability of the ego to handle stimulation and manifest anxiety of the signal type, which implies the ability to withstand tension. Zetzel (1955) feels that the ability to tolerate anxiety and to avoid denying it is a vital prerequisite for healthy character development.

The author has taken the liberty of going beyond the concept of anxiety and including other negative states of the organism in order to point out two unique and appealing positions taken by Lilly (1960) and Jacobson (1953).

Jacobson reconciles tension and discharge theories of affects (anxiety could be included here) by suggesting that affects are better understood in terms of energic flux on either side of a median line. This seems to imply, according to Kaywin (1960), that beyond a certain intensity, biological and physiological processes will *always* be perceived unpleasurably (anxiety?) or painfully and, in the extreme, lead to shock and death. Pleasurable perception is confined within conditioning limits. Kaywin states, "Whether it will or will not be pleasurable will be relatively determined, depending upon factors which may simply be described as the state of the organism relative to a particular reaction pattern at the moment" (1960, p. 638). It seems plausible that mild stimuli can be perceived as pleasurable, but when these stimuli are intensified, they are capable of arousing anxiety.

Lilly (1960) discusses reward and punishment systems in the brain, one subserving pleasurable sensations and activities, the other subserving punishments, painful and angry kinds of sensations, activities, and reactions.

In discussing a psychophysiological basis for two kinds of instincts,

Lilly lists several points in sequence that support his hypothesis: (1) When spots of extreme neuronal activity are introduced into these systems by emplanted electrodes, fully developed affects, emotions, and instincts are observed behaviorally. (2) Research has indicated that there are two-way connections between these reward and punishment systems and the cortex and also with systems lower down within the brain stem and spinal cord. (3) It is possible that sufficiently strong stimuli applied elsewhere in the brain will overflow into these reward or punishment systems to render them active in the same sense that weak electrical stimuli would. For example, it would be possible for a loud noise, by overflow into a punishment system, to create the feeling of fear.

In experiments with monkeys, death seemed imminent when negative systems of the brain were stimulated for too long a period of time, but behavioral reversal could be induced by stimulating a reward system. Lilly says, "One cannot conceive of any ego functions without some sort of rewarding and punishing going on concomitantly and continuously. . . . These rewarding and punishing systems must be continuously operative in greatly differentiated detail in all aspects of waking and sleeping life" (1960, p. 663).

This comparatively lengthy but still insufficient discussion of anxiety is introduced to stress the enormous complexity of the concept of anxiety. Readers should beware of closing prematurely on a simplified notion of anxiety or of allowing their thinking about it to be circumscribed by the influence of a particular theory.

One of the essential aims, then, of any psychoanalytically oriented theory is to reduce the anxiety of the client to manageable limits in order for the ego to function in a more discriminating and effective manner. The goals of counseling and the role of the counselor will be taken up in later sections. Now we are concerned with how the analytic process works, how anxiety is reduced, and how the ego is strengthened.

The position taken in this chapter is closer to Freudian psychoanalysis than to any of the other psychoanalytic schools. In terms of understanding how behavioral changes are effected by the use of psychoanalytic methods, it seems appropriate to give the reader an account—although greatly abbreviated and with many omissions—of the process as it would occur in full-scale analysis as opposed to adaptations of psychoanalytic principles.

The primary task of the client in therapy is to talk. Without productivity on the part of the client, the resolution of emotional problems is impossible, and the work of the therapist is effectively thwarted. In most instances, long and pointed silences will be identified as resistance in its most primitive form, with some few exceptions.

This is an outgrowth of one of the basic assumptions of psychoanalysis: the idea of intrapsychic conflict. This conflict is caused by a force or tendency residing in the preconscious that opposes direct and immediate discharge of instinctual energy. This element became manifest clinically in the resistance to recollection and verbalization and manifest genetically in the tendency to repress or censor thoughts, wishes, or other tendencies derived from the sexual drives.

Arlow says, "Verbalization is perceived as representing the substitutive discharge of quantities of controllable energies for the more massive discharge in action or symptoms of the highly mobile cathexes of the unconscious system" (1961, p. 46). Through speaking, the client weakens repressive forces in his personality and allows for the draining off of pent-up feelings and bound energy.

As the client becomes progressively desensitized to elements within himself that were previously sensed as threatening, less energy is used by the ego to maintain its defenses, and more energy is available for the cognitive and rational processes of the ego which are needed to grapple with reality and to meet the id demands for finding outlets for instinctual expression.

As new insights are formed and new emotional linkages are perceived, there is an increasing relaxation of ego defensiveness during which the person feels on better terms with himself and under less internal strain. The ability of the ego to use realistic and delaying tactics in dealing with unconscious emotional drives is increased as well as the ability to make fine, discriminative judgments. These judgments, generally negative in nature, have the character of indicating to the client that "this is different from that." For example, as therapy progresses and the meaning of the transference is understood, the client is able to tell the differences between a boss who is irritable due to a gruelling day and a punitive father on whom his economy of happiness used to depend. Or, that a coquettish young lady who flashes him an obscure smile does not harbor the predatory attitude toward men that he sensed in his mother.

With an expanding capacity to make discriminations of this sort, the client feels a growing ability to master problems in the real world that confront him as well as a lessened intimidation from unconscious urges, which are now emerging and more clearly seen for what they are—childhood residue.

Now more of the total energy of the person is enmeshed with the world outside his skin, he is finding a constructive use for his potentialities, and there is a constant discharge of affect into the real world that makes for a sharpening of the sense of reality, a clearer delineation of the boundaries of the ego (what is me and not me), and diminished feelings of morbidity.

The dislodging of a psychoneurotic condition ultimately requires a total emotional confrontation by the client of his psychoneurotic way of life and the masochism, agony, dulled awareness, predicaments, burning resentment, loneliness, etc., that are a part of it. Also required is a keen awareness of precisely what anticipated or real tragedy this psychoneurotic structure shielded him from. The high point in discrimination is reached when the client is capable of laying the past and present side by side and distinguishing the dead world from the live one.

Although this account of the process by which a client changes from poor to good mental health is short in the telling, the process itself will often require more than one hundred interviews with clients showing expected spurts of progress, backsliding, and lingering on plateaus that are unavoidably a part of therapy but that rarely make good reading. Therapeutic ascent is by no means steady, and the therapist who expects it should be aware of his own regressive and narcissistic anticipations.

The process by which persons are rescued from the doldrums of emotional ill health can be described in language easily understood by persons involved in counseling and clinical practice. At least, we think we understand it. If it is written lucidly enough, it should be understandable to nonpsychologically oriented persons also. We are sometimes caught in the dilemma of speaking a language that makes for clinical communication and at the same time feeling insecurity because the concepts are not couched in more scientific terms or conceptualized physiologically.

The position of aiming for a physiological translation of analytic hypotheses is expressed by Feigl

> Future scientific developments may be expected to couch such concepts as unconscious wishes, urges, or conflicts as postulated by such depth psychologists or psychoanalysts much more fruitfully in the language of neurophysiology and endocrinology. This certainly reminds one of some of the earlier statements of Freud on the relation of mental to physical phenomenon and is still heard today with remarkable frequency being promulgated as the foundation of the future program of the behavioral sciences (1960, p. 33).

An opposing point of view is indicated by Hoffman

> I am not sure whether those analysts who flirt with physiological conceptualization of analytic hypotheses realize that to some extent, at least, they

buy into a system the data of which is collected in a form altogether alien to that of their own science, and thereby throw a shadow over the validity of the work—that is, introspective and empathic, in which they are actually engaged (1962, p. 65).

There seems to be some justification, at this point anyway, for retaining a decidedly humanistic and personal flavor to counseling and therapy and to conceptualize it in terms that are the most communicative to both clients and other professional workers. Perhaps the language of psychoanalysis has been remiss in this respect.

Goals of Counseling

Counselors and counseling psychologists are found in various places such as high schools, university counseling centers, industry, mental hospitals, and community services, to name a few. Although some common counseling goals could be claimed by persons working in all these places, more often the individual setting will influence and delimit what the counselor can hope or expect to accomplish.

The type of problems the counselor is likely to encounter, the freedom with which the counselor may see clients with emotional problems over long periods of time, and the type of counseling that is "acceptable" will often be policy decisions made by the agency for which the counselor works.

Characteristically, high school counselors will not be as free as counselors in university centers to see clients over an extended period of time or for more serious emotional problems.[1] Counselors working in

---

[1] No distinction is being made here between personal adjustment counseling and psychotherapy, as the author feels that no line between these two concepts could be drawn on a reasonable and meaningful basis, and even if it could, it is beyond the scope of this chapter to attempt to make this distinction.

I feel that it is semantic nonsense to ask questions such as, "Where does counseling end and psychotherapy begin?" or "Are psychoanalytic techniques appropriate to counseling?" This implies that we know the limits or boundaries of what constitutes counseling, psychotherapy, or psychoanalysis, and of course there are no such clear delineations. All three concepts might be subsumed under the larger abstract of "helping people." One might facetiously ask, "Where does chemistry end and physics begin?" Both are subordinate to the larger concept of physical science. Few persons would lose sleep over such a problem. For example, at one end of a helping-people scale, a "helper" might be dealing with strong emotionality in the client, using free association or free imagery, interpreting behavior, inducing regression, etc. At the other end of the dimension, a "helper" might be dealing with cognitive reorganization, improving study techniques, providing information about vocational choices, coaching for social poise, etc. We should have little difficulty in labeling the first type of helping behavior, psychotherapy. The latter type we could easily label coun-

mental hospitals will find their efforts essentially focused on vocational problems, whereas counselors in community agencies find many opportunities to work with emotional problems as well as vocational.

The application of psychoanalytic principles will ordinarily have more relevance where personality factors are involved and where the counselor has the freedom to see certain clients for many interviews. However, psychoanalytic formulations of problems encountered by counselors in other settings and with other than emotional problems would seem to find some use.

People wend their way to counselors' offices because they are unhappy in some respect. The degree of this unhappiness varies from minimal to severe, and the things about which a person can be unhappy are apparently limitless—poor grades, trouble with parents, social awkwardness, sex, feelings of unworthiness, ad infinitum. Counselors, according to their theoretical positions, will choose to help these persons by using techniques with which they are most familiar and secure. A danger arises when counselors tend to perceive client problems in terms of their own special area of interest or capability, for example, the vocational counselor who perceives most of his clients as being unhappy because of vocational maladjustment or, conversely, the analytically trained counselor who feels that trouble on the job is invariably traceable to the client's troubled childhood. The predispositions of both counselors seem likely to do a disservice to the client.

A fundamental goal of counseling is to help a person solve a problem and to feel better after doing it. Analytically trained counselors tend to build up a case load of persons with minor emotional problems. These problems would ordinarily not be severe enough for referral to a psychiatrist and would be ones with which the counselor feels he could be effective within a reasonable time limit. A "reasonable time limit" often depends on the policy of the agency in which the counselor is employed. In some agencies, counselors find considerable leniency in the amount of time they are free to devote to a client, some of whom may receive as many as one hundred interviews or more. These clients are not typical ones, however. The twenty- to fifty-interview range for personal adjustment clients is more common.

---

seling. Where these two concepts merge somewhere in the middle, we are apt to experience semantic confusion and often try rigidly to define what one class of behavior *is* in terms of what the other *is not*. Reality rarely provides the opportunity for a nice fitting of this type of Aristotelian thinking or labeling. The dimension adumbrated above is that of "depth." This depth dimension should not be identified as a significance-nonsignificance dimension, nor should it be identified as a prestige-nonprestige dimension, etc. Dimensions should be evaluated on their own merits and not as integral parts of other dimensions, or adjuncts.

The analytically trained counselor would regard his clients in certain fundamental ways on which he would base his constructive action. Principally, he would view his client as having psychological processes of which he is unconscious as well as those of which he is conscious. He would feel that behavior is shaped in every moment of existence by an interaction of conscious and unconscious processes. He would pay particular attention to whether the unconscious factors in the personality were dominating or interfering with the client's behavior. He would feel that behavior could not be materially changed without ascertaining what these factors were. He would anticipate meeting resistances in the client that might require certain techniques to overcome. His aim would be to bring these unconscious conflicts under the domain of conscious control.

Kubie (1950) lists three types of psychotherapy: (1) Simple, nontechnical, nonanalytic psychotherapy which deals with conscious situational problems and conflicts. This will usually involve support, guidance, advice, or assistance in handling life situations. (2) Analytically informed psychotherapy, which may be both palliative and expressive. The therapist is alert to the interplay of unconscious forces and the way in which they affect the person's symptoms. (3) Analysis itself, The crux of which is an effort to share with the client full insight into his unconscious mechanism. A primary tool for this is the interpretation of transference.

Counselors with analytic training will usually operate between levels two and three. Some counselors will aim at bringing about a deep reorganization of the personality, which would require the client to recapture and express strong emotional feelings. This reduces the intensity of the repressed affect, and, if accompanied by emotional insights of sufficient depth, is capable of modifying and restructuring the personality.

Some counselors will aim at the goal of showing the person how to live within the confines of his psychoneurosis with as little discomfort as possible. With such techniques, the counselor ordinarily will not require the client to abreact his most deeply repressed feelings, although some emotional expression by the client is always sought for. The length of time required for this type of therapy is shorter. The overt behavior of the client will frequently be interpreted, and the symbolic meaning of his symptoms will be discussed. The counselor tries to give the client more cognitive control over his affect by siding with the ego, as it were, in its effort to handle the partially repressed primary process, rather than allowing the unconscious feelings to be expressed with full intensity.

In short-term therapy, the client's emotional transference to the counselor does not develop to the extent that it does in therapy that goes on for a longer period of time. Occasionally, the counselor will use techniques such as free imagery, hypnosis, or multiple therapy (discussed in the next section) to bring unconscious material to light that would ordinarily be revealed in transference phenomena, although the use of these techniques is not excluded when a more complete job of therapy is attempted.

Some university counseling centers and community counseling agencies provide the opportunity for clients to undergo deep, reconstructive psychotherapy in which the maximum therapeutic use of transference can be made.

Evan defines transference ". . . as a regressive discharge mechanism by which repressed impulses are repeated in the therapy situation and shifted via phantasy gratification from unconsciousness to consciousness where they are made accessible to the analytic work of transition from primary to secondary process" (1961, p. 28).

Although the principle goal of counseling is to help the person solve a problem, one of the most important subgoals is the establishment and working through of the emotionally transferred feelings that the client has for the counselor. The nonresolution of transference in the counseling relationship allows the client to maintain his infantile, narcissistic attitudes toward life and to continue his nonsatisfying relationships with people. The relationship between the counselor and client is the essence of psychoanalytic therapy and must be thoroughly understood in all its manifestations before the client can be expected to change fundamentally.

Transference in the counseling relationship never has to be created by the counselor but can be expected to develop spontaneously (Kubie, 1950). It appears to be a compulsive function of the psyche, and transference phenomena are observable even in the best adjusted individuals.

According to Ruesch (1955) it springs from early childhood situations in which experiences are overly intense and are more related to nonverbal than to verbal cues. It gathers momentum when the possibility of varied contact between individuals is reduced, when the exchange of messages becomes redundant, or when feedback phenomena cannot be relied on to correct distorted impressions.

One of the essential goals of therapy, then, is to improve the ability of the client to communicate and to reduce the inequality in the past development of verbal and nonverbal communication. Ruesch, in discussing some of the goals of therapy, says, "If the therapist's endeavor is directed at improving the patient's ability to communicate, the patient will eventually be able to relate with progressively lessening transference" (1955, p. 39).

The counseling process aims to disrupt the current life theme of the person and to establish a new and more satisfying one (Mullan, 1960). The deeply entrenched, habitual ways of adjusting that are unsatisfying will need to be interrupted and modified if the client is to improve. The therapeutic encounter has this as its purpose. There are several built-in aspects to the therapy process that effectively bring about this end. Although the client brings his history into the interview, the relationship is immediately spontaneous; it has no background. The atmosphere within the therapy hour is timeless: The past, present, and future are telescoped into one. The domain of the interview hour is all embracing (Mullan, 1960). Two persons are present, cloistered within the therapy room, each giving the other his total attention. There is the feeling of a fresh beginning. All of this acts to change the client's typical way of behaving, broadens the scope of his awareness, and gives him more living room.

Another goal of counseling would be the revitalization of the client, increasing his ability to get along with others. Meerloo (1962) says that one characteristic of almost every sort of growth is an alternating forward and backward movement rather than a continuous steady progress. It is seen in all phases of life, from the neurotic person enmeshed with his fixations to the repair of cellular damage due to pathology or disease.

The controlled regression that occurs during the counseling process has a revitalizing effect on the client. Often clients seem goaded to tear themselves down and resurrect themselves in a way that feels looser, more adaptive, and satisfying. Usually, this retrogenesis—this going back and putting things together anew—results in a reacceptance of people and an increased tolerance for their humanness. These effects are more easily seen in spontaneous regression that occurs when people take vacations, forget their cares, and renew their spirits. Human relationships during these times often take a turn for the better.

The Role of the Counselor

This section will indicate some of the general tasks of the analytically oriented counselor, showing his role during the interview hour and then demonstrating his functioning in more specific situations.

It is the responsibility of the counselor to engender an atmosphere of security, in which the client is able to discuss the most intimate matters with feelings of trust and confidence. The counselor should appear professional in manner without being formal or stiff. Although frequent expressions of empathic understanding are used by the counselor, it should not be perceived by the client or counselor as the mothering of a lonely child.

The task of the counselor is to keep the client at the job of producing material and actively attempting to uncover repressed or conflictful content. This does not mean that the counselor demands incessant conversation from the client because many occasions will occur when the client appears to "run dry" and is unable to produce anything relevant. These temporary lapses are understood by the counselor but are not allowed to continue for too long or to occur too frequently. The responsibility for the production of the material rests on the client, although when particularly strong resistances are met, the counselor may use special techniques to assist the client. The client should never get the feeling that the burden for his improvement rests with the counselor.

The counselor will make initial judgments whether the individual client is suitable for the particular type of therapy that he offers. Certain types of character structures are not suitable for analytically oriented counseling, and it is up to the counselor to protect his clients from long therapeutic encounters in which the client cannot be aided.

Nacht (1955) feels that clients whose anxiety is not too acute and whose anxiety has not been structuralized into phobic or obsessional symptons are most amenable to therapy. However, analytically oriented counseling could be considered effective with clients who present mild free anxiety, phobic symptoms, or symptoms of an obsessive-compulsive nature. Depressed clients and those with moderately severe marital problems in which the possibility of divorce is remote seem to respond well to therapy.

Therapy is contraindicated for clients who show schizoid personalities, paranoid states, or severe hypochondriasis, and the prognosis is guarded for persons with marked conversion symptoms. Sometimes persons in this latter group respond to more directive, supportive therapy, but results are often impermanent because of the plasticity of the ego. Treatment is rarely indicated for persons who have a history of habitual delinquency or drug addiction.

Although the counselor is warm, sincere, and understanding in his encounter with the client, he also maintains a therapeutic atmosphere that is, at the same time, depriving and nongratifying of some of the client's most basic aims. The counselor, in frustrating the direct gratification of these aims, becomes a loved but frustrating object. This lack of gratification for the client facilitates regression which is necessary for the reduplication of infantile conflicts within the therapy situation (Fleming, 1961). The client struggles for the fulfillment of his passive dependency needs with the therapist, and when these needs are not gratified, the client's urge to know himself and to communicate this to the counselor takes precedence. This need to know and communicate would seem to be an essential condition if the therapeutic process is to achieve its purpose.

The counselor will often have to make judgments about the use of special techniques and methods to facilitate the therapeutic work. Clients frequently encounter hard-shelled resistances that delay the course of treatment for extended periods. Although some clients simply need additional time for further exploration of these blockages for them to dissolve, others will require the use of special means to penetrate them. Free imagery, multiple therapy, and the setting of termination dates are techniques which help the client through resistant periods in his therapy.

Free imagery [2] is a technique that asks the client to relax as completely as possible and to report to the counselor the visual images that occur. The technique has the effect of reducing contact with reality, which diminishes the controlling functions of the ego and allows unconscious material to be expressed.

Multiple therapy ordinarily employs two counselors with one client. In this situation the dynamic complexity of the therapy relationship is enormously increased in such a way that the client finds it difficult to gear his old defenses to the new situation. Also, as the client usually accords superior status to the counselor, the original family constellation of mother and father is effectively reduplicated.

The setting of a specific termination date sometimes puts an end to the resistance to certain transference and countertransference phenomena with the result that the relationship gathers new meaning, and new insights are gained.

The counselor who uses such techniques will need to familiarize himself with indications and contraindications for their employment.

The counselor who does therapy has a paramount obligation to understand his own feelings throughout the therapeutic process as well as the feelings of his client. Colm (1955) feels that the essential part of therapy comes when the therapist is able to contact the center area of the field of experiences of the client, as opposed to contact with the client's defensive fringe area. This center-to-center contact can only be established if the therapist is aware of his own feelings about the

[2] The pioneering work in free imagery has been done by Joe Reyher, Michigan State University.

client. If center-to-center contact has been established, decidedly negative attitudes may be expressed by the therapist or the client without
damaging the relationship.

After the therapist has reached a point where the client is fully
involved in the transference relationship, failure of therapy from that
point on is usually traceable to the counselor rather than to some
inability on the part of the client. Such failures often arise from the
counselor's unawareness of and inability to handle his countertransference. Siegman (1955) points out that the client's perception of the
counselor as an omnipotent person or magician exacerbates the counselor's guilt-laden Oedipal wish to displace the awesome rival parent,
which can thus become a significant source of countertransference.

Positive transference can be more difficult for the counselor to handle than its negative counterpart because of the guilt that it produces
in the counselor. Such guilt will tend to make the counselor disturb the
positive transference by ill-timed interpretations and to look overly
hard for signs of negative transference. He might also divest himself
too early of the powers granted to him by the client, with an interruption of the therapy relationship. In psychoanalytically oriented counseling, the resolution of the emotional transference seen in the therapy
relationship is crucial.

The role of the counselor demands that he be aware of his function
and responsibility within the therapy hour. He should understand the
way in which he may be used within the interview to be of the most
service to the client—his therapeutic participation, in other words.

The counselor needs to devote all his attention to understanding the
productions of the client. To understand the client, he must have
access to his own unconscious but still fall short of regressive daydreaming to meet his own unfulfilled needs. His ego processes must be
available for use by the client, performing the function of subjecting to
reality the associations and productions of the person in therapy
(Fleming, 1961). Fleming says, "The therapist, then, must function in
two worlds simultaneously, the client's world and his own, a real world
and an unreal one, the past as well as the present. He must perform
this function while maintaining his own integrated position" (1961, p.
705).

The Link between Counseling and Psychoanalysis

The application of psychoanalytic techniques to counseling practice is
greatly restricted when the counseling is done in an educational setting. In a high school the restriction is even greater than in a college.

One may consider the application of psychoanalytic theory from two points of view. The first view would be that of therapeutic intervention, or the modification of the life adjustment of the individual by psychotherapy. To the extent that psychoanalysis attempts to deal with unconscious motives and conflicts that shape the person's behavior, many therapeutic interviews over prolonged periods of time are usually required. For example, a masochistic or self-defeating life orientation in a high school student will not be undone in a few interviews. As was mentioned before, some college counseling centers allow students to be seen for as many interviews as are required, but even these centers tend, in general, to discourage prolonged therapy. Consequently, if one looks for the application of psychoanalytic theory from the therapeutic intervention point of view—the doing of therapy —in education settings, especially in high schools, he will find it an inconvenient and unsought after technique.

If one considers psychoanalytic theory from a second point of view, that of providing a frame of reference for evaluating the behavior and personality structure of clients, then, even in educational settings, psychoanalytic theory can be useful.

Much seemingly inexplicable behavior in a student's interaction with teachers and school officials can take on new meaning when seen in the light of transferred attitudes carried over from the student's home life. A child who repeatedly displaces his original hostility toward his mother onto a teacher may enter a vicious downward spiral of rejection, bewilderment, and increased acting-out behavior unless the displaced and unconscious aspects of his conflict are explained, if only to the teacher. Of course, the counselor must have additional outside information on which to base his interpretation and must avoid the absurdity of labeling *all* hostile behavior as displaced and unconscious.

Inappropriate dependency or love attachments may be viewed in a similar manner—as expressing impulses whose original aims and objects have been unconsciously inhibited by the student for security reasons. When a counselor, sure of his information on the basis of repeated observations of such behavior and with test data and knowledge of the student's external environment, is able to interpret this behavior to the educator, a great deal of confusion may be eliminated.

Tactful discussions and cautious interpretations to the parents can often be helpful in easing the student's problem by giving them an understanding of his behavior. Counselors, acting as consultants, are often able to restore emotional equanimity to educators who have become involved in transference situations with students when these educators are able to perceive the *substitute* character of their participation. The anxiety and feelings of loss of control provoked by being intimately entangled in a relationship that they do not understand is thereby reduced. The counselor or school psychologist may wish to work with the student himself by nonanalytic techniques, but the help he can give significant persons in the student's environment may be considerable.

An understanding of personality or character structure can be useful in evaluating the constructive action that needs to be taken with certain clients, and the range of hit-or-miss remediation can be narrowed. It is not implied that only psychoanalytic theory can supply this understanding.

Suppose that a young high school student is unable to engage in activities that involve direct competition, any avenue of participation that remotely involves failure is scrupulously avoided, and mild obsessive-compulsive symptoms are evident. The counselor *tentatively* hypothesizes an early wound to the student's narcissism—an interaction with a person that prevented him from being able to continue to love himself—and he also senses the hostile undergirdings of the student's personality. He would be aware of the effectiveness of the student's obsessive-compulsive ego defenses and consequently would not expect to relate to the student easily and quickly. The counselor might arrive at a tentative dynamic formulation of the problem: The student seems to have equated opportunity for failure with loss of his parents' love and his own self-love with consequent fury at this anticipated deprivation. His meticulousness and compulsivity represent safety for him, as he uses them to bind back his aggressiveness toward others and toward himself. These defenses are therefore self-corrective in nature.

The counselor might then wish to set up some situations in real life where the student could risk competition with fear of failure minimized. Or the counselor might wish to set up a role-playing situation with several students in which the client may experience failure in a protected situation and thereby begin to reassess his attitudes about failing. There would be no attempt here to get the student to reexperience the original traumas or to reclaim the original affect.

The point of view that psychoanalysis provides a way of thinking about motivation, a framework in which troublesome behavior or feelings may be understood, would seem to be compatible with the aims of counseling psychology.

Place of Diagnosis

Screening interviews. The screening interview is used by the counselor as a means of arriving at a quick, initial impression of the client's suitability for counseling. During this first meeting, the counselor will judge whether the client falls within the limits of service offered by the institution for which he works, and within the bounds of his own personal competence. He will wish to avoid encouraging persons who are too emotionally ill to be seen, or who have problems of such a nature that his particular type of counseling would not help, e.g., signs of mental retardation or organic brain damage.

Part of his responsibility may be to find a place which offers appropriate help for the individual.

The client is allowed to tell the reason that brought him to the counselor, but ordinarily he is not permitted to go deeply into his feelings about the problem, as it is unlikely that the intake interviewer will also be the client's therapist.

The counselor tries to find out the obvious things in the person's life such as hospitalization for emotional illness, nervous breakdowns, periods of long physical illnesses in which the client was confined at home or in a hospital that will help the counselor decide about his suitability as a client. He will also want to know about the client's present ability to function in his environment. This will necessitate some inquiry into how much emotional pain and suffering the client is enduring and how he is trying to handle it. The counselor will wish to know any immediate plans or actions that the client is anticipating, e.g., leaving school, suicide, or delinquent episodes.

The client's mannerisms that would have some relevance to therapy are observed, for example, extreme posturing or nervous fidgeting. Mainly, the counselor attends to the client's way of relating to him as a person. Evidence of pronounced withdrawal, inability to communicate, indications of explosive hostility, or hints of acute panic can be used to help the counselor make his decision about the disposition of this client—to take him in therapy, refer him to a psychiatrist, request a neurological examination, etc.

If the counselor remains uncertain about what to do with the client, he may wish to see him again for a more complete social case history and psychodiagnostic testing.

Tests.   The analytically oriented counselor will find tests useful on many occasions, but most often he will gather his information as the client begins to unfold himself in the therapy process. The counselor will sometimes need to make a judgment about a client prior to accepting him for counseling. For example, there may be some question as to the emotional health of the client or some uncertainty as to whether counseling would be profitable for him. This would need to be assessed before he was accepted for therapy. Or, the counselor may be called upon to perform a diagnostic function where no therapy is involved. A client may be referred by an outside agency for a diagnostic evaluation to help that agency make the proper disposition of him. In such instances, the counselor would use tests in the typical diagnostic sense.

Recently, tests of the Thematic Apperception Test variety have been used as a means of getting the client to talk, rather than for its primary diagnostic use. Used in this manner, the test material is presented to the client and is used as a starting point to help him express some of his own problems. After the client is able to take off on his own without the use of the primers, the test material is discontinued.

The counselor uses his knowledge of the language of symbolism in understanding the protocols of projective tests, such as the Rorschach and the TAT. In general, the material elicited by the test will be understood by the counselor as expressing basic attitudes toward the client's parents, siblings, or himself or revealing instinctual wishes and impulses that have been, or need to be, expressed toward others, and attitudes toward his own body parts or zones.

It is not unusual and decidedly beneficial to have a two-hour interview with the client before the tests are administered. This gives the counselor some real-world knowledge of the client and a frame of reference in which to place the test material. Probably nothing is more untenable than a blind diagnosis of personality from a projective technique. Diagnostic testing and diagnostic interviewing are both subsumed under the general purpose of finding out about the client and each should be thought of as aiding and abetting the other.

Clients often transfer the emotional attitudes they had toward significant figures in their past toward the test and test interpretations. They will adopt passive attitudes and expect the test to reach immutable conclusions for them, pointing out courses of action. Or, they can feel resentful and oppositional toward the test as if they had somehow been deprived or scolded by it. Clients may feel fearful of the test as if they expected some sort of narcissistic injury from the results. Occasionally, these attitudes may be interpreted when the counselor feels that they are almost obvious to the client and are likely to be accepted.

These attitudes not only become attached to the tests but to the counselor as well. When these transferred attitudes dominate to the extent that realistic information given during the test interpretation is resisted and cannot be made use of, therapy is often indicated to reduce the symbolic and neurotic process so that factual information can be assimilated. If this is impracticable for some reason, one sterile interview is usually the result.

Case histories. Case histories, like tests, may perform a safety function for the counselor. Carefully collected case histories provide a thorough chronological account of the client's past as perceived by him and often will reveal periods of emotional instability or areas of conflict that may be useful in directing the attention of the therapist at a later date.

If the counselor feels a social case history is appropriate, he may wish to allow the client to tell his history in a manner that seems most natural to him, rather than interrogating him. When the client unfolds his past in his own way, it is the responsibility of the counselor to organize this information in a meaningful and chronological order and to fill in the gaps and omissions by unobtrusive questioning. It is prudent for the counselor to have his own goal, that of collecting information, clearly in mind during this process and to discourage this process from becoming a therapeutic one. In the event this happens, and if the counselor then decides that the client is not a suitable candidate for therapy, the client may feel already committed to therapy and suffer a wrench in his feelings when not allowed to continue. It is sometimes enough to tell the client that the decision about therapy will be made after the information is collected. This will occasionally protect the counselor from seeing a client for personal adjustment counseling who has spent several years in a hospital for schizophrenic illness and who may be a vastly unsuitable therapy candidate.

Interpretation, advice, and persuasion. It is most consonant with analytic theory for the counselor to feel that the client has the facts that pertain to his personal tragedy or problems and that he must be allowed to tell it in his own way. The prevailing attitude of the counselor is one of absorbed listening, while conveying to the client that the responsibility for the production of his life material resides with him.

Although the responsibility for therapeutic movement and self-betterment rests with the client, while the therapist remains passive and unobtrusive, there are times when he will choose to use the authority freely granted him by the client to perform certain therapeutic tasks.

One of the main functions of the therapist is to employ the rational, elaborative processes of his own ego to help the client understand the symbolic meaning of the material he has produced.

It is quite typical for the client well along in therapy to report the dreams he has had since the last meeting. If the client is unable to understand the meaning of the dream for himself, it is necessary for the counselor to use his knowledge of the client's dynamics, which has been gathered from previous dream material and the reporting of the client's life experiences, to help with the interpretation of the dream symbols. Good interpretations are those that are properly timed and gauged to the client's ability to assimilate them. The "when" and the "how" are beyond the scope of this chapter. An interpretation that reaches far beyond the client's awareness usually fortifies the resistance to this insight and delays the work of the therapist.

Interpretation finds its greatest use in helping the client resolve the transference that occurs during long-term therapy. The client's resistance is greatest to the understanding of the true meaning of his transferred feelings about the counselor. Continuous interpretation and explanation of every facet of the relationship between the therapist and client is required in order to dislodge the infantile neurosis that is reenacted during therapy.

Interpretation and persuasion may be used conjointly during the early stages of counseling when an effort is being made to get the client to suppress his symptoms in order that the conflicts underlying them may come to light. The counselor may use his authority to request that the client inhibit his usual symptomatic means of reducing his anxiety and sustain the discomfort that heightened anxiety entails. This will often produce a conflict in the client between wanting to obey the therapist and wanting to find relief from anxiousness by a reactivation of his old symptom complex.

If the client is able to grant the therapist's request and suppress his symptoms, this has the effect of withdrawing the libido from the symptoms (the symptoms tranference) and freeing the libido temporarily before it finds another anchorage on the person of the counselor. This makes for the development of the necessary transference relationship between the client and the counselor.

Advice finds little acceptance in analytically oriented counseling after counseling has progressed to any significant degree. Counselors will occasionally need to advise their clients in the management of life situations before the client has committed himself to therapy, if the counselor foresees that therapy could be wrecked by some imprudent action before it is really commenced. After a significant therapy relationship has been established, the interpretation of resistance to recovery would be substituted for advice.

Intrusion of values. It is not the task of the counselor to get the client to adopt the value system of another person, and this refers to the counselor himself. One of the most stultifying positions for a therapist to take is the one that urges the client to substitute the therapist's values for his own. The therapist's mode of adjustment would never fit the idiosyncratic life experiences of the client, and he should be spared from having this burden added to his other problems. In the course of therapy, it would be unusual, however, if the client did not come to view some things like his counselor. Indeed, the counselor may work actively to inculcate some particular value that he feels would implement the success of the counseling. One such value might be that emotional health is more satisfying than neuroticism and that the apparent gains of neurotic adjustment are spurious. The client may agree with the counselor verbally, but offer every resistance to surrendering his maladjustment; he acts as if neuroticism is more satisfying, although he professes not to believe it.

The counselor may also wish to stress for the client the idea of determinism and cause-and-effect as a way of thinking about his emotional troubles, which may soften the criticism that clients may visit upon themselves because of their poor adjustment.

Initial therapeutic contact. The first therapy interview is perhaps the most important one. The initial interview will occur after the counselor has made a decision on the basis of a screening interview or test data about the client's suitability for counseling. It is somewhat analogous to first dreams in therapy, in that it allows the therapist to see the basic elements of the emotional problem more clearly than they may be viewed for a long time to come. It is quite common for dreams to be reported during the first interview, as the client's knowledge of the approaching encounter with the therapist may understandably stimulate the dream.

At the outset of the counseling, when the impact of the fresh relationship with the therapist is extremely potent, the client will often reveal the basic roots of the problem before he is able to organize his defenses and ward off the unique and unaccustomed relationship that is forming with the therapist.

The first hour can make a deep impression upon some clients. For one thing, it is the beginning of hope for a new and better life. Symbolically, it can have a stronger, more primitive meaning. It may symbolize a deep wish to surrender all responsibility for coping with the world to the therapist, in a hope that the client may sustain nurturance, love and protection. Harbored in this magical wish is not the need to get well, but to continue the gratification of the infantile pattern of adjustment by dependency on the therapist. This rather complete dependency, easily observable in some clients, indicates a regression to the oral stage of development and may represent a wish to become one with the first cathected object, the breast.

The counselor is seen as offering hope, comfort, and the capability of solving the client's problems and, in this guise, the therapist may represent the pre-Oedipal mother—a person who is omnipotent, all-reassuring, and provident of total security as long as separation does not occur. This may partly explain the deep sigh of relief and freedom that some beginners in therapy give when the first therapy hour has terminated, although, in reality, their pain at facing themselves is just beginning.

The initial contact also allows the counselor to get some sort of therapeutic commitment from the client. The counselor may even remark that there is a lot of work to be done and that the road ahead will not be easy but that he (the therapist) will do everything he can to help if the client feels that he can make the same sort of investment.

Counseling style. To some extent the style and technique that is used depends on the individual counselor. Also, the attitude of the client will influence the counseling style to some degree. Some talkative clients will allow the therapist to adopt a more passive attitude, while the silent client will demand a more active intervention from him.

The prevailing atmosphere of the interview is one of alert listening, the counselor conveying to the client that he is totally absorbed in his verbal productions. He may have the client sitting vis-à-vis, or he may have the client turn his back to him in order to minimize the social carryover of a face-to-face relationship. The client must have the feeling that the main responsibility for progress in the interview lies with him, although he senses that the counselor is fully engaged in the helping process.

Most interviews begin with the client's recounting the significant experiences that have occurred since the last meeting and his feelings about them. Clients well along in therapy at this point will move into a relating of their dreams since the last session. If the client is not able to understand the meaning of the dream and the counselor feels he knows the meaning of the dream symbolism, he may wish to interpret (tentatively) what he thinks the dream means. Parts of the dream that are still unexplained or that seem significant may require free association or free imagery in order to discover what is being expressed. Frequently during this process the meaning of a dream the client was unable to grasp previously will become clear in the associative process of trying to understand the current one.

Some therapists will use the nonverbal cues offered by the client as a means of understanding his present emotional state. Such cues as pallor, sweating, posturing, preening, and undue relaxation can often furnish opportunities to tap some pocket of strong affect that would remain undetected if attention were focused solely on the verbal output. Care is required in interpreting these physiological reactions and defenses (they can be both) for the meaning of these preverbal reactions (reactions that were present before the child learned speech) can be far beyond the ability of the client to assimilate them when offered in an interpretation. Occasionally calling attention to the physiological reaction is enough to uncover the real feeling that lies behind it.

As the client relates the routine events that have occurred over the past several days, the counselor will listen for patterns of reaction that are similar to the early patterns revolving around significant happenings in the early years. For example, the counselor might sense the similarity between the feelings of shame followed by strangulated anger, recently experienced by the client, and an early episode with his mother which served as the prototype. This insight alone will rarely suffice to change his behavior very much unless he also understands the operations of this emotional sequence in his present life—the constant repetition of feeling furious because he has been made to feel guilty. There is a present-day trend toward an increased therapeutic use of interpreting patterns of reaction to the client rather than having him focus on dredging up forgotten traumas.

The counselor is customarily warm, human, and understanding in the relationship without gratifying the passive needs of the client to maintain his infantile neurosis and narcissism in his dependency on the counselor. The client will feel somewhat thwarted when these needs are not met, but deprivation induces the regression by which the childhood troubles are reencountered and the narcissism interrupted.

During the middle and later stages of therapy when the transference is strong, the therapist will expend the main part of his therapeutic effort in helping the client see the transference relationship for what it is: a recapitulation of attitudes and feelings that were unresolved with early figures in the client's past. During the efforts of the client to resolve his feelings about the therapist as a duplication of someone in his past life, the therapist will attempt to side with the client's ego as well as presenting himself in as realistic a light as possible. This helps the client make the discrimination between the therapist and the person whom he symbolizes. This frees the client's energy, which was absorbed in defending and maintaining this distorted relationship, for use by the client's ego in coping with the world. To effect this resolution, the counselor might set a termination date to bring to light some of the passive aspects of the transference that have lingered because of the faint hope that the relationship will never end.

Particularly strong resistances in therapy might have to be overcome by special techniques mentioned earlier, such as free imagery or an interruption of counseling for a period of time. Sometimes counselors will deliberately set a schedule of irregular appointments in order to upset the timing of the client's resistances, or perhaps he will schedule an early morning appointment (eight o'clock), hoping to arrive at some fresh material before the client's customary defenses are established for the day.

When the therapist senses that the end of therapy is approaching, he may wish to search in two areas of the client's life for lingering manifestations of the client's emotional troubles: (1) the client's terminating relationship with the therapist and (2) the client's ability to translate his newly found self into action in the world of reality. Some clients resolve one of these areas and fail to resolve the other. To feel that a "complete" job has been done, the client must be relating freely with the therapist, with transference at a minimum and also must be putting into action in the real world parts of himself (id derivatives) previously rendered inactive by repression.

Group procedures.   In analytic counseling with groups, the optimum number of persons is between five and eight. If less than five are in the group, and for some reason two persons are unable to come, the group flavor is destroyed. With more than eight persons, the dynamics of the situation and interpersonal involvement become so complex that it is beyond the ability of most counselors and clients to grasp the meaning of what is being expressed, with the result that some group members fall into oblivion and are "lost" therapeutically.

Kuhnel (1955) emphasizes the view that, in analytic group work, the transference the members have to each other is more important than the transference to the group leader. The leader promotes in an unobtrusive way the contact between the members. While communications between the members are given this small-scale publicity, the leader can more easily observe the underlying dynamics. He steers the transference away from himself and remains the representative of reality. This favors adaptation to reality and makes the resolution of transference easier.

Ordinarily, the material produced in the group sessions does not reach the depth that is achieved in individual therapy, nor does the transference get resolved to the same degree. There is the advantage of a more efficacious social desensitization by the client as he discusses his problems before others. This method avoids the defensiveness that is sometimes still present outside the therapy room, even though the client has overcome his resistances with the counselor. Consequently, insights gained in therapy find a smoother transition into actions in the world.

Special problems

(a) *The client who won't talk.* A great deal of counselor sweat and irritability has been engendered by the client who comes in and, after a quick relating of his troubles, refuses to go on in the discussion of his problem. This may happen on the initial interview, but it can also happen after several interviews when good rapport has apparently been established. Zeligs points out that therapists are too quick to conceptualize this silence as resistance when it can have various other meanings. He states, "When the patient's speech is inhibited and silence prevails, the ... analytic aim is not merely to get the patient to speak, but to try to make meaningful for him the unconscious reasons for his inability to speak" (1961, p. 11). Zeligs points out, in his analysis of a young woman, the different ways that silence was used by her during therapy. According to him, silence may be used as re-repression of thought, as a means of retreating from reality, as a struggle for power with the therapist, revenge against a parent, a wish to die, etc.

Loomie (1961) sees silence occurring with the greatest frequency in connection with resistance to verbalizing feelings about the transference, and he stresses the oral and anal sadistic impulses that are important ingredients in these transferences feelings. He also notes that their self-punitive life behavior is paralleled by the analytic propensity for negative therapeutic reaction and the continuation of spiral patterns of provocativeness and atonement.

Arlow (1961) points out the resistance aspects of silence, but also feels that silence can be an invitation to the therapist to participate in an acting out of primitive fantasies. In this instance, silence is used in the service of discharge rather than resistance. Silence here points at joint repetition, rather than recollection.

Silence always needs to be understood in some light, and chronically silent clients may be considered delinquent to a basic rule of analytically oriented therapy: The client must communicate his feelings.

(b) *The client who acts out.* The acting-out client is usually a source of concern to the counselor. For one thing, there is the possible danger or trouble that will accrue to the client as a result of one of his acting-out episodes. Also, the counselor knows that such behavior is gratifying to the client, yet defensive in nature, making emotional insights difficult for him to achieve. It is this very acting out that protects him from the insights that are so painful.

Most practitioners of psychoanalytic therapy forbid and discourage acting out, but Silverberg (1955) feels that such a procedure can have relevance only when the acting out is occurring in the therapy hour.

He cautions against the therapist's, in prohibiting acting out, assuming a disciplinary role and encouraging the client to react to him as an actual authority figure, rather than as an authority figure by way of transference. This change in attitude on the part of the client can make the interpretation of the transference difficult and confusing to the client, for he has evidence that the therapist, in actually becoming authoritarian, is the sort of person he judged him to be. The emotional insight that could come from an interpretation of the client's distorted perception of the therapist is obscured by the real-life behavior of the therapist.

Acting out may be understood as an overt and dramatized manifestation of the transference. It signifies the lingering on of a traumatic bygone experience, the memory of which is unverbalized. The acting out is seen as repeated efforts on the part of the client to rectify the helplessness of the original traumatic experience. Silverberg also points out that at stake for the client are his current claims to omnipotence as well as a test of the effectiveness of his aggression and the establishment of his self-esteem. The simple prohibition of acting-out behavior has the effect of heightening anxiety and creating conditions under which emotional insights may be expected, but it can also create a perception of the therapist that is unfavorable for the effective resolution of the transference.

(c) *Adolescent vicissitudes.* The adolescent years in this culture are marked by a definite instability in mood and an alternation of attitudes and behaviors. There will be shifts in interests, inconsistent progress toward goals, and many general indications of the state of flux and transition that is going on within the adolescent. Although adolescents are pronouncedly egotistical, they seem to be capable at the same time of extreme self-sacrifice and devotion (Strean, 1961).

Fountain (1961) says that adolescence is a time when psychic forces are disturbed and that new harmony is achieved as the adolescent gradually becomes an adult. He indicates that this restoration is accomplished by two processes: (1) the formation of new defenses, primarily against Oedipal and pre-Oedipal impulses and (2) the practice of continuously trying out these defenses, during which the ego learns which defenses are better and how and when to apply them.

The strain upon the adolescent psyche is partially traceable to the reactivation of Oedipal fantasies and impulses. At the same time, the adolescent is experiencing heightened physiological urges and changes which are disrupting the solidity and stability of his ego that he knew during latency. Mother, brothers, sisters, and father are imbued with these Oedipal colorings, and he is faced with the necessity of making nonincestuous object choices and integrating himself into the social order of others his own age.

The threat of reliving the Oedipal anxiety induces a partial regression that eases the discomfort for a while, but does not last long because of the deeper fear of emotional surrender and dissolution of the ego that would occur if regression were to continue (Geleerd, 1961). This situation makes for a constant alertness on the part of the ego, a forerunner of anxiety, in case the defenses are inadequate.

Geleerd emphasizes the constructive effect of this partial regression, feeling that the ego needs to withdraw from its various anchors of cathexis in order to prepare itself for adult object relationships.

With all these demands on the adolescent ego, it is still a time of growth and differentiation. The teen-ager wishes to be grown up, to have new experiences, and he is filled with anticipation of a better life awaiting him. There is heightened interest in artistic and scientific activities. The intellect appears more perceptive and grasping. Many ego functions receive a boost. It is a time for irreversibe change.

Fountain (1961) points out the impairment of the synthetic functions of the ego due to the adolescent's increased narcissistic attitude and regression to earlier stages of development. He pays particular attention to the adolescent's need for immediate gratification and his inability to accept life's subtleties and his intolerance of frustration. He says, in showing the linkage between castration anxiety and frustrations in the early life of a child, "To experience anxiety or to be frustrated in expected gratification represents to such children castration. The similar quality of adolescents is due to the same cause. Castration fears have a resurgence in puberty" (1961, p. 33).

To Fountain, the adolescent's need for quick gratification and his intolerance of frustration represents castration, abandonment, engulfment, or other misfortune depending on the nature of his pre-Oedipal experiences.

Some analytically oriented counselors feel that deep therapy for the teen-ager is contraindicated as the ego already has so many demands on it and so much change and conflict to harmonize.

Strean (1961) mentions the similarity between the adolescent and the adult schizophrenic, in that both manifest pronounced narcissism, mood shifts, extreme negativism, weak defenses, and hindering functions of the ego. Many adolescents see the therapist as a threat and are hesitant to seek treatment on their own.

Strean notes the suspicions that some adolescents have of friendly support on the part of the counselor. He mentions a paradigmatic technique sometimes successful with adolescents in which the therapist tries to mirror the personality of the client, feeling that many adolescents cannot tolerate a more serious therapeutic intervention because of the irrationality of their egos. The client, sensing that the therapist is a kindred spirit, becomes more interested in him, whereupon the therapist then strategically selects certain types of roles and offers himself as a likeness of introjection and identification by the client. The therapist might join in the client's fantasies by telling wild and fanciful tales about himself, as the client does, or by allowing the client to project his impulses and wishes upon the therapist, while the therapist remains nondefensive about it all, indicating by his attitude that these attributes are not too dangerous to live with. Such procedures increase the self-confidence of the client until, hopefully, the client's own problems and the tranference can be dealt with directly.

Scholastic achievement will occasionally take a turn for the worse when adolescents encounter counseling and therapy, and the counselor may often have to face the accusations of the referrer or the parent that the client made better marks before counseling began. This can usually be explained on the basis of the client's increasing preoccupation with material that had previously been repressed, with time consequently being taken away from his studies. Often, after therapy is over, the client's marks will get worse while holding up throughout therapy. Such clients will have been working beyond a limit that is comfortable for them and with more freedom to be themselves will set more comfortable goals.

Dependency on the therapist can be troublesome for both the client and the therapist. Extreme dependency can be intolerable for some adolescents and will lead them to terminate therapy prematurely. Counselors will want to be alert to such "flights into health" and search the transference relationship for new meaning. The client may unconsciously see the therapist as demanding total allegiance and self-sacrifice in return for allowing the client to depend on him, resulting in the client's fear of a complete loss of self—regression to a phase of undifferentiated object relationship in which the client confuses his own ego boundaries with those of the therapist.

The loss of ego boundaries in the disturbed adolescent client is more likely—though still rare—than in the adult client, because of the changing, taxed, unstable state of the ego.

In general, the counselor may rely on a strong need of the adolescent to grow up, master his problems, fulfill his destiny, and become an adult.

Illustrative Case Material

The following counseling interview took place in the counseling center of a large Middle Western university. The client is a nineteen-year-old sophomore, who announced to the counselor during the first interview that he had personal problems and wished the opportunity to discuss them.

The client had been suffering from pronounced feelings of inadequacy and tension for several years, although he felt he had never been happy at any time in his life. The feeling of being pent-up and not getting any enjoyment from life were the crucial feelings that urged him to seek help.

The client's mother and father are both living. The father is a professional man, and the mother is a housewife, with occasional part-time jobs that she seeks to relieve the boredom, rather than because the family needs the money. There is one sister, three years younger than the client, who still lives at home, which is about two hundred miles from the client's university. The client visits home only during holidays.

This is the eleventh interview. Prior to this one, most of the time had been used by the client to communicate his feelings of discomfort and unhappiness in an unproductive and repetitive way. The last three interviews were marked by a noticeable passivity, while he hinted to the counselor that he would be more satisfied if he would diagnose him and plot a course of action for him to pursue.

During the previous interviews, the client presented a sketchy account of his past with no elaboration and little feeling. The client had always been close to his mother, and although he and his father "got along well and without bickering," he always sensed a distance between them. He considered himself rather artistic and sensitive and easily upset. He and his sister were friendly but had drifted further apart in the last several years. He sensed that his family wished him to start out on his own, but felt, at the same time, that they would discourage any effort he made in that direction.

The therapist felt that the client had not committed himself to therapy and was using his passive ego defenses to block the release of emotional material and to prevent any real change in his neurotic attitude. He decided to use the technique of free imagery to circumvent some of the client's defenses by minimizing the controlling influences of the ego, as well as to try to give the client a feeling of therapeutic movement, which might result in a greater investment by him in the therapy process.

Free imagery had been described to him in the last interview and was presented as a method that might move therapy a little faster. He seemed nervous at the prospects of doing it but still wished to try.

The following is a verbatim account of parts of two free-imagery interviews. The comments in parentheses are the thoughts and feelings of the therapist during the hour. CO stands for counselor and CL stands for client. As this was the first time free imagery had been used with the client, the therapist had no previous pattern of images with which to compare the present ones. The picture of the personality ordinarily emerges through repetition of similar themes expressed by the visual fantasies of the client. In this manner, both the client and the therapist gradually build up an understanding of the basic emotional problem as it is operating in the present world and as it originated in childhood. Interpretations and hypotheses by the therapist may be confirmed, modified, or denied by the long-range patterns of recurrent themes played over in these highly symbolic fantasies.

CO: You'll remember last time I said we might try something different today. How do you feel about it now?

CL: Good. I'm ready.

CO: Okay. Why don't you lean your head back against the chair, close your eyes and report all the pictures and visual phantasies that occur to you. It's important that you tell me everything, regardless of how trivial or silly. Try not to censor anything. Also report all the feelings you have or any physical sensations you are aware of. Concentrate upon your body. Attend to the pressure of your hips and legs against the chair. Feel your feet pressing against the floor. Breathe deeply. Please don't open your eyes until I tell you. While you are talking I will not be speaking, and I will be very quiet, but I am here. Do you understand? This is an effective technique, and it will work for us.

CL: Okay. Are you ready? I'm looking down a valley or some sort of path, or something. It is lined with evergreen trees. It goes down pretty far. It's not cloudy or anything; the sun's shining real bright. A little village. I see a man with glasses on, an old man. He has a big head and a real small chin—kinda ugly. I see some sort of label or plate. I can't see what it says.

CO: (He mentions an old man. I wonder why the age is important. Then he is unable to read the printing on the label—resistance? Resisting something about the old man?)

CL: I see a football, a football player. There's a big shaft or a well. I'm looking down on it from above. There's dark water below; the walls are white. The walls are concrete. The dark waters below sort of fascinate me, yet they seem sort of . . . sort of . . . nasty. I'm within the shaft now, looking up from the inside, pretty close to the top of the hole. It's night time outside, and there's some sort of light shining over the hole or across it. I see a bunch of arrows, all together—just the points of 'em, and they're sticking into the hole. You said pay attention to what I feel, and I'm beginning to feel frightened, and sort of like I want to cry.

CO: (The therapist reaches over and touches the client lightly on the arm.) Too frightened to go on; if you are we'll stop now.

CL: No, let's go on. There's a big sewer, like a drain sewer. I'm tempted to walk inside. The sun is just beginning to set. It's dark inside that sewer, and I'm looking into it. I'm not going in there. I feel as if I'd like to run away from it, but I don't, or can't. I see a face, the nose, the eyes, forehead. There are some more eyes over on the right. They're kinda sad like they've been crying, like they're ashamed. There's a woman standing with her back to me. It's dark all around her. She's got her head down. There are the eyes again; they're closed this time, like they're asleep or dead.

CO: (The well shaft, then the inserted arrows—this suggests thinly disguised sexual symbolism. He felt quite anxious here. Some emotional conflict must have been "touched". This is followed by the sewer—this suggests filth to me. I wonder if this conveys his attitude about sex—that it's frightening and dirty? His fear continues, he doesn't wish to go into the sewer, and the sun is setting. This has sort of a morbid feel. He must feel guilty—the eyes are ashamed and sad. Has he seen some episode as a child? The woman has her back turned; he must not wish to identify her.)

CL: I see a tractor or a bulldozer pulling something real big. There are a lot of chains going back to this thing the tractor is pulling. It looks like a big block. Now the scene shifts. I'm looking up the side of a tall building. Now there's a bowl, a black bowl. It has a purple thing coming up from the middle, and it's turning around real fast. It looks like a hand or a gun pointing straight up. There's an alley, a blind alley. It's like it wouldn't do any good to go in there, it doesn't lead anywhere. I feel sort of hopeless right now. Here's a fence, it's all around me. I can't see over on the other side. Now I'm looking down into a basement garage. Cars are coming down a ramp real fast and piling up at the bottom. There's a sun, a big orange sun, like a painting. It's real colorful, red, orange, and purple. Now I'm sitting behind someone in an airplane. The plane's on fire. It's crashing. I feel I've got to get out of the airplane before it crashes. Now I'm back looking up the side of the building again—art work on the side of it, statues.

CO: (Again he expresses affect, he feels hopeless—right after the gun pointing straight up—potency?—and after he saw the blind alley. This might be his conceptualization of the masculine role, that sex and power just don't lead anywhere. The fence suggests his being bounded or inhibited. Cars piling up and the impending wreck of the airplane have a sameness quality to me. I sense strong emotional feeling and destructiveness—probably an outgrowth of his inability to solve the conflict and to activate his unused self. Then the artistic side comes in;

that's a quick switch. Is his artistic nature serving a defensive purpose for him rather than enriching his personality?)

CL: I see a night club singer or something. She's sitting on a piano. Can't see her face. It's dark all around her, just a spot light on her. She has on a shiny, black dress. All the guys in the audience have wolves' heads—human bodies, but wolves' heads. It's creepy. There's a big, long chamber or something, like a gun barrel. I can see somebody looking down the other end, through a hole in it. I see clouds again, light coming through them in spots. See the bottoms of someone's boots or something; they're brand new, and they're tan colored. There are some grapes in a basket and some slavegirls hanging around. There's another basket of peas and carrots, I think. There is something coming out of it, little green stuff, and it's bubbling up like there's something underneath there. It's growing, like. It just keeps bubbling up. I'm looking through a window, seeing the back of someone's head, but they've got their coat collar pulled up. I see a big eye. It's staring real hard. It's real big. Now it seems like someone has turned a room on its side, and the room became real long. And now everything is sort of falling down toward the bottom—table, chairs, spoons, and everything. There's a big mountain standing right below this room. I'm looking up. Its light on top, and there are clouds way up above, but it's light all around them too. It's light all the way up the mountain; nothing's hiding anything. I have the strangest feeling. Like I want to cry again. A few minutes ago if I had cried, it would have been because I was afraid. Now if I cried it would be because...I don't...I don't know...something about that mountain. It would be because I would be, maybe, happy. Like I might dare to climb that mountain. I do want to cry.

CO: (The counselor breaks his silence.) I do understand. (Again the woman is unidentifiable. Wolves' heads—that seems a significant distortion, and the gun barrel, more phallic symbolism? I wonder if wolves have to do with his being lustful. Or maybe they signify danger. The basket of peas and carrots, and the slavegirls seem to be in an early Greek or Roman setting. I get the feeling of emotional pressure—the bubbling up. Again the back of someone's head—he rarely sees faces. He must be threatened by whom he will recognize. Then a hint of spatial disorientation—the room on its side—I wonder if that implies emotional chaos? He was quite touched about the mountain. I feel strangely enthusiastic about that too! It seems like he is almost daring to hope that he might be different—to change. I feel he is moved; I share his excitement.)

CL: I'm looking up a ladder or a steel thing. It's light all around; the ladder goes straight up. I feel like I'm going to climb it or something. Climbing must be awfully important to me. (Laughs forlornly.) I see a tiger. He's got something in his mouth—a briefcase or books or something. He's kind of restless. Only it looks like a big cat, not a tiger. There's a telephone. A woman's hand came down to pick it up, and I don't know who she is. Her face is all white. She's yelling over the phone like she's scared. Her eyes are getting real little; her hair is all white—streaked like. She is afraid of something. Now there is a real big bunch of real high chairs alongside of a wall. They're inside a corridor or something, like in the Palace at Versailles in France. The chairs are propped against the wall, and there's a window right above them. As you walk by them, I don't know, the corridor gets foggy. I can't see anymore. I was walking down one side of the corridor, and I looked over on the other side, and there was something like a statue—it's all white. It's a marble statue. It seemed to come around a little corner so quick. It's real hard. It's like a monster or something, and it came around the corner. There are some people in a room; they have beards and mustaches, and they are working on something. They're working on somebody there, lying down. They've all got beards and mustaches. Somebody has lifted up a cover over a casket. Just lifted it up. I can't see anything. It's all just stopped. Everything is frozen. Nobody's moving. I'm looking down from a balcony. There's a light on the floor. There's a door opening just a little bit, and it's opening a little more. There's somebody there with white hair and a white beard. I don't know, he closed the door again.

CO: (All of this sounds significant to me. He appears lost in his production —no acting now. He seems very much a part of his phantasies: "I feel like I'm going to climb the ladder." He must feel freer. Again I sense fear—the tiger must have been too threatening—he reduced it to a small cat. I wonder if the freedom brings on the fear? Does the tiger symbolize a devouring mother who permits no freedom? Or is this castration fear of the father that follows self vigor? The woman is old, like the man. His people are always old or unrecognizable. That surely reduces some threat for him. He seemed almost afraid while talking about the statue—that was followed by the death scene with the casket. Does he wish someone to die? Has he destroyed someone in phantasy? Who? Is this a disguised death wish for himself? The resistance was intense here. Everything froze. The opening door—does that mean readiness for insight? He didn't wish to see what lay beyond. He hasn't gone this far before.)

The interview continues in the usual manner after the client has discontinued free imagery.

CO: How do you feel?
CL: Oh, everyway I guess. Puzzled about what it all means, sort of scared, yet there's also a feeling of happiness. I know it sounds goofy to talk about being scared and happy at the same time, but I do. You know, like I could go either way.
CO: Of course I do.
CL: I really felt ... felt deeply a couple of times.
CO: Yes, I sensed that. Good. It's sort of good to have feelings, regardless of what kind they are, isn't it? Or does that sound strange?

CL: No, that's true, that's really true. I think I was most frightened about the arrows at the first, remember? And then, near the end, about the casket and the old man opening the door. I really felt scared.

CO: Those two things seemed the most important then—more feeling about those.

CL: Yeah, that and looking up the mountain. You know, it sort of seemed like me in that casket, and then I wasn't there any more.

CO: You sort of had a quick flash of feeling about your own death then—saw yourself there for an instant. That does sound frightening.

CL: It was. You might be wondering if I wish to die, and there have been times when I didn't care, but this didn't feel like that. This felt like I *am* dead. That it's already happened. You know, I think I do feel that —that I am dead in a sense. Life sure hasn't had much meaning for me for a long time. I don't ever feel much anymore. Do you understand?

CO: Sure I do. Something inside died a long time ago. I understand.

After a few more remarks, the interview terminates. Several weeks later the following interview took place. Free imagery had been used during the intervening interviews. The client now is more at ease with the technique and has reported some loosening of his affect within and outside of therapy.

CL: I'm walking now alongside of a woods, and I'm holding my mother's hand. I feel content just to leave my hand resting in hers. I'm playing all around beside her, but I leave my hand in hers. Sort of like I have, well, just so much space to play in—just as far as her arm can reach. And I don't seem to pull away. We are walking beside the woods. It looks scary in there, big trees, dark, and I can see only a little way in. I wish to go in there, but I'm scared. I sort of want to explore, but I know she won't go with me. I'm turning loose of her hand and wandering into the woods alone. I'm just walking down this path—it's a very narrow path. I'm pretty far into the woods now, but I'm just standing there not doing anything. I want to get off the path, but I can't. I'm afraid. There's green grass on both sides of the path and I don't have on any shoes. I want to step over in that grass, but I feel like the ground beneath would be muddy and "oozy." I can't move. I just feel trapped. I feel like I'll stay here forever.

CO: Let something happen. If you need help, let help come. (The counselor breaks silence here in order to break the conflict and allow the imagery to proceed.)

CL: There's a man coming down the path toward me. It's very quiet; nobody's talking. He's very tall and has on a...sort of woodman's jacket. He's a lumberjack or something. He reaches down and picks me up. I'm sitting on his shoulder, way up in the air. He has on boots, so he can step off the path and not worry about the mud underneath. I'm just sitting there, feeling very secure. I'm sort of...like up among the branches. I let go of his shoulder and climb around on the branches.

He waits below. For some reason I'm peeling some bark off one of the branches. There's white wood underneath where I've peeled it away. He's still there below. Then I climb down on his shoulders again. We're going back to the path now, and he's putting me down. It's very quiet—not a sound. It's like we can't talk. It's real strange. We just can't speak.

CO: (The counselor again feels the need to pierce this resistance and understand the feeling behind this inability to communicate.) Keep your eyes closed, and relax as much as possible. I'm going to hand you a piece of paper and a pencil. Can you see the paper and pencil?

CL: Yes. I take it, but I hand it to the man. He's bending down, writing on it, writing on his knee, kind of. He hands it back to me, but the paper's folded. I can't see what it says. I want to open my eyes. It feels like I want to run out of here. It really seems like I want to run.

CO: I understand. (Soothingly) Keep your eyes closed. Can you still see the paper?

CL: Yes, it's still folded. But I have it in my hand. The paper is real white and clean. It looks like telephone pad paper.

CO: Let's open it and see what it says.

CL: It says "I need you!" (Long silence.) I feel like I want to scream. I feel sort of hot and tingly in my skin, all over. It seems like I could scream and cry at the same time.

CO: I understand how angry and hurt you must feel.

After more remarks in this same vein, the free imagery is interrupted, and the interview proceeds in the normal manner.

CO: Well?

CL: Jesus! We hit something didn't we?

CO: Yes, it seems like it.

CL: Do you know what it means?

CO: Not really. I guess I feel you have the answer to that. I am sure of one thing, you felt very intensely about something. If I'm getting it right, sort of real angry and real hurt—side by side.

CL: I think that's right. Where do those feelings come from? All of a sudden they're there.

CO: Something you've needed to feel for a long time, I suppose.

CL: M-hm.

CO: Was there anything that seemed important that you haven't told me about. So much happened it might be hard to say.

CL: Yes, there was (definitely). You know when the guy was waiting for me under the tree.

CO: Yes.

CL: He was tapping his foot. Just tapping it on the ground.

CO: Like he was irritated or impatient?

CL: No, he wasn't mad or anything; it was just a mannerism. Just something he was doing.

CO: I got it. Go on.

CL: Well, it's something my dad used to do a lot—just tap his foot. He wouldn't be mad or anything like that, but he just had the habit of doing it. Tapping his foot. I don't know whether you realize it or not but you do that a lot too. Do you know you do?

CO: I hadn't been aware of it, but now that you point it out, it seems that I do. Yes, I do. Isn't that odd? We are sort of a threesome then—the man in the dream, your dad, and me. It's something that sort of links us together, this foot tapping business.

CL: That's right. You know I always feel so uneasy when I bring you into things.

CO: Yes, I know. You want to keep me in place as just a psychologist and not have any human feelings about me.

CL: But that's goofy, isn't it. You are human. It's obvious you are.

CO: Yes. Indeed I am.

CL: You know, right at the start there was something about you that reminded me of dad. Even before the foot tapping. Something, I don't know what. But one time, when I was leaving, and you hit me on the back as I went out the door. Remember that?

CO: Yes.

CL: Well, I felt like I wanted you to put your arm around my shoulders, or give me a hug, or something like that. Does that sound too crazy?

CO: Not at all. Somehow it would have been very satisfying or reassuring if I could have responded to you like this. Is this sort of what dad used to do?

CL: Well, some, but not as much as I wanted him to—I wanted him to a lot more than he did. I always felt there was so much unsaid between us.

CO: You mean like in the dream.

CL: Yeah, just like that. I always wanted to feel ... I thought how nice it would be if dad wanted to be with me like I wanted to be with him, but he never did. Or he didn't seem to. (Sighs deeply.)

CO: You never could get the deep commitment from him that would have been so satisfying. That sort of explains the note, I guess. You wanted to be needed and loved as much as you loved him, but it didn't ever happen that way.

CL: Oh, Lord. I tried harder than you know.

CO: I know you did.

After a few remarks, the interview terminates. Much of the symbolism of the waking dream is explained in the interview after the free imagery has ended. The client's need for his father as a model for identification and his wish to be loved by him seem apparent.

The therapist by this time has made a tentative formulation of the client's problem, but always subject to modification as the client produces newer and deeper material. At first, the formulation of the problem is sketchy and incomplete. In many instances the therapist is uncertain of the meaning of the symbolism and the articulation of the various aspects of the maladjustment.

During the early stages, the therapist selects certain sequences in the imagery that appear to him to be important in the dynamics of the client. He attends to the male and female sexual symbolism scattered throughout the interviews. He is aware that this symbolism is often followed by scenes of catastrophe, danger, or morbidity. He is also aware that the client chooses to see in the imagery decidedly old persons who appear with their backs turned or situations in which their faces are unrecognizable. The therapist senses the frequent references to contrasting shades of light and dark throughout the production but does not understand the meaning of this symbolism. Fear seems to be a significant feeling for the client, and the therapist, at this juncture, wonders if it is connected with a wish for someone to die or a masochistic internalization of this wish—that is, a wish for himself to die.

By the time of the second recorded interview (there were six or seven unrecorded intervening sessions), an emerging picture of the client's personality has become clear. The therapist tentatively—and it should be repeated for emphasis, *tentatively*—formulates the problem as one in which repressed sexual elements play an important part, perhaps with incomplete sexual identification with the father and consequently with the male role. The client's attitude toward sex seems to be one of morbidity, guilt, and fear. Death seems in some way connected with this complex, either as an urge to self-destruction or, perhaps, at a deeper level, a death wish for someone else. The therapist conjectures the narcissistic personality makeup of the client's mother plus the unapproachability of the father which combined to keep the client dependent on his mother, fearful of exploring and pursuing masculine interests, and thereby unable to crystallize a masculine identification, as well as constantly searching for safety and support, and narcissistically regressed. The client is seen as fixated at the phallic stage of psychosexual development, suffering from anxiety centering around the Oedipal complex and his assumption of an independent and masculine life role. His diagnosis, at this time, would be that of psychoneurosis, anxiety reaction, mild, with no appreciable impairment, with dependent behavior.

Passivity and dependency on the therapist would seem to be the line the client's resistances will follow. The client wishes to solve his problems, and there are signs that he will achieve some significant insights soon in therapy in addition to those he already has. The therapist anticipates being used as a transference target for the feelings the client has for *both* his mother and his father. The therapist would expect the client, during the latter stages of therapy, to recapture the original feelings of fury and hurt when he as a child came to the dawning realization (later repressed) that the strangulation of his potential self and his adulthood was the price he had paid for his safety and continued union with his parents. The therapist would also anticipate an emancipation from his infantile dependency on adults (parent surrogates), the resurrection of his own values, and a reincorporation of the parents with an acceptance of their neurotic limitations—a human understanding, in other words.

To make significant gains on his emotional problem, the therapy process will probably require not less than weekly interviews for an academic year.

Research and Validation

Few theoretical disciplines have captured the imagination of men more profoundly than psychoanalysis, yet the psychological researcher, for all of its dramatic appeal, sees it as a system in which it is abysmally hard to do research. Freud's theories, some of them at any rate, almost seem beyond investigation. Little research can be done on the death wish, as it is practically impossible to derive any empirical propositions from it. Almost as exasperating is his concept of reaction formation, which permits the analyst to explain behavior in terms of a direct expression of forces within the id or the polar opposite of these forces. Research is difficult when opposite behaviors can be explained in terms of the same unconscious impulse. Scientifically trained psychologists attempting to do research in the field of psychoanalysis have been exasperated and impeded by such knotty problems.

Attempts to validate psychoanalysis have developed along two lines. The most obvious one is the clinical validation of the postulates of psychoanalysis, which are observed by the analyst during the therapy hour. This usually takes the form of interpretations offered by the analyst and confirmed by the patient, which reduces his anxiety and allows him to put to use parts of his personality that were lying dormant and ungratified. This is usually enough validation for the practitioner.

The other method is by subjecting psychoanalytic hypotheses to experimental investigation, and here, researchers run into the problems mentioned earlier, as well as opposition from the analysts themselves, who are decidedly nonexperimentally oriented, and who are accused of being frightened by any attempts at quantification.

In general, there have been four kinds of attention given to researching psychoanalytic principles. One sort of attention has been the actual doing of research, most carried on by clinical and experimental psychologists who have been familiar with Freudian theory. The majority of these studies have unfortunately emphasized repression and its derivatives, with other postulates of the system suffering neglect.

A second kind of attention has been that of defending the reasons research has not been done, and this comes from the analysts themselves. They point out the idiosyncratic development of the individual, the ethical problems that arise in research, and the superior means of understanding behavior afforded by the introspective method.

A third sort of attention comes again from the analysts. Some of them recognize the need for research and even mention ways in which research on psychoanalytic theories might be methodologically improved, but they wish that psychologists indoctrinated in analytic methods would do it.

The fourth sort of attention also comes from the analysts, who examine their own motivations for wanting to do, but not doing, research. They find that the doing of research is an expression of more basic aims within the researcher, and they are apparently freed from the need to do research after this insight.

Difficulties with Validations

If one is attempting to validate psychoanalytic assumptions, one probably should do so within the framework of analytic theory, which requires the acceptance of certain hypotheses as valid from the outset (Brenner, 1955). These are: (1) the existence of unconscious mental process, (2) the characteristics of the operation of the primary process, and (3) the separation of the functions of the mind into the ego, superego, and id. If confirmatory evidence is not forthcoming within this frame of reference, then the more basic hypotheses need to be challenged.

For the analytically oriented therapist the validation of unconscious processes meets its acid test when an interpretation has been offered to the patient who then responds in such a way that the validity of the interpretation can be assessed. In general, the response to a correct interpretation is a reduction of the ego's fear of the id, a relaxation of the ego's defenses, and the emergence of a derivative of the id impulse that was being defended against (Brenner, 1955).

The use of psychoanalytic interpretation as a validating tool for unconscious processes occurs mainly in two fields. The first field is that of the practitioner, previously discussed, who has repeated opportunities to test the accuracy of his interpretation as therapy progresses. In the second field psychoanalytic interpretations are applied to other techniques or sciences, as in biography, history, or anthropology. Interpretations applicable to biographies do not afford an oncoming opportunity to confirm or negate hypotheses, for example, when the subject is dead and no further insights are possible (Schmidl, 1955).

Still with validation, when an interpretation is based, for example, on an Oedipal conflict, two things must hold for the interpretation to be valid: The Oedipus complex must be shown to exist in a prevalent form within the culture, and its specific application to this particular client must also be validated (Schmidl, 1955). Sources of error may creep in at both levels.

Further difficulties in validation occur because trivial incidents in the unconscious may be seized upon to convey special meaning, which in time may come to seem more significant than the seemingly catastrophic incident. Also different symbols may be in converse order of import in one patient to the same symbols in the experience of another. This appears to make the most potent validation of psychoanalytic interpretations necessarily confined to therapy, where there is the opportunity to modify interpretations under the individuating influence of the patient.

Psychoanalysis formulations and concepts are nothing if not dynamic, ever-changing, and interrelated. Research that measures end results and outcomes somehow miss the essence of analysis. Suggestions to measure health and increments of health at serial points during therapy are being heard. Are there changes in the functioning of the ego that process research would uncover that pre- and post-research occlude (Bellak, 1961)?

Investigations of Repression

Most of the experimental studies in the field have been done on repression, partly because it lends itself to investigation more easily than some of Freud's other fundamental concepts.

Defining repression has been troublesome. Freud mentioned two kinds of repression: (1) primal repression, which occurs when archaic ideas linked to instinctual strivings are denied entrance into consciousness; and (2) after-expulsion, which is the removal of anxiety-laden material from consciousness. Primal repression is a childhood phenomenon and is generally considered inaccessible for experimentation. By far the largest amount of work has been focused on after-expulsion repression. The investigations that have been done on this area are partly justified by the fact that it is a basic cornerstone for the later elaborations of Freudian theory.

According to some authors the experimental evidence for repression is far from convincing. The techniques employed have been criticized on the grounds that they are not measuring repression but the subjects' ability to recall material under stress. Attempts at methodological refinement have been frequent and sincere. Guidelines for doing research in certain areas have been published with subsequent improvement in experimental design. In general, studies on repression have followed a pattern advocated by Zeller (1950) in which material was learned, then repressed, and recalled later when the effects of repression were removed. Hypnosis fits this paradigm nicely and is being used more frequently in recent studies.

The gathering of the basic data in analytic experiments is under scrutiny. It makes a difference, some say, because analysts who hold different theoretical positions not only differ in their conjectures about data but attain different *kinds* of data (Marmor, 1955).

Researchers have understandably been preoccupied with what sort of material (feelings, ideas, concepts) is apt to be repressed. Freud makes it quite clear in his writings that unpleasant and appalling thoughts are anxiously repressed, and many experimental efforts have attempted to test this hypothesis. Most studies have found that unpleasant material is recalled less easily than pleasant material or that a threat to the ego is essential for repression to occur. In the same vein, unsuccessful performances or incompleted ones are difficult to remember. Sex differences come in and complicate the picture. Men and women do not repress the same sorts of things. Men tend to repress sexual material, while women favor the repression of aggressive material, with much obvious overlap (Rosenstock, 1951). Later studies reinforced the findings on sex differences and repression and also pointed out that men, more than women, distort and repress Oedipal material, as well as evidence of weakness and inadequacy in themselves (LaForge, Leary, Naboisek, Coffey, & Freedman, 1954).

There are some indications that persons easily hypnotized and suggestible tend to emphasize the repression mechanism in the avoidance of anxiety. Emotional conflict per se does not always occasion anxiety, the anxiety being contingent on the completeness or incompleteness of the repression. Emotional conflict accompanied by complete repression does not ordinarily disrupt behavior (Bobbitt, 1958).

Some evidence for the unconscious mind is revealed by investigations of repression, but not so narrowly defined. These experiments might be more properly concerned with behavior without awareness rather than with repression since repression carries the implication of ridding the mind of something unpleasant, which is not accurate in these particular experiments.

Subjects have been able to make discriminations about lifted weights (although they thought they were guessing) and also to identify geometric figures better than chance when exposed subliminally. Other experiments using subliminal techniques have offered additional evidence of judgments and perceptions taking place on unconscious strata of the mind. For example, subjects can match previously learned associations to stimuli exposed at illumination levels too weak for correct identification and can identify letters of the alphabet better than chance at subliminal levels. Subjects commonly are unaware of the important factors that have led to vast improvement in special experimental tasks such as writing in unusual ways or multiplying large numbers.

Experimentations and the Clinical Atmospheres

Some experiments have captured the clinical atmosphere nicely. Subjects found neutral sentences previously paired with sexual and aggressive aims toward parents more difficult to perceive than ordinary material under various conditions of illumination. Still in the clinical vein, subjects who observed tachistoscopically exposed landscapes and had the opportunity to tell about and draw what they had seen, had the omitted material appear in their dreams the following night (Poetzl, 1917).

Much of the criticism directed at the nonchalance with which psychoanalysis views research is justified. The most demoralizing barrier to research has been the tendency of psychoanalysis to obscure the relationship between external event (to which a person reacts) and behavioral change by postulating internal constructs (guilt, ego, cathexis, etc.) which have no dependable behavioral referents in space and time (Lundin, 1963).

Although Skinner (1954) has been understanding of the use in psychoanalysis of these metaphorical constructs as symptomatic of the initial stages of any science, some experimenters have excitingly tackled some hard-to-verify hypotheses. Two of these experiments dealt with "unconscious" behavior of a sort. McGinnies (1949) found subjects had longer recognition thresholds to tachistoscopically exposed taboo words (whore, Kotex, bitch) than to neutral words and to have *greater* GSRs (galvanic skin response) during *prerecognition* trials when taboo words were shown. He interpreted this as suggesting an unconscious detection of anxiety-producing stimuli.

Hefferline (1962) was able to condition minute thumb twitches to terminate aversive auditory stimuli. The interesting part of his experiment was that the subjects felt they had been passive victims to the onset and duration of the loud stimuli and were unaware that they had controlled the sound with their thumb twitching. Hefferline points out the relationship between such subliminal conditioning and "unconsciously" motivated behavior advanced by psychoanalysis.

These two experiments among a few others, seem to be much "in the spirit" of psychoanalytic theory, whether by accident or design, and are suggestive that some of the difficult models of psychoanalysis should not be eschewed as hopeless and unproductive.

Few people who familiarize themselves with psychoanalytic theory accept it with neutral candor. Most are fervently opposed or gullibly embracing. The criticizers relentlessly attack the vague, untestable referents of the theory and point out the analysts' dereliction of scientific responsibility in not offering empirical evidence of their hypotheses. The clinicians often feel that no other one theory is capable of explaining so much behavior observable during the therapy hour or provides such a useful frame of reference for thinking about personality and motivation.

During introspective moments, most of us are able to sense in ourselves the dark and mysterious elements of which Freud wrote, lying somewhere in the depths of us, to be aware of the vigilance of parts of ourselves to ward off threat, and to feel the defensive maneuvering we maintain to ensure our self-regard. We are alternately despairing and elated, confident and cringing, self-loving yet feeling tender for others, and, for many people, Freud's clear identification of such things that were heretofore only half sensed and suspected provides a basic validity for the system.

BIBLIOGRAPHY

Arlow, Jacob A., M.D. Silence and the theory of technique. *Amer. psychoanal. Assoc. J.,* 1961, 9, 44–56.

Baura, M. Freud and Horney on anxiety and neurosis. *Samiksa,* 1955, **9,** 93–103.

Bellak, Leopold. Research in psychoanalysis. *Psychoanal. Quart.,* 1961, **30,** 519–548.

Bobbitt, R. The repression hypothesis studies in a situation of hypnotically induced conflict. *J. abnorm. soc. Psychol.,* 1958, **56,** 205–213.

Brenner, Charles. Panel on The validation of psychoanalytic techniques. *Amer. psychoanal. Assoc. J.,* 1955, **3,** 496–505.

Colm, Hanna. A field theory approach to transference and its particular application to children. *Psychiatry*, 1955, **18**, 324–326, 339–352.

Evan, Sarah. The compensatory work of transference. *Psychoanal. Rev.*, 1961, **48** (2), 19–29.

Feigl, H. Mind-body: Not a pseudo problem. In Sidney Hook (Ed.), *Dimensions of mind*. New York: New York University Press, 1960.

Fleming, Joan. What analytic work requires of an analyst: A job analysis. *Amer. psychoanal. Assoc. J.*, 1961, **9**, 719–730.

Fountain, Gerard. Adolescent into adult: An inquiry. *Amer. psychoanal. Assoc. J.*, 1961, **9**, 417–434.

Geleerd, Elisabeth R. Some aspects of ego vicissitudes in adolescence. *Amer. psychoanal. Assoc. J.*, 1961, **9**, 394–406.

Hefferline, R. F. Learning theory and clinical psychology—An eventual symbiosis. In A. J. Bachrach (Ed.), *Experimental foundations of clinical psychology*. New York: Basic Books, Inc., Publishers, 1962.

Hoffman, Martin. On the relationship between psychoanalysis and the philosophy of mind. *Psychoanal. Quart.*, 1962, **31**, 62–72.

Jacobson, E. The affects and their pleasure-unpleasure qualities in relation to the psychic discharge processes. In R. M. Loewenstein (Ed.), *Drives, affects, and behavior*. New York: International University Press, Inc., 1953, pp. 38–66.

Kaywin, Louis. An epigenetic approach to the psychoanalytic theory of instincts and affects. *Amer. psychoanal. Assoc. J.*, 1960, **8**, 613–659.

Kubie, Lawrence S. *Practical and theoretical aspects of psychoanalysis*. New York: Frederick A. Praeger, Inc., 1950.

Kuhnel, G. Transference in group analysis. *Acta Psychotherapeutica Psychosomatica Orthopaedagogica Suppl.*, 1955, **3**, 196–200.

LaForge, R., Leary, T. F., Naboisek, H., Coffey, H. S., & Freedman, M. B. The interpersonal dimension of personality. Part II. An objective study of repression. *J. Pers.*, 1954, **23**, 129–153.

Lilly, John C. The psychophysiological basis for two kinds of instincts. *Amer. psychoanal. Assoc. J.*, 1960, **8**, 659–671.

Loomie, Leo S. Some ego considerations in the silent patient. *Amer. psychoanal. Assoc. J.*, 1961, **9**, 56–79.

Lundin, R. W. Behavioristic psychology. In R. W. Heine, & J. Wepman (Eds.), *Concepts of personality*. Chicago: Aldine Publishing Company, 1963.

McGinnies, E. Emotionality and perceptual defense. *Psychol. Rev.*, 1949, **56**, 244–251.

Marmor, Judd. Panel on The validation of psychoanalytic techniques. *Amer. psychoanal. Assoc. J.*, 1955, **3**, 496–505.

Meerloo, Joose A. M. The dual meaning of human regression. *Psychoanal. Rev.*, 1962, **49** (3), 77–86.

Mullan, Hugh. The existential matrix of psychotherapy. *Psychoanal. Rev.*, 1960, **47**, 87–99.

Munroe, Ruth L. *Schools of psychoanalytic thought*. New York: Holt, 1955.

Nacht, S., & Levovice, S. Indications and Contra-indications for psychoanalysis. *Rev. Française Psychoanal.*, 1955, **19**, 135–204, 279, 304–309.

Poetzl, O. Experimentelle erregte traumbilder in ihren beziehungen zum indirekten sehen. *Zfl. ges. Neural. Psychiat.*, 1917, **37**, 278–349.

Rangell, Leo. On the psychoanalytic theory of anxiety: A statement of a unitary theory. *Amer. psychoanal. Assoc. J.*, 1955, **3**, 389–414.

Riviere, Joan. *Freud's introductory lectures.* New York: Liveright, 1958.

Rosenstock, I. M. Perceptual aspects of repression. *J. abnorm. soc. Psychol.*, 1951, **46**, 304–315.

Ruesch, Jurgen. Transference reformulated. In J. Fiasch, & N. Ross, *Annual survey of psychoanalysis.* Vol. 6. New York: International Universities Press, Inc., 1955.

Schmidl, Fritz. The problem of scientific validation in psychoanalytic interpretation. *J. Psychoanal.*, 1955, **36**, 105–113.

Siegman, Alfred J. A reaction to positive transference. *Psychoanal. Rev.*, 1955, **42**, 172–179.

Silverberg, William V. Acting out versus insight: A problem in psychoanalytic technique. *Psychoanal. Quart.*, 1955, **24**, 527–559.

Skinner, B. F. Critique of psychoanalytic concepts and theories. *Scient. Mon.*, 1954, **79**, 300–305.

Strean, Herbert. Difficulties met in the treatment of adolescents. *Psychoanal. Rev.*, 1961, **48** (3), 69–80.

Zeligs, Meyer. The psychology of silence: Its role in transference, countertransference and the psychoanalytic process. *Amer. psychoanal. Assoc. J.*, 1961, **9**, 7–44.

Zeller, A. F. An experimental analogue of repression: Part I. Historical summary. Psychol. Bull., 1950, **47**, 39–51.

Zeller, A. F. An experimental analogue of repression: Part III. The effect of induced failure and success on memory measured by recall. *J. exp. Psychol.*, 1951, **42**, 32–38.

Zetzel, Elizabeth R. The concept of anxiety in relation to the development of psychoanalysis. *Amer. psychoanal. Assoc. J.*, 1955, **3**, 369–388.

chapter 4

LEONARD D. GOODSTEIN | Behavior Theoretical Views of Counseling[1]

The scientific study of learning, or the changes in behavior as a function of experience, has been and continues to be a major concern of experimental psychology. Psychologists' interest in the phenomena of learning can be traced back to the pioneering work of Ebbinghaus (1885), Bryan and Harter (1897, 1899), and Thorndike (1898). Thorndike's later work (1911, 1932) in demonstrating the crucial importance of rewards and punishments in the learning process, particularly his statement of the "law of effect," has become one of the most significant factors influencing the development of contemporary experimental psychology. Thorndike proposed that learning occurred because responses that were accompanied by or resulted in a satisfying state were "stamped in" and consequently were more likely to be repeated in the future. This statement of the empirical law of effect or principle of *reinforcement* marked the introduction of concern and interest in motivational variables into theoretical conceptualization of the learning process, a concern and interest that characterizes many current behavior theories of learning.

A great deal of contemporary psychological research also stems from the work of the Nobel prize winner Ivan Pavlov (1927), who demonstrated that the simultaneous presentation of an unconditioned stimulus (meat paste) and a conditioned stimulus (sound of a tuning fork) would eventually result in the conditioned stimulus eliciting the response (salivation) which previously could only have been elicited by the unconditioned stimulus. This phenomenon, termed *conditioning*, together with Thorndike's research on the law of effect became the basis of an objective psychology which dealt only with observables and avoided the subjectivity and intuition which characterized much of the then current psychological approaches.

John B. Watson (1913, 1919) was the foremost proponent of this

[1] The author is indebted to a number of his professional colleagues for their careful reading and critical comments of earlier versions of this chapter. The author would like to especially thank Drs. I. E. Farber and Janet T. Spence for their considerable expenditure of time and effort.

vigorous objectivity based on conditioning, a position which has been labeled *behaviorism*. While the original meaning of behaviorism was at one time rather clear to virtually all students of psychology, the many changes, modifications, and alterations in contemporary *behavior theory*, or neobehaviorism, have obliterated this clarity. As Bergmann (1956) has pointed out, almost all contemporary psychology reflects Watson's influence by demanding objective scientific evidence for elucidating psychological theories, but no contemporary psychologists are true Watsonians. While much of Watson's methodological behaviorism underlies current American psychological theories, few if any of such theories have adopted his original extreme position in rejecting the significance of inferred motivational states and the importance of constitutional factors. Indeed, it was noted above that an emphasis on inferred motivational state, following Thorndike's seminal work, is characteristic of much current behavior theory, particularly that of Clark Hull.

The work of Clark Hull (1943, 1951, 1952) may be seen as the most highly developed and comprehensive theory which follows in the tradition of an objective, empirically based science of psychology. His work, primarily based on the *stimulus* (S) and *response* (R) concepts of Pavlovian conditioning and the motivational concepts of Thorndike's reinforcement principle, is better anchored in objective laboratory investigations than any other current theoretical position. This position has been extended by some of Hull's colleagues, especially Dollard and Miller (1950), to the field of personality and to counseling and therapeutic relationships. The work of Dollard and Miller thus represents a comprehensive attempt to apply the behavior-theoretical approaches developed in the experimental study of learning to the understanding of the complexities of human personality development and personality change.

Most current behavior theories stem more or less directly from the laboratory tradition in psychology and have their empirical roots in Pavlovian studies of conditioning and Thorndikian studies of reinforcement and have their methodological roots in the objectivity advocated by Watson. Since, however, they tend to deviate from Watson's original position, the terms *behavior-theoretical* or neobehavioristic are probably more appropriate. The former term, behavior-theoretical, will be used throughout the remainder of this chapter in the interests of simplicity of presentation. It can be noted that the singular importance of the terms *stimulus* (S) and *response* (R) in such approaches has also led to their being labeled S–R *theories,* while the emphasis on learning has led to labeling these *learning-theory* formulations. Finally it should be noted that there is no single behavior-theoretical

approach or S–R formulation of behavior (or of counseling), but
rather there are several theories. All resemble each other to a greater
or lesser degree especially in their emphasis on the importance of
learning and in their attempt to explicate the learning process in
objective and quantifiable ways. The interested reader will find Hilgard's *Theories of Learning* (1956) a useful summary of the most
prominent of these behavior-theoretical positions as well as of those
that have quite different orientations.

The Nature of Current Behavior Theory

The basic assumption of most current behavior-theoretical conceptualizations is that behavior is a function of its antecedents and, consequently, that behavior is lawful. Although constitutional or innate
factors are not ignored, the emphasis is almost always on the effects of
prior experiences or happenings on the events under scrutiny. It is
taken for granted that these antecedent events are identifiable by some
observational procedures and that the relation between antecedents
and behavior is regarded as investigable by the procedures and methods of the other natural sciences. The study of the relationships between antecedents and behavior is seen as the major task of psychology
in these behavior-theoretical approaches, and it is assumed that such
relationships, that is, the laws of behavior, are potentially discovera-
ble by such an approach. Such an assumption does not presume that
these laws or relationships are currently available but merely that they
should be and will be available as the body of empirical information
relating antecedents and behavior is built up. Once these laws of
behavior are available, human behavior can then be predicted and, to
the extent to which the antecedents can be manipulated and controlled, human behavior is potentially controllable.

It is important to note that such an assumption does not involve a fa-
talistic view of human behavior, a view that human destiny is irrevers-
ible. While it is assumed that certain determinants or antecedents do
lead to a certain behavior or a particular consequent, it is always further assumed that changes in the antecedents, that is additional antecedents, may lead to changes in the consequences. The influence of later
events may always change the consequences of some earlier event. This
modification by later events of the effect of a particular antecedent on
behavior does not deny the validity of an observed law but would
simply suggest that the operation of a particular determinant of behavior is complex and interacts with other determinants. As a hypothetical example, let us suppose that it has been found that early

weaning (antecedent) leads to thumb sucking (consequent) but that the psychological climate of the home, the affection and respect of the parents for each other and the child, may also affect the amount of thumb sucking. Early-weaned children from happy homes, those with a warm psychological climate, were thus found to suck their thumbs less than those early-weaned children from psychologically cold homes. The latter finding would not destroy the validity of the former law, that early weaning leads to thumb sucking, but only suggests that the law is rather complex in its operation, as it is dependent also on the psychological climate of the home. Most of the laws of human behavior will almost certainly include such complex relationships involving several determinants of behavior which interact with each other rather than just simple one-to-one relationships.

It is often argued that such lawfulness in human behavior is somehow forced or coercive because the antecedent is seen as requiring or forcing some particular behavior. This notion usually results from a confusion between the nature of scientific and legislative laws. While enacted or legislative laws may have the effect of forcing or requiring certain behavior, scientific laws are seen as merely statements of observable relationships among events in the natural world. In our hypothetical example the observation of the relationship between weaning and thumb sucking did not make the child suck his thumb; this would have occurred with or without the relationship having been observed or known. The statement of the law in such cases simply makes explicit certain relationships which help the scientist understand the natural relationship betwen antecedents and behavior. It can be noted in this example that manipulation of the age of weaning would provide some measure of control over thumb sucking, suggesting the practical utility of having such behavioral laws available.

There are some who insist that this behavior-theoretical or S–R view of human behavior is too mechanistic, too deterministic for them to accept. They argue that such a view of behavior reduces man to the level of an automaton with no active role in the choosing of his own destiny, a robot merely responding to changes in the environment over which one has no control. These critics insist that such a view is inconsistent with man's experience of his own behavior in which he sees himself as actively deciding what responses to make and what courses of action to follow. While these protagonists may accept the validity and usefulness of such a naturalistic approach for understanding the physical world, they argue that the complexities of human behavior, particularly the intricacies of human personality functioning, defy such a simple-minded and direct analysis. While granting the strength of the emotional appeal of the opponents' arguments, the behavior theorist insists on the usefulness of his approach in the understanding of human behavior and, as noted above, insists that this approach includes ways of comprehending the complexities of human behavior and personality.

One aspect of these objections to a behavior-theoretical view deserves special consideration, namely, the contention that human behavior is a function of active decision making, of higher mental activity, on the part of the behaving person. Farber (1964) has noted that there is disagreement among behavior theorists as to whether or not such decision making or thinking responses are important determinants of much human behavior, but at least some behavior theorists, including Dollard and Miller (1950) and Farber (1963) insist that these *mediational* responses, thinking or higher mental activity, do importantly influence human behavior. Much of Dollard and Miller's theory of both personality development and personality change is concerned with the nature and operation of these mediational or thinking responses. It should be noted that the acceptance of the importance of such mediational responses in these behavior theories does not change the thoroughgoing deterministic nature of the theories. These mediational responses are regarded by Dollard and Miller as having antecedents, some of which they attempt to identify; they do insist that such higher mental activity or decision making partially serve as a determinant of other, subsequent behaviors.

The Role of Language and Thinking

Dollard and Miller, following Hull, distinguish two types of responses, those which are direct and instrumental and have some immediate effect on the environment, and those which have no direct effect on the environment but rather mediate or lead the way to another response. These mediational, cognitive, or thinking responses frequently involve language behavior, although the language may not be spoken or overt.

Labeling or naming aspects of the environment, labeling particular events or certain experiences, is an important aspect of these mediational or cognitive processes. Giving two aspects of the environment the same label or name, for example, labeling or identifying two situations such as crossing the street and playing with a ferocious dog both as "dangerous," increases the probability of the person's responding the same way, with caution, timidity, avoidance, and so on, in these two rather dissimilar situations. Conversely identifying two rather similar aspects of the environment with different labels, for example, naming two similar appearing men as "father" and "uncle," increases the probability of a dissimilar response. These examples illustrate the role of mediational language or labeling responses in enhancing *generalization* and *discrimination* in behavior, respectively.

Another important property of language, not directly related to its mediational function is the capacity of language responses, both by the responding person and by others, to reward or reinforce responses. Verbal rewards, praise, commendations, and approbations serve to enhance the frequency of occurrence of responses in the manner suggested by Thorndike's statement of the law of effect. Such statements as "That's a good thing to do" or "You've done the right thing" after a particular response, whether made by others or by the person himself, have important consequences for the repetition of that response by the individual. How such verbal statements acquire reward or reinforcement value is itself an important theoretical problem with which behavior theorists have concerned themselves (cf. Brown, 1961). In general, it may be noted that behavior theories typically attempt to explain acquired motivation as a consequence of the socialization of organic drives, but a presentation of such conceptualizations is beyond the scope of this chapter.

Still another function of language is to facilitate the incentive or potential reward value of events which will occur in the future. Generally, the effectiveness of a reward on a response is dependent on the time intervening between the termination of the response and the delivery of the reward, with lengthy delays diminishing the reinforcing value of the presumed reward. Anticipatory language responses maintain the effectiveness of delayed rewards which would otherwise be dissipated over time. Thus language can mediate the reward value of such events as a candy bar to be received later in the day and the diploma to be received at the termination of school. It is these primarily human language responses which make human behavior so sharply distinct from that of the lower animals and simultaneously make human behavior so complex and difficult to explain.

Thinking or reasoning is the substitution of internal mediational responses for more overt behavior. The adult human can utilize his reasoning for more efficient solutions to his problems. He can rehearse his responses symbolically rather than overtly, anticipating at least some of the consequences of alternative responses. He can both plan his future behavior, anticipating some of the difficulties that various responses will pose and the rewards such responses can perhaps yield, and he can also analyze his past behavior, recognizing the limitations in effectiveness posed by his prior responses as well as his successes. The application of efficient higher mental processes can do much to eliminate responses which raise more problems than they solve and responses which may be temporarily satisfying but ultimately lead to undesirable consequences for the individual. The inability of the individual to think straight and to use his higher mental processes in this way is one of the primary identifying characteristics of the maladjusted person in our culture, according to at least some behavior-theoretical points of view (Dollard & Miller, 1950; Shaffer, 1947). Such failure of thinking to yield adjustive solutions to one's problems can frequently be explained in terms of the inhibiting effects of fear or anxiety on the higher mental processes, a problem to which we shall return later.

The above emphasis on the far-reaching effects of the mediational aspects of language behavior or thinking on other behavior provides one basis of the behavior-theoretical view of the counseling process. Shaffer (1947) has presented a relatively explicit statement of such a view of the counseling process. His formulation suggests: (1) that an outstanding characteristic of the maladjusted or disturbed person is his inability to control his own behavior, (2) that normal persons control their behavior by the use of a variety of language signals, or mediational responses, including subvocal and gestural ones, and (3) that counseling or therapy can be seen as a learning process through which the individual acquires an ability to speak to himself in appropriate ways so as to control his own behavior. Human behavior is seen as partially dependent on the individual's mediational or self-signaling language responses which can be changed in therapy or counseling with a resultant change in other behaviors.

One set of mediational or self-signaling language responses that is very important in both current personality theory and current counseling theory is the *self-concept*. Within a behavior-theoretical framework one can conceptualize the self-concept as those organized mediational or language responses that a person uses in describing the continuity of his motivational patterns, the underlying or genotypical pattern of his motives, and his prevailing interpersonal relationships (Hilgard, 1949). In such a conceptualization, such specific self-concept or mediational responses as "I am a failure" or "I am a success" are regarded as important determinants of the subsequent behavioral response. To the extent that such expectations of success or failure are generalized and constitute an organized set of expectancies about the consequences of one's behavior, they operate as a part of a person's self-concept.

In one recent study (Aronson & Carlsmith, 1962) those subjects who expected to do poorly on the experimental task (had an initially low self-concept) but who were told that they had performed well on the task were found to be surreptitiously lowering their performance records, while those subjects who had expected to do well on the task (had an initially high self-concept) and who were told that they had performed poorly surreptitiously raised the record of their performance. On the other hand, those subjects whose performance was in line with their expectations or self-concept made few changes in their records. Although there are obvious additional reality considerations such as aptitude or skill also involved in determining the adequacy of the consequent response, these would not preclude the importance of the self-signaling language responses also affecting such responses. Such an interpretation of the role of the self-concept in behavior highlights the importance of counseling-induced changes in the self-concept without the necessity of accepting a phenomenological view of the self-concept advocated by the Rogerians (Rogers, 1951; Combs & Snygg, 1959).

The counseling process is thus seen as focusing on the verbal language or symbolic behavior of the client, not because of some intrinsic interest in verbal behavior per se, but because of the profound and far-reaching consequences of modifications in the mediational language system or thinking processes of the client. It is assumed that these changes in cognitions initiated or acquired in the therapeutic situation will be generalized or applied in other situations, just as the effect of all educational experiences are expected to transcend the narrow confines of the situation in which they were acquired. Thus the client, as a function of counseling, learns to reason better, to analyze more carefully, to see new relationships between antecedents and behavior, to modify his self-concept, etc., and to use these new understandings not only in discussing his problems with his counselor but in changing other aspects of his life.

The Role of Fear and Anxiety

While the concept of fear or anxiety has long been of interest to psychologists, most of psychology's contemporary interest in anxiety as an important determinant of behavior stems from the work of Cannon (1929) and Freud (1936).[2] Mowrer (1939) appears to have been the first to translate their notions of anxiety into the language of S–R reinforcement theory. According to Mowrer, fear or anxiety is a learned or acquired emotional reaction to originally neutral stimuli which were presented a number of times together with a noxious or painful stimulus. Thus anxiety is the acquired capacity by new stimuli

[2] Much of Freud's work on anxiety precedes 1936 but this 1936 book is his most widely cited English-language reference on this topic.

or cues to evoke strong affective reactions, reactions acquired according to the classical conditioning conceptions of Pavlov. This conceptualization of anxiety as learned emotionality or affectivity plays a central role in several behavior-theoretical views of human motivation and behavior (Brown, 1961; Dollard & Miller, 1950) partially because of the clearly observable and profound effects of fear or anxiety on behavior and also because acquired fear is better understood than any other learned motivational state.

Both the controlled experimental research with animals and clinical reports with humans clearly indicate that the cues or stimuli that have been previously paired with painful or noxious stimuli now themselves can elicit the emotional reactions previously aroused only by the original or unconditioned stimulus. It may be further noted that this anxiety may be generalized or transferred to other than the original stimulus or cue and that this generalization can be enhanced or inhibited by labeling in the fashion discussed above. For example, a child may have been badly frightened by a particular dog, and the acquired fear of this dog can then generalize or spread to all similar appearing dogs (large, black, or growling ones), to all dogs, to all animals, etc., depending on the labeling or mediational behavior that follows the original experience.

Fear or anxiety can be attached in this way to virtually any stimulus or cue, and the socialization process presents innumerable opportunities for humans to acquire anxiety or fear reactions to a variety of cues. Dollard and Miller (1950) and Whiting and Child (1953) present analyses of the socialization process and of how anxiety is acquired through early childhood learning experiences to a variety of social stimuli. Fear or anxiety, acquired in this way, is characteristic of the maladjusted individual, and an understanding of how these anxiety reactions were acquired is crucial to an understanding of maladjusted and neurotic behavior. The "inexplicable" or "silly" fears of the neurotic, his fears of success, of studying, of making decisions, and so on are explained in terms of learned anxiety reactions to the cues involved in these situations. It is our inability to observe the circumstances of learning involved in the acquisition of these fear and anxiety reactions that makes much neurotic and maladjusted behavior difficult to comprehend. The maladjusted person himself cannot recall the occasion of acquisition because of the inhibiting effects of anxiety on thinking, a problem which is discussed more fully below, or because the learning may have occurred early in life, before the language or mediational responses were sufficiently developed to permit such verbal recall.

A very important theoretical consideration is that anxiety or fear operates as a secondary or acquired drive. Increases in activity level are characteristic of individuals in the presence of drive cues, and there is considerable evidence (cf. Brown, 1961, pp. 144–168) that anxiety cues do function precisely in this way. The presence of acquired anxiety cues operates both as generalized energizers of behavior and as cues for particular responses. It is beyond the scope of this presentation to differentiate between these two functions.

Not only does anxiety appear to function as an instigator or energizer of behavior, but its prompt reduction after a response leads to facilitation of that response (a case of the operation of the previously noted empirical law of effect). The elimination or cessation of an anxiety-arousing cue thus has reinforcement value and leads to the repetition of any response which has led to anxiety reduction. Anxiety cues lead to increases in activity, and provided that the initial response made does not lead to anxiety reduction, a variety of responses are made; such variable or trial-and-error behavior will continue until a response is made which reduces the anxiety. The nature of the response which results in anxiety reduction will depend on a variety of factors, including the particular situation.

It should be clear that there are many potential anxiety-reducing responses in any situation and that there will be considerable variability among individuals as to which response is acquired. Some individuals will leave the situation and avoid it in the future, some will deny the existence of the anxiety cues, and so on, covering the entire gamut of the so-called "defense mechanisms" or responses to anxiety. These responses which serve the individual best as anxiety reducers become acquired as an important part of his behavioral repertoire or personality. It can be noted that many anxiety-reducing responses have later undesirable consequences, although they do serve as immediate anxiety reducers. Such responses as compulsions, hysteria, and alcoholism can be seen as strong immediate tension or anxiety reducers, although they later raise difficulties for the individual. Symptoms are those responses whose immediate anxiety-reduced effects are outweighed by their later nonadaptive consequences.

It might be asked why individuals do not simply avoid these anxiety-producing cues and thus avoid the possibility of developing such self-defeating responses. In some situations, as in the case of phobias, this is exactly what does occur. If the anxiety-producing cue can be easily avoided, as in not swimming or not flying in airplanes, the individual has little difficulty in arranging to avoid these cues. However, many of these cues are not so easily avoided because they are highly generalized fears such as fear of people, fear of competitive situations, and so on, and because adequate functioning in such situations is regarded by society as essential for normal daily life. Persons who are successful in interpersonal relationships or in competitive situations are highly reinforced for such success, and persons with acquired fears of these situations are in strong conflict between their incompatible desire to function effectively and their strong fear of the situation. Thus, fears lead to conflicts that are also very characteristic of the neurotic in our society.

In summary it can be noted that certain cues or stimuli can acquire the capacity to serve as the signal for complex emotional responses, called anxiety, and these responses then themselves serve as cues or stimuli for still other responses. Anxiety is therefore both a response and a signal for other behavioral responses. Anxiety operates as a drive, instigating or impelling the individual to respond, and its reduction will reinforce those responses associated with the reduction. Those responses which have led to the prompt reduction of anxiety will be repeated even though they may lead to later maladaptive consequences.

Unconscious Processes

We have previously presented a conceptualization of the important role of cognitive or mediational responses, language and thinking, in behavior. Such mediational responses, especially those involving foresight and planning, are regarded as important in determining the adaptive quality of the individual's behavior. Those responses which are not under language control or where the language control is faulty are important in maladjustment of behavior pathology. These behaviors which are not under mediational or language control are regarded as *unconscious,* a formulation which is quite consistent with psychoanalytic notions.

It is possible to differentiate two different types of unconscious responses in behavior theory. The first of these includes the responses acquired early in life, prior to the development of language behavior, and for which there are no adequate cultural labels provided such as kinesthetic or visceral responses. Our inability to label accurately such complex motor behavior as that involved in driving an automobile or playing tennis partially accounts for the difficulties we encounter in teaching these skills to others. The second type of unconscious process, which is far more important for understanding maladjustive behavior, involves those responses for which anxiety or fear prevented the acquisition of labeling responses or for which the mediational responses were available but could not be used because of the inhibiting effects of fear or anxiety. Fear and anxiety can become attached to thought or language responses in exactly the same way that any previously neutral cue can acquire anxiety value; this process has been labeled as *repression* by Dollard and Miller (1950, pp. 198ff.). Repression is thus seen as the avoidance of certain thoughts which have acquired anxiety effects and the response of not thinking or repression is reinforced by drive (anxiety) reduction in exactly the same way as the other symptoms discussed above. Memories of painful events are thus avoided because of their capacity to reevoke the pain or anxiety experienced in the original situation.

This repression of the antecedents of behavior, the inability to recall the circumstances of how certain behaviors were learned, is one of the elements that make maladjusted behavior appear silly or unreasonable. The individual evidences responses which are clearly maladaptive, frequently even to himself, and cannot explain why he is responding in this fashion. For example, this occurs in phobias where the individual cannot remember, i.e., has repressed, the original learning experience leading to the phobic reaction although the resultant reaction is clearly present. Recall of the original learning situation is not necessary for the effects of learning to be present, although in ordinary social intercourse we almost always expect persons to be able to offer some acceptable reasons for their behavior. It is suggested here that the person's inability to justify behavior involving repression may actually raise his anxiety level, for he is now viewed by others as peculiar or stupid because of his inability to explain why he is behaving in this fashion. This state of affairs often gives rise to the development of socially acceptable but often either incomplete or inaccurate explanations of one's own behavior, the so-called "rationalizations." Such faulty labeling or inadequate thinking may be self-satisfying and socially acceptable but inhibits adequate self-understanding.

It should be noted that in our culture we tend to punish others not only for overt acts but also for having the thoughts or impulses that led to the overt act. This type of punishment is particularly evident in our child-rearing practices where we sometimes punish children more severely for the "dirty" thoughts that led to the aggressive or sexual behavior than for the behavior itself. Because we frequently punish children more for such "evil" thoughts than for the deed or act itself, we may actually inhibit the thinking response without inhibiting the overt response. Thus an individual responds sexually or aggressively without being able to adequately label his own behavior as such. In such cases the anxiety has been attached only to the verbal or mediational responses and not to the overt ones.

The tendency to avoid certain anxiety-producing thoughts varies along a continuum depending on the strength of the fear involved. Strong fear may result in a complete inability to think about particular topics and is evidenced by blocking and generalized avoidance of the subject, while milder fear will result in a weaker tendency to avoid the anxiety-producing topic. We frequently see instances of this type of avoidance of anxiety in group discussions of illness or death when one member of a group suggests, on a more conscious level, that the topic be changed to a more pleasant one.

The avoidance by an individual of thoughts about certain responses will also lead to a failure to see connections between responses or patterns of behavior. For example, an underachieving high school student may not be able to see that his scholastic failure serves as a way of expressing his hostility toward his father. All previous direct expressions of hostility as well as the thoughts underlying such expressions previously may have been severely punished. The youngster, while recognizing that the father is upset and angry, can deny any direct responsibility for his father's upset, blaming his academic difficulties on a variety of other circumstances. Since the son is unable to correctly label his own failure as a subtle form of hostility because such an admission would be anxiety arousing, he continues to fail, much to his own dismay as well as that of his teachers who find such behavior inexplicable. The father, although himself upset and angry, is typically not able to punish the adolescent for his hostility but only for his underachievement. These unconsciously determined responses are typically seen by the psychologist as maladaptive because of the long-term consequences of such responses, although they may have short-term reinforcing properties.

In still another example of the interfering effects of repression on thinking, a vocationally undecided college junior is unable to choose among several major fields for which his aptitudes and interests would qualify him, although he has available considerable information about the fields and the opportunities these fields present. The counselor to whom he turns for assistance with this problem recognized that the client is unable to take responsibility for making any important decisions which affects his life and, further, that there is a pattern of such responsibility avoidance running through the client's self-reported history. The client, however, is unaware of this pattern and is consequently unable to conceptualize remedial courses of action. Under such circumstances the counselor would be concerned about the client's dependency problems and how the client's anxiety about dependency was presumably interfering with his seeing the pattern of his own behavior.

In both examples we can observe that repression, that the avoidance of certain thoughts that are anxiety producing, leads to the failure by the individual to label adequately his own maladaptive behavior and see certain connections among his responses or between environment events and his responses. This failure to develop adequate mediational or language responses, the inability to "think straight," can lead to the failure of any response to appear, to the making of inappropriate responses, to faulty generalizations or discrimination, to an inadequate or unrealistic self-concept, and to the entire gamut of maladaptive and neurotic behaviors.

Counseling and Psychotherapy

Thus far this chapter has been concerned with an explanation of maladjustive behavior, using the concepts and terms of traditional general or experimental psychology. It is this methodological behaviorism that characterizes the behavior-theoretical approach to all problems and, naturally enough, extends to the behavior-theoretical views of counseling and psychotherapy. Behavior theory regards human behavior as primarily rooted in the experiential history of the organism, as having been learned, and as susceptible to modification by psychological means. The emphasis of behavior theory is thus on the nature of the learning processes that underlie this behavioral change, and these processes are regarded as essentially identical to those involved in any other kind of complex human learning. Such an approach not only does much to remove the mystique surrounding counseling and psychotherapy but also permits the application of understanding gained through traditional laboratory and educational psychology to the therapeutic interaction.

It should be noted in this context that there is no single behavior-theoretical view of counseling or psychotherapy but rather that there are a number of such views. Just as there is no single behavior-theoretical view of learning, even in the case of rather simple learning phenomena, there is no single behavior-theoretical view of the process of therapy or counseling, which is more complex and far less understood than the general process of learning. What characterizes such divergent views as behavior-theoretical, or S–R, is their conceptualization of counseling as a situation involving the application of the general laws of learning. Behavior-theoretical analyses of the therapeutic interaction use the same constructs and language derived from laboratory psychology that were used in the earlier section of this chapter to describe the development and maintenance of nonadaptive responses and behavior. Thus a behavior-theoretical view of counseling is one characterized by methodological behaviorism and by rigorously defined concepts and operational language rather than by any particular counseling or therapeutic technique.

Contemporary behavior theorists interested in the area of counseling and psychotherapy are currently advocating two quite dissimilar approaches to the problems of therapeutic change. One group of these behavior theorists (Shoben, 1948; Dollard & Miller, 1950; Murray, 1964) has advocated the use of procedures and techniques typically used in the rather traditional, psychoanalytically oriented approaches to counseling and psychotherapy. Each of these writers has attempted, more or less successfully, to translate the concepts of traditional psychoanalysis into the language of behavior theory and regard such a *rapprochement* as both feasible and desirable. Another group of writers (Wolpe, 1958; Eysenck, 1960; Bandura, 1961), stemming from a similar behavior-theoretical orientation, has advocated the direct intervention in and manipulation of the client's behavior, following closely the procedures typically regarded as traditional directive therapy. These latter theorists argue that an acceptance of the full implications of conceptualizing counseling and therapy as a learning process must lead to a therapeutic system which is very different in its procedures from the typical one-to-one verbal interchange of traditional therapeutic interviews. Both groups, although they advocate apparently dissimilar approaches to the process of therapeutic change, are consistent with behavior theory; rather amusingly each set of theorists tends to argue that its position is *more* consistent with behavior theory than the other. The more significant question, of course, is which approach has more potential for therapeutic change, an empirical problem that can only be answered by research studies. Adequately controlled studies comparing the efficacy of such different therapeutic approaches have not yet been done, and the lack of empirically derived data heightens the controversy.

Throughout the remainder of this chapter an effort will be made, whenever appropriate, to contrast the implications for therapeutic practice of these two approaches. The former, with its emphasis on verbal reports of behavior and changing mediating responses, will be termed the *indirect* approach, while the latter, with its emphasis on the actual overt responses and the direct control of behavior, will be termed the *direct* approach. The theoretical roots of both of these approaches in current behavior theory should, however, be recalled.

Although there has been no systematic attempt to translate client-centered or Rogerian concepts into behavior-theoretical terms, Murray's (1956) behavior-theoretical analysis of several published client-centered cases suggests that this could indeed be done. It should appear equally feasible to translate virtually any psychologically based theory of therapeutic change into behavior-theoretical terms but, it would be noted, such translations are typically far more satisfactory and rewarding to the translator than to the original proponents of the system who almost invariably claim that the translation has damaged the original theory beyond any hope of recognition. The client-centered approach with its emphasis on the verbal interaction between client and therapist and on the resultant changes in self-concept is far closer to that advocated in the indirect approach than that of the direct approach. One common element involved in both the direct and indirect approaches is a concern with anxiety as an important factor in maladjustive behavior and its modification.

Anxiety as a Counseling Problem

One general characteristic of the client who requests therapeutic help, be it called counseling or psychotherapy, is the presence of anxiety. In general, diffuse anxiety or the so-called "free-floating" anxiety typifies the anxiety neurotic, or, on the other hand, it may be more delimited anxiety which is anchored in some rather circumscribed area, such as vocational or educational choice, marital, educational, or occupational adjustment. Even when the anxiety cues can be crudely identified by the client, he usually has difficulty in precisely delineating or differentiating the circumstances of anxiety arousal. The client may also have developed a variety of mechanisms for attempting to cope with his anxiety, obsessions, compulsions, rationalizations, denials, and so on (see Dollard & Miller, 1950, p. 157ff., for a behavior-theoretical analysis of how such mechanisms are learned), but these mechanisms are always operating ineffectively, or the client would not voluntarily seek help. The mechanisms may not be operating efficiently, and the individual is thus still experiencing anxiety; or the anxiety level has suddenly been increased by some new threat, and the mechanisms cannot handle the additional load; or the mechanisms are themselves maladaptive and anxiety producing. Compulsive or obsessive defenses that actually interfere with a person's attempts to study, work, or play are examples of this last type of failure of the mechanisms to work.

There are two general reasons for the nonadaptive behavior seen in counseling, both of which involve anxiety. In one instance, the individual has never had sufficient opportunity to acquire or learn adaptive or adequate responses, and his inadequate behavior stems from a limitation of experience. Thus a client may be seen as having poor social skills, no vocational plans, or inadequate study habits, simply because of the failure of his prior experience to provide adequate opportunities for the learning of such responses. In such cases the anxiety observed in counseling is regarded as stemming from the failures which have resulted or can result from this lack of skills, skills which the client recognized that others possess but that he does not. This anxiety coupled with shame and guilt stops the client from seeking assistance from nonprofessional sources, friends or relatives, and turns him instead to the counselor or therapist. The person who is not anxious about such inadequacies rarely seeks professional help, while the anxious client turns to professional help because of the paucity of social resources available to remedy such personal inadequacies. The popularity of such skills-oriented self-improvement courses as public speaking and social dancing partially attest to the social need for such resources. In such cases, once the anxiety due to not having the skills available is alleviated, the skills can typically be promptly acquired.

Rather typical vocational guidance may be seen as an example of this type of treatment. The client's initial anxiety about not having made a vocational choice is quickly alleviated, and the counselor then sets about to provide information about the client's abilities and interests and also about the world of work so that the client can now integrate these data into a vocational decision. In such a circumstance, the client's failure to have previously acquired such information is regarded as stemming from a prior lack of exposure to such educational experiences. The very interesting problem of how persons can avoid such experiences in the normal course of events is ignored and the focus is on the client's acquiring the necessary skills. In this first instance the anxiety evidenced by the client is seen as a consequent of the client's failure to have developed the appropriate skills. The anxiety is seen as playing a rather minor role in the etiology of the problem, being primarily responsible for the client's not availing himself of the other noncounseling resources available for problem solving.

In the second instance, anxiety is regarded as playing a central role in the development of the problem. In this instance, the client's failure to develop or learn the appropriate response is not regarded as resulting from the failure of opportunity but rather from the failure to use the opportunities which were provided because of the interfering effects of anxiety. Thus the client who is vocationally uncommitted is undecided not simply because of lack of information either about himself or the world of work but because making a decision or commitment is strongly anxiety arousing. He may have such information but be unable to utilize it, or he may not have such information, his anxiety preventing him from taking advantage of opportunities to acquire it. For example, making a vocational decision may involve breaking away from parents or defying them; it may represent an act of independence for which the client is not yet ready; it may mean a commitment to an academic career for which the client may feel inadequate, and so on. In each of these hypothetical examples the client avoids the anxiety by avoiding making a decision. But there are strong social pressures on adolescents and young adults to make a vocational choice, at least on the verbal level, and the client cannot completely avoid this anxiety-producing situation as can the phobic individual who is made fearful by airplanes or bodies of water. In the case of the vocationally indecisive client, there are strong pressures to symbolically approach the source of his conflict. Simply consider as one example of this social pressure the number of times adolescents and young adults are asked, "What are you going to be?" It is often this *conflict* of opposite tendencies, one to avoid the anxiety involved in a decision and the other to yield to the social pressure and decide, that serves as the drive that brings the client to counseling or therapy. If the situation that arouses the anxiety could easily have been avoided, the client would have avoided such situations and the anxiety arousal and never come for help.

In this latter instance it is the anxiety which has been previously attached to otherwise neutral cues (see above for a more detailed discussion of how anxiety acquisition is typically explained by current behavior theorists) that prevented the client from using the previously available opportunities to acquire the skills which he now lacks. One of the goals of diagnosis in counseling and therapy with such cases is the identification of the cues that arouse this anxiety so that the anxiety can be eliminated or reduced, permitting the client to now learn appropriate skills. The counselor's mere provision of current opportunities for learning the skills is not sufficient in this latter instance since the anxiety will still be aroused by the cues in the learning situation. In this latter instance the anxiety is regarded as a cause of the client's problem. But, as noted in the first instance, the lack of such adequate responses is itself anxiety arousing, and the client is often only able to discuss this consequent anxiety without noting the interfering effects of the antecedent anxiety. Indeed, since discussing the type of experience, even in counseling, involves anxiety-producing thoughts, repression or the avoidance of such anxiety-producing thoughts may operate, producing a distorted or incomplete picture of the development of the client's problem. It is, therefore, sometimes rather difficult for the counselor to decide exactly how anxiety did enter into the etiology of the client's problem.

For example, a twenty-one-year-old male college junior applied for counseling help with a presenting problem of very poor social skills, especially in heterosexual relationships, a history of rather limited heterosexual experience, and considerable anxiety and concern about the implications of this problem for his general adjustment in the future. A diagnostic problem which confronted the counselor was the assessment of the role of anxiety in this case. If he decided that the client's lack of heterosexual skills was the result of a lack of opportunity to develop such skills, an example of the first instance, he might have encouraged the client to avail himself of the several opportunities for acquiring social skills now available to him. The counselor might have arranged for the client to take social dancing lessons at the campus Y or join a social group that would permit the client to develop some social skills. The counselor's role would have been to reduce the client's initial anxiety, provide the opportunity for the skills to be acquired, and wait for the development of more adequate social behavior to be reinforced by society. If, however, this was a case of the second sort, where anxiety initially interfered with the acquisition of the response, the client would still become extremely anxious when confronted with the opportunity to learn how to dance or interact with girls, and unless the cues arousing the anxiety were identified by the counselor and this anxiety eliminated or reduced, the client could not profitably use these counselor-provided opportunities for social learning. This was indeed the case with this particular client who, upon contact with girls, became sexually aroused which, because of his particular learning history, served as the cue for strong anxiety. Thus, for this client the opportunity to develop heterosexual social skills only served as an opportunity to become extremely anxious. Only when the anxiety was reduced through counseling was this client able to acquire the skill he previously lacked in this area.

A diagnostic problem confronting the counselor is the assessment of the role of anxiety in the etiology of the problem. In the above example the decision that anxiety was an important antecedent to the problem was based on the counselor's ascertaining that the client had many opportunities for heterosexual relationships throughout high school and college but never used them because he felt tense and anxious when confronted with such opportunities. Further he evidenced strong anxiety and powerful repression when asked about his sexual interests in females, explaining that his puritanical religious background would never permit him to think about girls "in that way" prior to marriage, if even then. The counselor therefore reached the diagnostic decision that anxiety had led to the development of this client's problem and must be weakened or eliminated prior to the acquisition of any new skills.

It should be noted, however, that the mere elimination of anxiety does not directly or invariably lead to the development of these previously unlearned responses, even when anxiety is the antecedent of the failure to learn. The extinction of anxiety now makes the client teachable, but the acquisition of skills, particularly such complex social skills as dancing or dating, still requires specific learning experiences directed at the development of such skills. The failure of counselors and therapists to help the client find such opportunities, especially in a culture with few such opportunities generally available, leads to less effective counseling results than would otherwise be the case. The resolution of the client's problem in the above example involves not only a reduction of his anxiety but also an acquisition of the proper skills. While it is obviously beyond the interests and perhaps even beyond the skills of the average counselor or therapist to provide these learning experiences himself, he should not overlook the client's need for finding and using such opportunities to achieve an adequate resolution of his problem.

In actual counseling practice, the two processes of reducing the interfering anxiety and initiating the acquisition of skills frequently overlap in time. The counselor continuously evaluates the changes in the client's anxiety level. When, in the counselor's judgment, sufficient anxiety reduction has occurred so that the client may now approach the anxiety-producing cues without severe discomfort, some counselors will urge the client to test his freedom from anxiety by entering into a program of acquiring new socially adequate responses. The client can regularly discuss his progress in these real-life situations, with the therapist serving both to reduce the antecedent anxiety further and to reinforce the reported gains.

The previous discussion takes the view that neurotic or maladaptive behaviors are responses to internal and largely hypothetical states of emotionality which are typically called anxiety. Following Dollard and Miller (1950), it was argued that counseling typically requires some elimination of anxiety before desirable patterns of behavior can be learned. Some behavior theorists (e.g., Eysenck, 1960), however, would contend that such anxiety elimination should not be the counselor's primary concern but rather that therapy should be directed at the elimination of nonadjustive behavior pattern and/or providing conditions for learning more adjustive responses. In actual practice, however, it is often difficult to decide to what extent a therapeutic procedure involves anxiety extinction along with retraining. It would also appear that there may be some cases in which anxiety extinction is necessary prior to retraining.

The Elimination of Anxiety

Anxiety has been previously defined as a learned or acquired emotional reaction to an originally neutral stimulus. Earlier sections of this chapter have highlighted the central role of anxiety in the etiology of maladjustment and have discussed the importance for reducing or eliminating anxiety in order to effect behavior change in counseling. The issues, both theoretical and practical, involved in a behavior-theoretical analysis of such anxiety elimination or modification are highly complex and beyond the scope of this chapter. The following is a necessarily abbreviated attempt to elucidate the process of anxiety elimination, especially as it applies to the therapeutic interaction.

Anxiety, like other learned responses, may be weakened or extinguished when the response is made to occur without any primary reinforcement. The fear or anxiety was originally acquired by pairing a previously neutral stimulus or cue with a painful or noxious stimulus. Such learned fear or anxiety can be weakened by now presenting the learned anxiety cue without the primary reinforcement of the painful or noxious stimuli. The child who has learned to be frightened of a large black dog because he had been bitten or knocked down by this dog will have his fear reduced if on his next meeting with this animal, he is not bothered by it.

In comparison with many other responses, however, fear or anxiety is extremely resistant to extinction. The experimental research on fear reduction in animals as well as clinical reports on anxiety reduction in humans offer unequivocal support for this contention. Explanations of the resistance to extinction of fear or anxiety responses is based on empirical observations that fear is a strong drive and that fear reduction is a powerful reinforcer (see Brown, 1961, p. 144ff.). The strength of responses or habits learned as a function of the reduction of such a powerful drive should themselves be quite powerful and consequently very resistant to extinction.

There is the additional element that many responses can serve as anxiety reducers, and because the anxiety is temporarily reduced, these responses operate to prevent any final extinction of the acquired anxiety response. Thus, the learned anxiety cue elicits the anxiety, and the anxiety, in turn, elicits some maladaptive but anxiety-reducing response. This vicious circle prevents any permanent extinction of the anxiety-arousing properties of the cues.

Further, the resistance of anxiety to extinction is affected by any circumstance that would serve to enhance the anxiety, such as reinforcement by a more painful stimulus or additional reinforced trials, particularly if these reinforced trials occur after extinction has started. This process is an instance of *partial reinforcement,* where the primary-reinforcement is not paired on every trial with the learned or conditioned stimulus but occurs together less frequently and leads to responses that are exceedingly resistant to extinction. Thus, in the example of the boy and the dog, if the dog were to again knock the boy down or bite him after several experiences where the animal had appeared harmless, the boy's resulting fear of the dog would now be very much more difficult to extinguish than it had originally been. If it is assumed that most human fear responses are acquired under exactly such conditions of partial reinforcement, the resistance of such anxiety to extinction becomes more understandable.

Guthrie (1952) notes that, in general, there are three ways of presenting a stimulus or cue that are likely to lead to extinction of a learned response, such as anxiety, to that stimulus. The first of these, termed *adaptation* or *desensitization,* involves the presentation of the stimulus at very weak strengths so that it will not be strong enough to actually elicit the response. The strength of the stimulus is then gradually increased, always taking care to keep the strength of the stimulus below that required to elicit the response, until even the presentation of the stimulus at full strength is no longer an effective cue for eliciting the response. One way of reducing the effectiveness of the stimulus in such an adaptation process is to present the stimulus at some distance from the organism and then gradually decrease the distance. In the example of the boy and the dog, the dog could be brought into the boy's sight and gradually brought closer each time but never close enough on any occasion actually to elicit an anxiety response.

The second method of extinguishing anxiety is called inhibitory conditioning or *internal inhibition.* The present view of this process of internal or reactive inhibition involves presenting the anxiety-producing cues in sufficient strength to elicit the anxiety response, and these cues are either continuously presented or are presented for periods of time, without any additional primary reinforcement, but with only brief intervals of rest interspersed between their presentation. The continual or very frequent presentation of such stimulation will result in a virtually continuous response; such continual responsiveness will in turn lead to fatigue and other changes in the organism, which will eventually lead to the cessation of the response despite the continued presence of the anxiety-arousing cues. An important factor in extinguishing anxiety through internal inhibition by frequent presentation of the anxiety cues is the length of the interval between the presentation of the anxiety cues. If the interval between these presentations is very brief, more technically termed the *massing of trials,* the internal or reactive inhibition builds up quite rapidly and extinction of the anxiety response is facilitated. This procedure is the *experimental extinction* process of classical Pavlovian conditioning and can be applied to any conditioned response, presumably including anxiety.

If, on the other hand, these rest periods are sufficiently lengthy or distributed in such a way as to permit dissipation of the reactive inhibition, then little extinction will occur. Simply stated, extinction of anxiety will occur as a function of internal inhibition if the stimulus-arousing anxiety is continually presented to an organism with only brief time intervals between these continual presentations.

One reason for the failure of anxiety responses to extinguish through internal inhibition in the natural course of events is that individuals tend to avoid anxiety-provoking cues in real life, particularly if they have recently been exposed to such cues. The massing of extinction trials, with no opportunity for internal inhibition to dissipate, rarely occurs naturally when fear or anxiety is the drive involved. For example, the individual who has a phobic fear of heights rarely will continually ride up and down the elevator in the tallest building in town to rid himself of his anxiety by such a massing of trials. Quite the reverse is more likely to happen: If he can bring himself to ride the elevator once, his relief at arriving safely on the ground will lead to a quick leave taking of the premises. In the example of the boy and the dog, for internal or reactive inhibition to lead to the extinction of anxiety, the boy would have to be presented with the sight of the dog again and again with only brief lapses of time intervening between these presentations, although he would probably evidence signs of strong anxiety and make several attempts to withdraw from the situation. The difficulties in arranging for extinction to take place under such circumstances, especially if a protective parent was present, should be readily apparent to the reader, although there is little question that such a procedure will often be efficacious in eliminating the anxiety.

The third procedure discussed by Guthrie, *counterconditioning*, involves the presentation of the anxiety cue in sufficient strength to elicit the anxiety response but when the organism is making some other response that is incompatible with the anxiety response, *counterconditioning*. For example, eating and the satiation of hunger are partially incompatible with fear, provided that the fear is not too strong. In a now classical experiment using this method of *competing responses*, Jones (1924) eliminated a young boy's fear of a rabbit by showing the boy a rabbit while the boy was eating. Under these circumstances, the child did not evidence any fear, although it was evidenced under other circumstances. The rabbit was kept at a distance during the early phases of the extinction process so that the responses involved in eating inhibited the anxiety responses rather than the reverse occurring. One of the dangers inherent in such procedures is that the opposite result may occur, and the child may learn through a process of higher-order conditioning to become anxious at the sight of food.

It should be recognized that these three methods are not clearly distinguishable from each other, especially in practice. Most attempts to eliminate anxiety involve some combination of these methods, and it is difficult to find instances of a pure approach. All three methods are aimed at eliminating the acquired capacity of a cue to arouse the anxiety response by somehow interfering with the capacity of the previously neutral cue to elicit the emotional response originally elicited only by the noxious stimulus. Unfortunately for contemporary counseling practice, there have been few studies of the relative effectiveness of these three procedures of extinguishing anxiety. Further, since the mechanisms underlying these procedures are not clearly understood at this time, it is not possible to decide on their relative efficacy on theoretical grounds.

Anxiety Reduction in Counseling

While most behavior theorists would tend to agree with the foregoing analysis of the principles of anxiety reduction, they would not necessarily agree on how to implement these theoretical considerations in the actual process of counseling or therapy. The advocates of the direct approach to counseling and therapy generally attempt to reduce anxiety through a direct manipulation of the environment, either in the therapist's office or in the real world, to produce anxiety reduction, rather than through a symbolic representation of these cues. Eysenck's (1960) collection of readings on behavior therapy presents a representative cross section of the rather straightforward techniques of anxiety reduction recommended by the proponents of the direct approach. The techniques generally recommended in this approach include such procedures as adaptation or desensitization based on the actual physical presentation of the anxiety-producing cues, such as ambulances, animals, baby buggies, and so on, to the client in order to eliminate the anxiety. This desensitization is very frequently accompanied by a process of counterconditioning.

Lazarus (1960), for example, has reported treating a child's strong fear of moving vehicles by reinforcing each of the child's "positive" comments about trains, cars, buses, and so on, by giving him a piece of candy. After the child was able to talk about moving vehicles without experiencing anxiety, the child and the therapist began to play with toy cars and, during the play, the child was again reinforced with chocolates. He then was fed chocolates in a stationary auto until he no longer experienced anxiety and finally was driven in a car to a candy shop where he was fed chocolate. At the conclusion of this series of treatments, the child was sufficiently free of anxiety to be able to go driving with his parents, although, for a time, he insisted on being fed chocolates during such drives.

Another recommended procedure is the elimination of responses which are anxiety reducing, but otherwise maladaptive responses, by means of internal inhibition. Yates (1958), following the early research of Dunlap (1932) on negative practice, has offered the following which he regarded as an example of the application of the principle of internal inhibition: If tics are voluntarily evoked by therapist's instructions under conditions of massed practice followed by periods of prolonged rest, these tics are extinguished, and this extinction is generalized beyond the therapy situation.

Nonadjustive anxiety-reducing responses may also be treated by a process of counterconditioning, using pain or other noxious stimulation, so-called *aversion therapy*. In such counterconditioning the maladjustive responses, which previously served as anxiety reducers, now become the cues for anxiety increments. Blakemore, Thorpe, Barker, Conway, and Lavin (1963) report successfully treating a male transvestite by systematically providing a very unpleasant electric shock at irregular periods to the patient while he was dressed in woman's clothing; the series of shocks were terminated only when he had removed all of these clothes. Thus, being dressed in women's clothing became the cue for anxiety, which was reduced when he divested himself of these clothes. Under such circumstances the transvestism became anxiety producing, and the patient gave up this maladaptive response.

Still another set of recommended procedures involves the direct reinforcement or reward of those emergent behaviors which the therapist regards as appropriate with little concern about anxiety extinction. Peters and Jenkins (1954), Lindsley (1956), and King, Armitage, and Tilton (1960) have all reported increases in socially appropriate behavior by hospitalized schizophrenics when such responses were initially promptly rewarded by candy or cigarettes. Ferster and DeMeyer (1961) have reported increases in reality-oriented behavior in autistic or schizophrenic children by the use of similar *operant-conditioning* procedures. Brady and Lind (1961) report curing a patient suffering from hysterical blindness by this method. In all these studies, changes in behavior in the direction of greater social adjustment resulted in the patient's promptly receiving a small but tangible reward, and all therapists report the continuance of this behavior outside of the therapy situation as culturally available secondary reinforcers now sustained the new responses.

Not all the procedures recommended by advocates of the direct approach are quite as impersonal as those discussed above. Indeed, one of the most widely used and strongly recommended techniques is that of desensitization coupled with counterconditioning by relaxation. Wolpe (1958) recognized that the responses involved in relaxation were incompatible with those of anxiety. If, therefore, thte anxiety cues could be presented while the patient was in a state of more or less complete relaxation, the capacity of these cues to elicit anxiety would be consequently reduced. Wolpe also used sexual and assertive responses in his *reciprocal inhibition* therapy since such responses are also physiologically antagonistic to and therefore inhibitory of anxiety, but the use of relaxation appears to be the most widely adopted of his procedures (see Eysenck, 1960). The relationship of these procedures to the concept of counterconditioning should be obvious to the reader.

On the basis of his examination of the patient, particularly his assessment of the current sources of the patient's anxiety, Wolpe develops a list of the cues that elicit anxiety in rank order of strength, the anxiety hierarchy. The patient is then taught relaxation procedures, frequently involving the use of hypnotic suggestion, and is then told to think of or imagine situations involving a very weak anxiety-producing cue. If anxiety is evidenced, a still weaker cue is chosen until the client can imagine the anxiety-producing situation without experiencing anxiety, while still in a state of relaxation. In later sessions stronger and stronger anxiety-producing cues are presented until the entire anxiety hierarchy can be imagined without disturbing the patient's relaxation. Thus, through reciprocal inhibition therapy or counterconditioning, relaxation rather than anxiety is attached to the cues in the anxiety hierarchy.

The proponents of the direct approach to behavior-theoretical counseling and therapy emphasize its rather impersonal, highly manipulative, ahistorical, symptom-reducing orientation. In this approach, with its reliance on mechanically delivered reinforcements frequently based on primary drives of hunger, thirst, pain avoidance, and so on, the relationship between client and therapist is not central to the treatment process, although several writers, especially Wolpe (1958), point out the need for establishing a good interpersonal relationship in the treatment process. The focus of this general approach to treatment is the elimination of the client's symptoms with considerably less attention to anxiety elimination. Although it is clearly recognized that both the anxiety and the mechanisms of handling anxiety have been acquired through learning, it is argued that the direct treatment of these conditions does not ordinarily require any specific knowledge by the therapist of the historical events to identify the anxiety-arousing cues or to retrain the client. These conditions or symptoms are not regarded in this direct approach as resulting from any underlying historically based neurosis but rather as "simple learned habits" (Eysenck, 1960, p. 9). Since there is no neurosis or conflict underlying the symptom but merely the symptom itself, the elimination of the symptom should be the therapist's only concern, at least according to Eysenck. In such a conceptualization there is little concern with the learning of the symptoms, only with their unlearning or reconditioning. This lack of concern with the etiology of the client's problem typically extends to the cognitive or language responses that mediate the client's anxiety and his attempts to reduce anxiety. Thus, not only is there little or no exploration of the client's psychological development and his personal history, there is also little or no exploration of his current intrapsychic life, his self-concept, or his other cognitive responses which serve as mediators of his behavior. The proponents of this direct approach believe that the elimination of the symptoms is the crucial element of counseling and therapy and that appropriate changes in the cognitive processes will follow the elimination of the symptoms.

In contrast, the proponents of the indirect approach take the view that changes in the cognitive or mediational processes that direct or steer human behavior must first be accomplished, and changes in the more overt responses will typically follow these cognitive changes. These changes in cognition or self-signaling language systems may be termed as "developing a more realistic self-concept" or "the growth of insight into one's personality," etc., depending on the particular frame of reference of the therapist. In the indirect approach, the counselor's efforts are concentrated on changing these cognitive habits or responses, particularly those which have been blocked or inhibited by anxiety, with the expectation that changing these mediational processes in the direction of clearer thinking will lead to more effective behavior. Thus, the indirect approach views changes in overt behavior as following changes in the mediational responses, while the direct approach views the changes in mediational responses as following changes in overt responses. The problem of whether changes in the direction of a more positive self-concept must precede or follow satisfying experience is a case in point. The advocates of the indirect approach argue for an initial attention to such mediational responses in therapy prior to having the client attempting more overt responses in real-life situations.

Although it is sometimes argued that counseling or therapy with this indirect orientation is overly intellectual and pays too little attention to motivational or emotional factors, it should be noted that it is precisely these emotional factors that are conceptualized as interfering with the adequacy of the cognitive processes, and it is on this anxiety that the indirect behavior-theoretical counselor concentrates his efforts. The process of anxiety reduction in the indirect approach involves the presentation of the anxiety-arousing stimuli on the verbal, symbolic level, through a discussion of the client's problems and how they developed, rather than the presentation of the actual physical stimuli, as was advocated in the direct approach.

The question of the efficacy of these two approaches, the direct or the indirect, in the elimination of anxiety, especially the problem of the necessity of reexposing the client to the actual anxiety-arousing cues, as part of counseling is quite complex. Some anxieties are highly generalized, such as anxiety about authority relationships or heterosexual interactions, and because of repression, the client cannot identify the original source of the anxiety. Further, it often would be impossible to provide the original anxiety-producing cues in counseling because of practical considerations, for example, the cues involved in anxiety learned on a battlefield in wartime or those acquired in an interaction with a deceased parent. Such considerations would appear to limit the application of such direct reconditioning procedures to fairly circumscribed anxiety reactions to relatively common objects, the so-called phobic reactions.

Under such circumstances the question of the relative effectiveness of these two approaches is an empirical one still to be answered by research. In one experimental study dealing with this problem, Peck (1951) compared the effectiveness of counseling on anxiety reduction, both with and without the actual anxiety-producing cues being present. She found that the relative efficacy of these two procedures depended on the general anxiety level of the client, with those persons originally classified as nonanxious showing anxiety reduction only when reexposed to the original anxiety-arousing cues as part of counseling. On the other hand, anxiety reduction in those persons originally classified as anxious occurred when only the verbal cues were presented. For these anxious subjects, reexposure to the actual anxiety cues in counseling tended to intensify rather than reduce the anxiety. This single study is, of course, not definitive but does suggest that the question of the adequacy of these procedures is more complex than is typically suggested by advocates of either approach.

In the indirect approach, it is argued that the client's anxiety has its roots in his socialization experience and is, therefore, interpersonal in nature. Maladjusted individuals in our culture learn to be anxious about their interpersonal relationships, in particular about expressing such thoughts as hostility, dependency, and sexuality. Such interpersonal anxiety can best be extinguished in an interpersonal relationship with a warm, permissive counselor who provides an opportunity for the client to desensitize these anxiety-producing thoughts by not punishing the client when such thoughts are expressed. The extinction of the client's anxieties in his relationship with the counselor may thus well be seen to some extent as a direct reconditioning experience. For example, a client with anxiety about dependency may have such anxiety reduced as dependency responses occur in his relationship with the counselor in such a way that they elicit anxiety which is identified or labeled but not reinforced by the counselor. Thus, desensitization of dependency anxiety is occurring in a kind of direct reconditioning, even though the counselor is an advocate of the direct approach.

The process of anxiety extinction through the indirect approach is even less well understood than that of the direct approach. Most conceptualizations tend to emphasize the processes of adaptation or desensitization and of counterconditioning. Shoben (1948, 1949), in an analysis based on counterconditioning, has pointed out that the non-anxiety responses of acceptance, warmth, and security experienced by the client in working with a counselor can now become attached to the verbal symbols which previously elicited anxiety. Such an analysis is by no means inconsistent with one based on desensitization, where the client is conceptualized as symbolically approaching anxiety-producing material in the counseling session through the discussion of his symptoms and their etiology. This may involve the discussion of hitherto unverbalized thoughts, the recall of unpleasant experiences, the vicarious rehearsal of anxiety-arousing behavior, and so on. The choice of language in permitting the client either to approach or avoid the emotionality or anxiety is noteworthy is this context. The client may discuss the same material on a very abstract, impersonalized level or on a highly specific, detailed, personal level which is far more likely to arouse anxiety. Consider the differential consequences of having the client say "My father and I don't get on" versus "I hate my old man." Anxiety elimination can only occur when the client is able to discuss anxiety-producing material with emotionality actually occurring in the counseling situation. The similarity of this conceptualization to the psychoanalytic notion of *catharsis* can be noted. It has been frequently noted, most recently by Hobbs (1962), that the therapeutic development of "insight" or a change in cognitive behavior that does not also involve changes in emotionality or anxiety is not likely to be very useful to the client in modifying his adjustment pattern.

The client thus approaches anxiety-arousing material in his counseling sessions, and the counselor, either implicitly or explicitly, encourages this approach behavior by his interest, sympathy, and concern. Anxiety extinction begins to occur when the client experiences anxiety while approaching these cues and while the anxiety is not reinforced by the counselor. The permissive, accepting counselor does not punish or intensify the client's anxiety under these circumstances, but he reflects or interprets the feeling and attempts to clarify the relationships between the emotional response and the precipitating thoughts.

It must be recognized that extinction would not ordinarily occur with a single experience, even when rather intense feelings are expressed. The relatively permanent extinction of anxiety is thought to require several exposures to the anxiety-arousing material, in this case on the verbal or symbolic level. The similarity of such extinction procedures to the psychoanalytic process of "working through" may be apparent. One practical problem involved in this desensitization of anxiety-arousing cues is the frequency with which such cues can be presented or discussed in the counseling sessions. The previous discussion of internal inhibition would suggest that a massing of such desensitization sessions, with only relatively brief periods of time intervening between counseling interviews, might maximize the anxiety reduction.

On the other hand, the counselor must be continuously concerned lest the client's anxiety level become so high during counseling sessions that he withdraws from counseling because it has become too painful for him to continue. The client-centered counselor (Rogers, 1951) takes the extremely cautious position of giving the client the major responsibility for setting his own dosage of anxiety, although Murray (1956) does point out that such counseling is by no means "nondirective." Most indirectly oriented counselors take a somewhat more active role than Rogers in the dosing of anxiety, but care must be exercised to promote extinction without losing clients because of the overdosing of anxiety.

Another important function of the counselor or therapist, in addition to anxiety extinction, is teaching the client to distinguish better or differentiate the cues that elicit anxiety. As noted above, anxiety learned to specific cues can be generalized to an entire class of cues so that the person is fearful of all dogs rather than a particular dog, is made anxious by all members of the opposite sex rather than a particular person, is anxious about any dependent relationship rather than a specific one, and so on. The counselor not only helps extinguish such anxiety but also helps the client learn that the anxiety has been generalized and is inappropriate in some of the instances in which it occurs. The counselor may point out that all dogs do not bite, that all heterosexual or dependent relationships do not necessarily lead to rejection. This discrimination learning, coupled with some anxiety reduction, should lead to attempts by the client to try out in real life responses which were previously inhibited by anxiety. The client may attempt to approach a dog, secure a date, or become involved in a dependent relationship outside of the counseling situation.

Too often it is these tentative and fumbling attempts by the client to try out new responses that lead to a failure of counseling. If these tentative attemps result in a reinforcement rather than a reduction of the anxiety—if the dog does bite, or if the date is a monstrous failure or if the dependency leads to rejection—then, because of this additional reinforcement, the resultant anxiety will be more difficult to extinguish than was the original anxiety. Some discussion of the possibility of failure, some vicarious rehearsal of the consequences of failure, can be attempted by the counselor. Successful counseling, however, usually involves the positive reinforcement of the emergent responses by society rather than the enhancement of the anxiety. Fortunately, these tentative responses are usually ones that are regarded by our society as socially appropriate and useful and are typically more likely to be rewarded than punished.

One type of discrimination learning involved in the indirect counseling process deserves special consideration, namely, discriminating between thoughts and actions. The anxiety which has been previously acquired because of prior punishment inhibits not only the overt behavior but the thoughts and impulses which mediate the overt responses. This repression interferes with the client's higher mental processes, his thinking about his internal state, and how he should respond as a consequence of this internal state. Not only are aggressive behaviors inhibited by anxiety, but even the recognition that one is angry or aggressive under conditions of frustration or conflict may be inhibited. This type of repression leads to inappropriate and maladaptive behavior because the individual is unable to correctly label or identify how he feels. The counselor's task under such circumstances is to help the client recognize and correctly identify such feelings but at the same time discriminate between having such aggressive feelings and acting aggressively. The counselor will attempt to point out that such aggressive feelings are natural and acceptable but that aggressive behavior is not usually regarded as acceptable. Thus, the counselor attempts to teach suppression rather than repression, again emphasizing the role of the client's cognitive behavior in mediating his overt responses.

Still another important function of the counselor in the indirect approach is that of a reinforcer of certain client behaviors. As the therapeutic relationship develops, the responses of the counselor, his interest, attention, and approval, or contrariwise, his disinterest and disapproval become increasingly important to the client. The positive reinforcers may range from statements of direct approval such as "I'm glad you told me (or did) that," to such indirect or subtle procedures as head nodding or the client-centered "Mm-Humm." The negative reinforcers range from a failure to make any response to direct verbal disapproval to threats to discontinue the therapeutic relationship. These reinforcers are interpersonal and social in nature and involve the language behavior, verbal or gestural, of the counselor in contrast to the material rewards primarily used in the direct approach.

These secondary reinforcers help sustain the client's behavior both in the counseling sessions and in real-life situations. In the counseling sessions, the therapist tends to reinforce the client's approaching anxiety-producing material by his interest and sympathy, if not by more direct verbal approval. The counselor especially rewards talking when the client is anxious or afraid because, as noted previously, it is the experiencing of anxiety while verbalizing about the anxiety-arousing material in a permissive situation that leads to the extinction of the anxiety. Murray (1956) has demonstrated that the behavior of client-centered counselors can be analyzed as reinforcing client behavior by subtly approving the discussion of the topic of independence, while disapproving, primarily through disinterest, the topics of dependence, sex, and intellectual defenses. Those topics which were rewarded tended to occupy a greater proportion of the client's attention during counseling, while those which were "punished" tended to decrease in frequency of verbalization. On the basis of a behavior-theoretical analysis of the counseling relationship, the empirical studies of the counseling interaction (e.g., Murray, 1956), and the recent research on verbal conditioning (see Krasner, 1958, and Salzinger, 1959, for systematic reviews of these studies), it must be concluded that the counselor, consciously or unconsciously, does influence the content of the counseling sessions.

The counselor not only reinforces the client's behavior in the counseling situation, but this control tends to extend to the client's extra-counseling behavior as well. The counselor rewards certain responses that the client reports performing in real-life situations and punishes others. These rewards are still the secondary reinforcers of approval, interest, and sympathy which stem from the counseling relationship.

Such reinforcement would be especially important during the period when the client is trying out responses that are not being regularly reinforced by other agents of society.

It should be noted that what is being reinforced under these circumstances should not merely be the client's verbalization about his extracounseling behavior but the behavior itself. Krumboltz (1963) has demonstrated that the counselor's reinforcing client statements indicating that student clients were asking relevant questions or intended to seek information pertaining to their occupational or educational choice actually led to information-seeking behavior. The clients who were reinforced for their interest in seeking information by such counselor remarks as, "It's good that you are thinking about it now because you should find this out before you make a decision," actually were found to be making significantly more use of the occupational information in the library, etc., than the noncounseled group. This study is rather significant in that it demonstrates that the indirect changing of the client's mediating or thinking responses, in this case the client's thinking about post-high school plans, actually resulted in a change in the client's more overt behavior. The more direct approach of actually taking the client to the library and directly reinforcing the overt responses of reading and information seeking does not seem to be necessary under such circumstances.

The Counselor and the Therapeutic Relationship

It would seem appropriate in this final theoretical section to recapitulate and elaborate on the role and function of the counselor and the therapeutic relationship in this behavior-theoretical view of the counseling process. This reanalysis will largely be concerned with the counselor's function in the indirect approach where the counselor and his therapeutic relationship with the client have primary importance rather than with the direct approach where no special significance is attached to the counselor or the counseling relationship.

Almost all conceptualizations of counseling which advocate the indirect approach emphasize the counselor's role as a permissive and accepting one, particularly with regard to what the client may feel or say. The extinction of anxiety through counseling requires that the counselor be nonpunishing and nonpunitive, especially of the client's feelings and thoughts. The counselor should be, however, continuously aware of society's values and must help the client recognize the sanctions that society can apply to those who act in defiance of its commonly accepted standards. The counselor must facilitate the utterance of anxiety-arousing thoughts while the client is actually experiencing anxiety in the counseling session. It should not be surprising to learn that Bandura (1956) has shown that counselors who are themselves anxious are less competent to do this than are nonanxious counselors.

It was previously noted that many of the client's difficulties involve his interpersonal relationships, including problems of aggression, affection, dependency, and so on. As the therapeutic relationship is an interpersonal relationship between two persons, many of the client's interpersonal difficulties may be activated in this relationship with the counselor. Indeed, the permissive, accepting atmosphere of counseling probably facilitates the direct and overt expression of thoughts and feelings that are partially inhibited in more typical social interactions. The counselor thus has an opportunity to observe directly some of the client's interpersonal behavior and the problems involved in such behavior in addition to having the typical indirect knowledge based on the client's discussions and analyses of his own behavior. The diagnostic usefulness of such direct behavioral observation, for example, seeing the client when he is angry or depressed or dependent, over relying entirely upon the client's report of such behavior should be immediately apparent. Such a firsthand understanding of the client should greatly facilitate the counselor's attempts to modify these behaviors as well as extinguish the underlying anxiety which may motivate these responses.

The counselor must help the client develop a warm, close, and rather dependent relationship wherein the counselor becomes the dispenser of important secondary rewards. The counselor becomes a significant person to the client, and his approval or disapproval become important factors mediating the client's behavior. Snyder (1961) has concluded that the client's positive feelings for the counselor, feelings that the counselor respects the client and is attentive, warm, and empathetic are essential for successful counseling to occur. Snyder has further noted that such positive feelings must be reciprocal, that is, the counselor must indeed like and respect the client, for the counseling to have a successful outcome. While undoubtedly some of the reward value of the therapist's behavior stems from his cultural role as a professional expert, his reinforcement value would appear to be substantially enhanced by a close interpersonal relationship with the client.

The therapist or counselor must also play a diagnostic role, assessing the role of anxiety in the client's symptoms, evaluating the client's capacity to handle anxiety, and then dosing the anxiety in the counseling situation by symbolically exposing the client to anxiety-arousing cues. The counselor must have considerable understanding about the various sources of anxiety in the culture and how it may be best extinguished. He must be able to facilitate the client's psychologically approaching anxiety-arousing materials without becoming anxious himself. Bandura, Lipsher, and Miller (1960), using anxiety about aggression as the case in point, were able to demonstrate that counselors who were themselves anxious about aggression avoided discussing the client's feelings about aggression, while the counselors without anxiety in this area encouraged such discussion. The avoidance of discussion by the former counselors of both the client's aggressive impulses and his anxiety about these impulses precluded any extinguishing of the client's anxiety, vitiating the usefulness of the counseling interaction in this area.

The counselor not only exposes the client to anxiety cues, but he also reinforces, directly or indirectly, consciously or unconsciously, the client's behavior both in the counseling sessions and in extracounseling situations. It should be clear that an awareness and understanding by the counselor both of the client's need for these counselor-dispensed secondary rewards following certain responses and of the importance or reward value of such counselor behavior would greatly improve the efficacy of such reinforcing behavior. For example, there may be a need for the counselor to reinforce the client for discussing some particularly anxiety-provoking topic or for attempting some especially fear-arousing response in a real-life situation. The experienced counselor would, however, refrain from such attempts to reward the client until he was reasonably certain that, on the basis of the therapeutic relationship, his approval would have some reward value to the client.

In addition to extinguishing anxiety and differentially reinforcing client behavior, the counselor also attempts to teach the client to think more effectively, to approach situations with a problem-solving attitude, and to substitute vicarious problem solving for overt trial-and-error behavior whenever possible. As the counselor helps the client to discriminate more accurately between realistic and unrealistic fears, between thoughts and actions, he enhances the client's capacity for developing intelligent, rational solutions to his problems and reduces the client's need to discuss new problems with the counselor as such problems arise in the future. Such an approach emphasizes the client's problem-solving ability rather than simply providing the client with the solution to a particular problem.

There are at least two additional, but not unrelated, elements of the therapeutic interaction that deserve brief mention, namely, the counselor as a role model for the client and the transmission of the counselor's values and philosophy of life to the client. As noted previously, the counselor has become an important person to the client and can often become a model for the client to imitate. The counselor is typically seen as a well-adjusted, successful professional person who is well rewarded, both intrinsically and extrinsically, for his efforts. The therapist's nurturance of the client would ordinarily facilitate such social imitation in a manner not unlike the classical conception of *identification* (Bandura, 1962). While certain aspects of such imitation are undoubtedly healthy, for example, appearing well-adjusted, other aspects may be more worrisome, as for example, the client's deciding to become a counselor or therapist himself, although he has low verbal aptitude. The counselor must recognize that he provides a high prestige model for the client and should be prepared to help the client discriminate which aspects of this model are reasonable for this particular client to adopt.

During the course of the counseling interaction, the counselor continuously, if inadvertently, exposes the client to his own values, attitudes, and philosophy of life. The counselor's manner of dress, the way he keeps his office, and most importantly, his verbal remarks to the client reflect his own personality. For example, in a vocational counseling case, the question of how the client's family feels about his vocational decision may reflect the counselor's values about the importance of family ties and may suggest to the client that how they feel ought to be taken into account in his planning. In a marriage counseling session the question of whether the client has discussed a particular problem such as finances with his wife again may reflect the counselor's values about the importance of such discussions. While such questions undoubtedly do reflect general middle-class cultural values, these are the values of the counselor and are communicated to the client as the counselor's personal attitudes toward such situations. The counselor or therapist apparently cannot avoid providing cues about himself as a person since these are manifested in almost all of his behavior. All that can be reasonably expected is that the counselor be aware of his own values and attitudes and attempt to weave these values into his therapeutic techniques on a conscious rather than unconscious level.

Illustrative Case Material

This is a case of a twenty-six-year-old female graduate student who was self-referred to a counselor because of emotional upset stemming from her psychological problems. Physically, this client was rather short, quite attractive, and well groomed. Her manner of dress was quite flashy and somewhat out of place for a small Middle Western university town. The client's speech was very precise, although the rate was extremely rapid; she tended to exaggerate both her problems and the

changes that occurred between the interviews. While she appeared
initially to be sincere, open and friendly, the more lasting impression
created was that of a shallow, histrionic, immature, quite dependent
person who lacked much real warmth or emotional depth. Diagnos-
tically, the impression was initially of a classical hysteroid personality
with the rather tenuous, superficial adjustment often found with such
persons.

Initial interview.   The client had telephoned for an "emergency" appointment early one afternoon to discuss a "problem of life and
death." She specifically requested an appointment with this particular
counselor as she had once heard him give a public lecture and felt that
he was the "ideal man for the job."

When the client arrived for her appointment later that afternoon
she began by stating that she had been extremely upset during the past
nine weeks, primarily over her relationships with two men, Bob and
Tom. It was the pressure of these relationships that was the precipitating factor leading to her seeking help at this time. Symptomatically,
she had become tense and restless and somewhat insomniac with mod-
erate loss of appetite. She felt that the situation had become intolerable and was concerned about her ability to continue her graduate
work. She appeared obviously distraught, quite anxious and tense during the early portion of this interview but did seem less upset and
anxious at the end of the hour.

The client conceptualized her relationship with these two men in
the following fashion: Bob was a somewhat older man (forty) whom
she had begun to go with the previous summer shortly after his divorce
from his wife. She pictured Bob as an unemotional, prudish, restrained person who treated her in a very fatherly, tender fashion.
While she initially felt very secure in this relationship, Bob's overpro-
tectiveness and stodginess began to pall on her and she began to rebel.
While discussing this aspect of her relationship with Bob the counselor
had the strong feeling that the client was rebelling against what she
saw as a parental authority figure but had little or no understanding
of any etiological factors involved in her ambivalent feelings.

During one of the several arguments that she had with Bob, she met
Tom who is approximately her own age (he was twenty-four). Tom,
who was also a student, fitted many of her needs in that he "treated
me as a woman," expected her to assume responsibility, made sexual
demands, etc. She began to lose interest in her relationship with Bob
and entered into an intense love affair with Tom. When Bob learned
of this, he "reentered my life" and for the first time proposed marriage.

For the past several weeks the relationship between the client and these two men had become more intense and more complicated. Both of the men knew about the other and were angered by the client's inability to decide between them. Each had begun to threaten to take some sort of action, possibly physical, against his rival, and it was these threats that had alarmed the client. She felt that she must make a decision and that unless this decision was forthcoming fairly soon, they would "take matters into their own hands." It was quite obvious that the client actually believed that this might happen although it did seem somewhat improbable to the counselor. It was clear, however, that the client was under rather strong pressure, and this pressure had begun to adversely affect her adjustment. Somewhat more realistic was the client's fear that both men would simultaneously break off the relationship and that she would be left completely alone.

The client related that she has had adjustment problems for some time and had undergone a similar experience three years ago, which she described in some detail. The client frequently interspersed through this interview derogatory remarks toward her parents. She sees them as "very old-fashioned" and nonunderstanding of her and her problems. Many of her statements suggested that she blamed her parents for her present difficulties but for rather nonspecific reasons. The parents are seen as quite concerned about her, particularly about her failure to marry as yet.

Throughout the initial interview the counselor's role was a relatively inactive one. The client spoke volubly, without any hesitation, and the counselor only occasionally interjected a question aimed at clarifying a point or getting additional pertinent information. At the conclusion of the hour the counselor suggested overnight hospitalization at the student infirmary as the client had been quite distraught, anxious and tense, particularly early in the hour. The client refused this suggestion, stating that she felt "very, very relieved" after this initial interview and was certain that hospitalization was not necessary. As it was obvious to the counselor that the client was indeed more composed and relaxed at the end of the hour, he did not insist on hospitalization, although he did suggest that the client stop back the following morning for a brief talk.

Second interview. The client was seen briefly the morning after the initial interview, primarily as a check on her condition and also to discuss the prospects for additional counseling contacts. The client was quite composed and seemingly more able to deal realistically with her problem. In discussing additional contacts she was somewhat hesitant, in marked contrast to her eagerness of the previous day. The therapist suggested that an appointment be made for the following week, and in addition, arrangements would be made for psychological testing and psychiatric consultation.

Diagnostic formulation and therapeutic strategy.   The counselor decided that the client was in strong conflict with either of the alternative goals, Bob or Tom, each arousing powerful ambivalence. Bob, who represented security and nurturance, was paternalistic and over-controlling, while Tom, who represented youth and affection, demanded maturity and an active involvement in the relationships on her part. She was unable to decide between the two because of the inhibitory effects of anxiety on her thinking and vacillated back and forth between the two. The counselor decided to focus the client's attention on the conflict, on her avoidance of thinking about the negative elements in her relationship to both men, on her unwillingness to resolve the conflict, and on the secondary gains involved in maintaining the conflict. In view of the intense level of anxiety present, the nature of the client's manner of handling her anxiety, the rather inadequate capacity of this woman for effective dealings with her environment, and the long-term pattern of neurotic interactions, it was decided to avoid historical material which would exacerbate the anxiety but rather to concentrate on the immediate conflict situation, her role in the maintenance of the conflict, and the implications for the future of the various courses of action open to her. The following are excerpts of a verbatim transcript of the third interview with this client. The parenthetical comments are explanatory and were not verbalized during the hour. The attempts of the counselor to focus on the client's conflict, her avoidance of the negative elements in both relationships, and her inability to think constructively about her situation should be noted as well as the counselor's attempt to reduce the client's anxiety in the counseling situation.

Third interview
Cl-1: Well, fantastic things have happened since I last talked to you. (long pause) Ah, Bob, you see, in the first place Bob didn't expect to miss me as much as he did. Do you remember?

Co-1: Uh huh. (pause) The triangle. (The counselor here begins to focus upon the relationship which is anxiety arousing.)

Cl-2: (laughs) The triangle. Gone for glory. (pause) Oh well, and passed through various stages of pride being hurt and certain things, but he never wanted to let me go, you know, uh, all kinds of things which he didn't even know himself came to the fore. I don't think he felt anything at that point that he had not felt before. It was just a sudden realization, the way he felt about me and—

Co-2: In a sense your decision to leave him kind of crystallized—

Cl-3: That was the way I—Yes. Oh yes, because you see since then he had done a great deal of thinking about this. He's really a *very fine* person, you see, and was terribly badly hurt to the point where he had to operate in a marriage situation where he was continually rejected, and he had to do something because he refused to get out. This was something he had done, and he would stick with it. This is the sort of person that he was, you see. So the only way he could take out his—the only way he could get any relief from this was, of course, first of all to shut off his emotions completely; he must not feel anything, you see, and of course the second thing was to slowly delve into his work. I have every admiration for the way he took it. I mean he didn't go around with other women, and I believe that he didn't take to drink, and he didn't do all kinds of things like this. He very well could have got very emotional and so ... (pause) (sighs) Uh, I'm trying to catch this up to date. But here is a person who is terribly proud of—he never admitted to me—oh just in many ways ran me down; I must conform to this standard, and when I didn't, he would get out of the relationship or he would have blasted out of it, but I never let him get out because I needed him. So I'd do anything, you see, at this point and he would say, "I'm leaving, this won't work out." I would do anything to get him back. My motives were *not* of the best at all. It was simply that I didn't dare to be alone, just didn't dare be alone. Heavens, I thought I'd fall through with something ...

Co-3: Your needs were pretty intense. (A labeling of her underlying psychological condition.)

Cl-4: (long pause) He was a person who came along, and I could talk to him, he was older, uh, I have always relied on him as far as his judgment is concerned, as far as what he says is concerned. What he says is true, and I have never found it otherwise, this kind of thing, and I've been in a situation where I had to—should have and had to actually told him to sit back and say, "I wonder if this person knows what he needs. I wonder if this person really will see this other situation, will he get a divorce?" He says he'll get one. Will he? Uh, trying all the time very hard to believe and further and further convincing myself that this person really did mean what he said. I knew him very well, and I knew that he did not have a great deal of strength, you know, of character, and I recognized it and completely allowed for it, and so of course you see, but here was somebody that I boomed right out of it, I suffered through the bitter stage of the business as far as he told me he was getting a divorce when he wasn't. He got to the same stage I guess where I am in this ...

Co-4: That was this fellow in Chicago? (While this counselor response is concerned with historical material, he was confused by the client's verbosity and is asking for clarification.)

Cl-5: Yes. Well this, this, uh huh. Yes. And so I went along trusting away here frantically because he said he would, you see, and, boy, I was going to be loyal to the end. I'd just sit there and sit there, you see.

Co-5: This was pretty important then in your relationship with Bob that he had been as stable and as trustworthy as he had been. (The counselor identifies a positive aspect of the relationship with Bob.)

Cl-6: Very important. I liked very many things. I liked the fact that he told me before he ever took me out exactly what his situation was, that he had been married, that he had just recently got a divorce, that if I cared to accept this, you know, people knew this; he told me his exact situation with regard to the church, all these kinds of things. Bob is a very honorable person, to the extent, that he, well, this always comes first. He doesn't handle people always as well as he should because he is more concentrating upon his principles than anything else. I mean this is not the cagey thing a man would do the first day out with a girl, who I think, to him, looks rather young, very attractive and that he wanted; he needed somebody to go out with but, under no circumstances would he say, uh, you know, well I'll wait to give her a chance to like me a bit and then I'll tell her this.

Co-6: He's frank almost to the point of bluntness. (A negative element.)

Cl-7: Uh huh. Uh huh. Sometimes almost too much so.

. . .

He is very blunt and forthright but, and his general reputation among his friends, and I know this very well, and it's uniform right down the line. They don't all like him as a person particularly. I mean they don't all—not his close friends. His close friends would *die* for him. You know? (Continues to talk about Bob's virtues.)

Co-8: I wonder why you're telling me all this about Bob rather than about yourself and your relationship with him? (Another counselor attempt to focus on the anxiety-arousing relationship.)

Cl-9: I don't know. (pause) I guess because I, here I am at the present time I've let this thing go on; this thing has been able to go on with people getting out, people getting back in, you know. Since I last saw you . . . Here has Tom stayed in this relationship believing that I loved him. I told him that I didn't. He would believe me, he would trust me, and he'd be so . . . He saw over this business of going back to Bob, going away from him emotionally is what he thought at first. Very sensitive person. You aren't always with me; I can't count on you but I know you'll come through. You are good for me. We believe and believe and believe on no basis whatsoever except we felt this way. He's never seen it. He's never seen any loyalty, anything like this from me, you see. I got into that relationship with him, I told him I was madly in love with him, and he felt the same way and what happened? I had evenings when I missed Bob to the point where I can't stand it.

Co-9: When you're with Tom? (Another attempt for clarification.)

Cl-10: When I'm with Tom. I can't be totally and completely with him at all times; I mean he feels this, you see, and I've never been able to.

And then I've let myself in for Bob talking to me. Bob has investigated, for Heaven's sake, Tom at this point, as to what people think of him. And the general opinion about him and certain other things. These things have come up and I, instead of dealing with them, have brought them up to Tom and he has had to prove himself and explain to all these things.

Co-10: You keep comparing one with the other? (A focusing upon the conflict.)

Cl-11: (pause) Constantly and endlessly. And at this particular point in time (pause) I—this has been such a completely destructive thing for Tom. He has just gone down and down and down. (There follows a critical analysis of Tom's immaturity and emotional instability.)

· · ·

Co-13: In a sense you're testing the two of them in this way demonstrated to you that Bob is more adequate of the two. (Still another focusing on the conflict.)

Cl-14: (pause) That was my first thought. Then I thought because Bob pointed this out to me last night, uh, Tom just got so—Tom had a complete emotional collapse as it were last night; he was just gone somewhere. I was continually comparing him with this person, he couldn't stand it any more. To his detriment, you see, constantly to his detriment. And then all of a sudden this just came over him that this thing he had believed in, he is very idealistic, you see, this love that he believed in—I didn't love him the way I should; not only that, but I left him nothing to combat this feeling that he was something low, he was something not to be desired, he was, uh, you see the reports on him were that he was rather egotistical and that he had chased after women and all kinds of things, you see.

Co-14: It seems to me from what you've said before that in these situations where you have compared them, Bob came through as the better possibility. He seems stronger and more mature, more stable of the two. (An interpretation of how she has evaluated one element of the relationship. An evaluation of which she seems rather unaware.)

Cl-15: Yes.

Co-15: Then when I suggested this, you immediately started to point out Tom's assets. (The counselor here begins to label the client's vacillation which was assumed to be symptomatic of her conflict.)

Cl-16: I suppose it just shows how torn I am. I'm dealing with extremes here. I know I am. The thing I started to tell you that after I'd had this reaction, then I sat down and I thought Bob said to me, he said I can come through like this to you without recriminations, without feeling my pride hurt, and so on because I realize now what you did for me during all those months. I realize that the things you put up with me, the faith you had in me that I would be all right, that I would come through to you, all these things you had for two months when I can't figure out anybody else who would have had them...

Co-17: In all of this it's really easier for you to talk about Bob and Tom and their feelings rather than what you feel and what *you* did. (Counselor labels the client's avoidance of the conflict.)

Cl-18: Well, I guess it is because I'm so confused, I don't know, I've got myself to the point I don't know what I think (crying), and I don't know how I feel. I've divided myself so completely. When this person needs me I run. Last night I ran to Tom, in the middle of the night, Doctor, in the middle of the night! I ran to this person. (pause)

Co-18: Could you tell me about this? (A request for clarification, but its permissive quality and implicit acceptance would lead to anxiety extinction.)

Cl-19: Well, I phoned him, he didn't phone me, and he was there all alone and he was just terribly upset about everything. And terribly upset, terribly disillusioned, he didn't want to talk to me and so on and . . . Well, he was just reduced to—well, it was just terrible. I mean he cried, and men just don't do things like this. He was so ashamed of himself. So, you know, and all I could think of, *all* I could think of at that point was that I must go to him. I just must go to him.

Co-19: When you found out that he was in trouble you felt that you had to give yourself to him? Extend yourself? (An attempt to clarify, and reinforce, the client's evaluation of positive elements in her behavior.)

Cl-20: I don't know how much it was that I felt I should do this and how much of it was that I knew that this was what a woman would do. You know? (sobbing) And I'm trying very hard, you see, to . . . (pause) I've got to get on one track or the other, or get out of this. I can't be like this anymore. I've been able, I've been able, in the past, to really love somebody. It's a wonderful feeling. To *really* love somebody, so that if anybody on earth said something about them, anybody, you'd say well, I'm sorry but I care for this person and I'm not able to do this either way, Doctor.

Co-20: You're too torn between the two. (Labeling the focal conflict.)

Cl-21: I'm just too torn, and each time I think, well, I'll be able to go completely one way, and I try it. That's what I'm doing. (sobbing)

Co-21: Is one of the reasons why it's so hard for you to talk about your own feelings in this situation that it's too upsetting? (An attempt at identifying or labeling one of the underlying reasons for avoiding the conflict.)

Cl-22: My feelings are so completely bound up with these things.

Co-22: Yes, but I think you can talk about them. (The counselor here reinforces the client's approaching the conflict.) Let me put it this way. When you talk about Bob and Tom and what kind of people they are, you can do this pretty calmly without very much emotion. When you talk about yourself and the way you feel, you're pretty close to tears. (pause) Are you ashamed to cry? (An effort to facilitate an emotional reaction so that anxiety extinction can occur.)

Cl-23: No, I'm not ashamed to cry, but it doesn't do *any* good. (crying) It doesn't help or anything. I've put myself in the position now where I, there are so many things, Doctor, there are just so many things. One day I feel one way, and the next day I feel the next. In one minute I feel one way, and the next minute I feel the next, and I don't want to give up anything. Obviously I'd rather kill myself than give up anything. There's something wrong with that. I know there is.

Co-23: Something wrong with your not being able to make a decision? (A clarification of what the client has said in an effort to highlight the conflict.)

Cl-24: Yes, something wrong with not being able to give up something. This is a fantastic thing I don't want to lose any of the things I get from Bob. I don't want to lose any of the things I get from Tom. And either way I go I'll lose something, and I don't want to (petulantly). And I don't know what's the matter with me that I don't want to. I can't stand the thought of Bob going with anybody else. I can't stand the thought of Tom going with anybody else, uh, I must have everything. I'm like some kind of deprived something or other that must have everything, have everything, have everything. And usually I'm quite capable of giving when I want something. Sometimes I've given too much, for something that wasn't worth it, you know.

Co-24: In this case, though, you feel that choosing one is giving up the other. (A labeling of one aspect of the conflict.) (There follows a long and confusing analysis by the client of her views of the nature of love.)

. . .

Co-29: I want to try to contrast the present relationships with the past ones because I'm not sure I understand them. You feel in some way each time you fell in love in the past it never worked out because of circumstances or for some reason or other. And now the present situation isn't working out either. But *it's* different. (pause) How do you see it as being different? (The counselor attempts to help the client recognize that she is actively involved in the conflict.)

Cl-30: It's different because the only thing that's causing trouble in it is me. There is no outside circumstance. This person is not attached to anyone else. This person has offered me a ring. This person wants to marry me.

Co-30: Both Bob and Tom.

Cl-31: At this point both Bob and Tom. I was speaking of Tom in this case because I was comparing him with past people I have fallen in love with.

Co-31: In a sense then what you're saying is that it's clear now that you have no one to blame for your failure to bring this to actualization but yourself. (Focusing on her active role in maintaining the conflict.)

Cl-32: In that you mean the case of Tom?

Co-33: (nods affirmatively) I wonder if this means something to you, the sequence of events. (The counselor hopes the client can herself identify her active role in the conflict.)

Cl-33: Well, the part of it means ... The only thing that I can add it up to is Bob and the combination of myself and Bill scared the life out of me for an entire year. Bob has said to me "Now this is the type of person you go for, my dear. Here he is, the Cornell type. This boy that I ... This is the type you go for. Are you going to go on doing this the rest of your life? What is going to happen for you? Are you going to go on going out here? For people who aren't worth it, whom you can't rely on and so on and so on."

Co-33: He was talking about Tom? (A request for clarification.)

Cl-34: Uh huh. "Here's just another case. Here you've gone and done it again. That person is no more wanting to marry you than fly a kite somewhere. He isn't worth this, he isn't worth that, he isn't up to the standards *we've* set, he isn't any of these things. And you just see what happens to you. Why you don't make any critical evaluations of people. You don't have any ability to make this critical evaluation. You never have in the past. You're not making it now. I hear these reports on this person. He's not a nice solid citizen type person, this is somebody who has done this and that and the other thing and is completely not the type of person you should be interested in at all, who is going to provide you with stability that you need," and he exaggerated it and exaggerated, and every day there has been something new come up ... To the point where I realize that I didn't make this kind of critical evaluation in the past so what have I done? I went in with both feet and then I said, "Oh, no, I won't do this. I won't do this. I mustn't ... I must investigate."

Co-34: When the relationship with Tom almost worked out, you allowed yourself to be talked out of it ... by Bob? (How she permits the conflict to be continued.)

Cl-35: I have allowed myself to be alternately talked out of this relationship ever since it began. And last night, of course, you see when, at the point where somebody is about to pull out.... Oh boy, I'm all there.... You see, I don't want to lose it. This is what it amounts to.... I don't want to lose this person. I can't stand it. So there I am and a yard wide I'll love them until my dying day.

Co-35: That's what you told Tom last night?

Cl-36: Except that Tom can't come back like that. He can't do it. I've told him this before. He thinks that I mean it when I say it. Both of them do because in both their interpretations you mean what you say when you say it. But how do I know I'll mean it tomorrow and the next day? There's no consistency.

Co-36: Whenever things seem to be changing so that one or the other now takes the lead in this rivalry, you hop back on the other side so as to rebalance it. (Again focusing on her conflict behavior.)

Cl-37: That's right. I just get Bob settled, and what do I do? I come in last night and I phoned Tom. Tom would never have bothered me in a million years, feeling the way he did last night. I know it. I phoned *him.* There I was feeling quite organized, about ready to go about my work, I thought, well, I finally decided this thing.

Co-37: You know what it sort of sounds like to me, and I wonder if it makes any sense to you.... You prefer things in this kind of chaotic state of balance, you prefer things not to work out. (The counselor must label her behavior because the client has not been able to do so.)

Cl-38: (pause) That's what it's beginning to seem like to me. It really is.... And this, this is what particular counselor, whoever it was Bob talked to, pointed out to Bob about me. I was furious. Anybody talked about me, not even knowing about me, he came right out and said things you wouldn't say, I'll tell you. But you know, on short notice like this, it is a lot to say about me. I could have gone right up there and said something, you know, to them, but I'm afraid it's true. "One or the other of you is going to have to make it because she doesn't want to. She needs you for this, she needs this person for this, this girl does not want to make up her mind."

Co-38: And you regard this as rather unflattering. (A labeling of her implicit negative reaction to Co-37.)

Cl-39: It is. Of course it is unflattering. It is a terrible thing, and it's killing me. I'm letting myself be.

Co-39: It is a little bit disconcerting to you that I see it this way, too. (The counselor is not dissuaded by the client's defensive maneuver.)

Cl-40: It's disconcerting to me because I don't know what it means. (sobs) I don't know what it means. It means that I... (crying) I'm *never* going to be able to think I'm through for somebody. I'm not going to but I—I—we ended up before in this relationship that I had with the psychiatrist that I talked to, and he said to me that the only conclusion he could come to was that I'm terrified to get married. "You're just terrified to get married. Marry somebody for heaven's sake and you'll come through." He said, "You'll come through when the chips are down. You don't have any trouble doing that." (pause) Excuse me. I'm just going to have a piece of gum, Doctor, because my throat's getting...

Co-40: Tightening, hmmm.

Cl-41: (sighs) Tight, and you see the only thing, Doctor, that I can pride myself on, even vaguely at this point, is that I know what I'd really like to do is to have a nervous breakdown because this would solve everything. (taps for emphasis) And this... this would solve it. This was the way I solved *my* problems the last time. I just sat down and had a nervous breakdown. I didn't have any control. Not because I didn't know what would happen, I didn't know *anything* about it but I knew, when I started to feel that way, started to feel the fear, feel my heart going and 101 other things, I thought, my heavens, I'm going to have this again. I said to myself, oh no, you won't. You will do something but you will not... solve your problems this way. If you have to take a train to Chicago, if you have to do this or that or the other thing, you have to do it because you're not going to have to face that this is the way you solved your problems. This is too much for me to face, Doctor. I couldn't lift my head again.

Co-41: If what happened? (A request for clarification.)

Cl-42: If I had a nervous breakdown. I get to the point where all I wanted to do was go to bed, cover my head up somewhere. I could go through the state. I went through that stage before. I didn't go to work. I didn't get my work done, I didn't do anything. Pretty soon everybody was looking at me as if to say, what's the matter with you? This same pattern is starting again. Everybody over in my department who has thought *so* much of me, why they've just done everything for me. They are being *so* kind and so nice; and "My dear if there's anything we can do for you. The only thing we want to know is if you're not going to be able to continue with your work, we'd like to be able to bring in a replacement before you fall through. We'll be glad to take this away from you temporarily." This just isn't having any gumption at *all,* Doctor.

Co-42: Seeing yourself as really being afraid of marriage and really not willing to make a decision is terribly upsetting to you. (pause) Even though you can see it fits the circumstances both immediate, in the present situation, and what's always happened in the past. (A summary interpretation confirming the immediate trend of the counselor's remarks, largely ignoring the client's implicit threat.)

Cl-43: I can see that it's very safe to give your love where you know perfectly well before you ever get into it that it won't work out. Because you're expecting too much here. Then that's safe.

Co-43: And it's safe as long as Bob and Tom are there, betwixt and between. (A labeling of reinforcement value of continuing the conflict.)

Cl-44: (pause) But once one of them pulls out . . .

Co-44: Then you're going to have to produce.

Cl-45: Produce or be alone again. I don't want to be alone either.

Co-45: Sort of out of the frying pan, into the fire. (Note the use of the non-technical description of the client's conflict.)

Cl-46: (pause) I don't want to be alone. I think I want to get married, but I obviously don't. It was such a nice feeling, such a nice feeling last night to feel even for a few minutes that this is what I'll (pause) you see I've had the proper feelings with regard—I think. I don't know. Maybe they're not—with regard to a man, you know? Really being in love with somebody, only under the wrong circumstances. I think this is probably the thing that has resulted in my having as many relationships as I have. Because I think perhaps men sense, they send me—I mean I have an awful lot to give and do and when—a very warm responsive person, you know? And why at one point I was silly enough to think that men didn't like me or something. Until the psychiatrist pointed out that he had never seen as many—I've had eleven proposals, you know that sort of thing, and it's just horrifying, Doctor, it's just horrible because what does it mean? It means that you walk around with something people apparently want and ...

Co-46: Can't give it.

Cl-47: I can't give it. When the chips are down in that way, I apparently can't (pause) can't do it. Now what I could do, you see, is that I could tell Bob I'm sorry, this won't work out. Because what's happened over here? I've got to prove something, here. This will take time. I will still have this person to some extent because he isn't ready to get out. I can be sufficiently upset apparently to satisfy myself, maybe I can't feel calm, cool and collected. I can stay in this relationship and prove *my great love* and sit around and think I'm hoping that this person will come through. And what will happen when this person if he comes through says, "Well, now I believe that you will be true to me and everything that I have never seen before and become disillusioned about. Now I believe this and we will get engaged and be married." Doctor, unless I can change I'll do that again. This has been offered to me. Two or three times now and what happened? I feel like a crouched animal up against a wall. All I want to do is get up.

Co-47: Perhaps coming to see me is one of the ways of trying to get out of the situation. (A labeling of counseling as conflict maintaining.)

Cl-48: (sighs) Yeh, we'll delay living a little bit longer.

Co-48: Delay making a decision because I have to talk about this ...

Cl-49: (sighs, pause) And even then perhaps I'm realistic because at this point things are at the stage where, I mean if I go into Bob tonight and say I can't come through, that *will be it*. He can't take this any more. He has given all he can. Every last inch of it. (pause)

Co-49: There's a lot of pressure on you to make a decision pretty quickly. (A labeling of the reality situation and its pressures.)

Cl-50: Mm uh. No pressure from Tom. He's just thoroughly disillusioned. If I want to stay around and he can't stop loving me. He wished he could. Just give anything if he could. This is upsetting; it makes him unhappy; that's no good, but he can't stop it. So if I want to get in there and prove this and prove that and prove the other thing, I guess maybe he'll stick. This I don't know. But Bob has come through to me now to the extent that he can't. Magnificently, I can't go in again and say I can't go through with this. I must have said it fourteen times. *Easily,* Doctor (pause). And I have put things off, I'll probably, if I can't make a decision tonight, what I'll probably do is, see, what you can always do is be too tired. I've just been too tired too many times. I'm just too tired to see you. Terribly sorry, I wish I could. Just give anything, can't you believe in me. Oh, it's just nauseating, Doctor. (cries) It's just nauseating. Getting out and declaring this and that and the other thing, and you know it isn't true, you know it isn't true. And being that convincing because you want to hang onto somebody. (sobbing)

Co-50: It's pretty easy for you to lose your self-respect at times like this. (A labeling of what is implicit in Cl-50.)

Cl-51: Easy, I'm afraid it is. How could anybody have any (sobs), I've nothing to respect myself for. It's one of the things I suppose that endears me most to Bob because it's a very comfortable feeling to know that a person knows as much about you as Bob knows about me and can love you just the same. I don't have that feeling about Tom. I'm just scared and I suppose I've been scared from the very beginning in this relationship that I wouldn't be, what he thought I was, I wouldn't be, I couldn't be. Because, as you pointed out to me, this is a man who, who wants a, a woman. He's not completely mature ... and so on, but he doesn't want this. He told me one day, "I didn't take you on to raise, my dear." You know? I've tried to get him—I regret, somehow, in a way, that I didn't ever do with Bob ... He must do things for me, you see. I don't bring my money, so he must provide me with some money to get my lunch. This is Tom. He must do this and that just make fantastic demands on him all along because maybe I'm trying to show him that really, if you can accept me like this because I won't be any worse than this. He's gotten me through my exams, done my studying for me, all on the belief that this is the temporary situation. And the thing is that I've gone to an extreme. I'm not like this. I never have done any of this with Bob. I've always been organized and had my money, and he thinks I've sort of sat back and said, really, doing all this stuff for me. You see? This is—I'm at a point and have become through this relationship with Bob much, much more dependent, Doctor, than I've made myself. Why I've gone through things by myself, very nicely before, you know, I've done all these things. Why do I feel now that I would go down the drain?

Co-51: There is a lot of pressuring, of course, now and it is certain that the pressure to make decisions, to make a decision here ... helps contribute to your present concern and upset. Our time is just about up and I just want to make sure we work through some of the mechanics of this.

(Time arrangements for reappointment.)

Some concluding comments. Hopefully, the reader has noted the active role played by this young woman in the development and maintenance of the conflict that brought her into counseling. While the client initially reported that she was torn between the two men and wanted to choose between them, a further analysis of her behavior would suggest that she was avoiding any resolution of the conflict by strengthening the position of whichever suitor was losing at that particular time. While the conflict in which she was enmeshed caused her considerable psychological discomfort, this discomfort was considerably less than that which she would experience as a consequence of its resolution.

There were two ways in which the client's present conflict could have been resolved: she could select one of the two men, or she could select neither and, symbolically speaking, leave the field. The former solution could occur either through the client's active choice of Bob or Tom or through one of the two suitors' permanently extricating himself from the situation. This resolution of the conflict would necessitate a psychological consummation of the relationship with one of the two men, and the client's anxiety level was sharply increased by her awareness of the psychological demands implicitly involved in such a consummation. She had told the counselor in the initial interview that she had been engaged to be married some eleven or twelve times previously; even if this number represents a considerable exaggeration, it can be regarded as strong evidence that the client was avoiding the psychological demands of matrimony. On the other hand, the simultaneous withdrawal of both Bob and Tom would also lead to an increase in anxiety since she would be again alone, seemingly unwanted, with strong parental pressure to settle down, marry, and raise a family. Thus any resolution of the client's conflict would result in an increase in anxiety rather than in anxiety reduction.

The client seemed largely unaware of her own role in maintaining this dilemma, and this aspect of her behavior may be regarded as unconscious. Her failure to adequately recognize or label this conflict-sustaining behavior increased the likelihood of its continuance. The client, in these circumstances, was not able to mediate her own behavior by adequate labeling or self-signaling language. The counselor, throughout the interview, attempted to increase the client's awareness of how she was actively, although unconsciously, avoiding any resolution of her conflict. He also began what was planned as a systematic attempt to extinguish the client's anxiety about entering into close heterosexual relationships.

In the client's original presentation of her problem, she emphasized the positive attributes of both Bob and Tom and how difficult it was to choose between them. She gave little if any weight to their limitations or the problems posed by a continuing relationship with either. Dollard and Miller (1950, p. 352ff.) have noted that this avoidance of thinking about or labeling the negative elements is characteristic of the individual caught in a double approach-avoidance conflict where the alternative goals are simultaneously both desired and feared. The person caught in such a conflict finds resolution difficult because his evaluation of the alternatives is grossly deficient, with little or no weight given to the negative elements. To assist in conflict resolution, the counselor should help the client to label the negative elements involved in the conflict and then evaluate their resultant weights.

The reader is left to judge for himself the success with which the counselor was able to apply the behavior-theoretical approach developed throughout this chapter to the particular case excerpt. The reader may be interested to learn, however, that the client did eventually resolve her conflict with a hasty decision to marry Tom.

BIBLIOGRAPHY

Aronson, E., & Carlsmith, J. M. Performance expectancy as a determinant of actual performance. *J. abnorm. soc. Psychol.*, 1962, 65, 178–182.

Bandura, A. Psychotherapist's anxiety level, self-insight, and psychotherapeutic competence. *J. abnorm. soc. Psychol.*, 1956, 52, 333–337.

Bandura, A. Psychotherapy as a learning process. *Psychol. Bull.*, 1961, 58, 143–159.

Bandura, A. Social learning through imitation. In M. Jones (Ed.) *Nebraska symposium on motivation.* Lincoln, Nebr.: University of Nebraska Press, 1962.

Bandura, A., Lipsher, D. H., & Miller, P. E. Psychotherapists' approach-avoidance reactions to patients' expressions of hostility. *J. consult. Psychol.*, 1960, 24, 1–8.

Bergmann, G. The contributions of John B. Watson. *Psychol. Rev.*, 1956, 63, 265–276.

Blakemore, C. B., Thorpe, J. G., Barker, J. C., Conway, C. G., & Lavin, N. I. The application of faradic aversion conditioning in a case of transvestism. *Behav. Res. Ther.*, 1963, 1, 29–34.

Brady, J., & Lind, D. L. Experimental analysis of hysterical blindness. *Arch. gen. Psychiat.*, 1961, 4, 331–339.

Brown, J. S. *The motivation of behavior.* New York: McGraw-Hill, 1961.

Bryan, W. L., & Harter, N. Studies in the physiology and psychology of the telegraphic language. *Psychol. Rev.*, 1897, 4, 27–53.

Bryan, W. L., & Harter, N. Studies on the telegraphic language. The acquisition of a hierarchy of habits. *Psychol. Rev.*, 1899, 6, 345–375.

Cannon, W. B. *Bodily changes in pain, hunger, fear, and rage.* New York: Appleton-Century-Crofts, 1929.

Combs, A. W., & Snygg, D. *Individual behavior.* (Rev. ed.) New York: Harper & Row, 1959.

Dollard, J., & Miller, N. E. *Personality and psychotherapy: An analysis in terms of learning, thinking, and culture.* New York: McGraw-Hill, 1950.

Dunlap, K. *Habits, their making and unmaking.* New York: Liveright, 1932.

Ebbinghaus, H. *Memory.* (1885) H. A. Ruger and C. E. Bessenius (Trans.), New York: Teachers College, 1913.

Eysenck, J. H. (Ed.) *Behavior therapy and the neuroses.* New York: Macmillan, 1960.

Farber, I. E. The things people say to themselves. *Amer. Psychologist*, 1963, 18, 185–197.

Farber, I. E. A framework for the study of personality as a behavioral science. In P. Worchel and D. Byrnne (Eds.) *Personality change*. New York: Wiley 1964.

Ferster, C. B., & DeMeyer, M. The development of performances in autistic children in an automatically-controlled environment. *J. chron. Dis.*, 1961, **13,** 312–345.

Freud, S. *The problem of anxiety*. New York: Norton, 1936.

Guthrie, E. R. *Psychology of learning*. (Rev. ed.) New York: Harper & Row, 1952.

Hilgard, E. R. Human motives and the concept of the self. *Amer. Psychologist,* 1949, **2,** 374–382.

Hilgard, E. R. *Theories of learning*. (2nd ed.) New York: Appleton-Century-Crofts, 1956.

Hobbs, N. Sources of gain in psychotherapy. *Amer. Psychologist,* 1962, **17,** 741–747.

Hull, C. L. *Principles of behavior*. New York: Appleton-Century-Crofts, 1943.

Hull, C. L. *Essentials of behavior*. New Haven: Yale University Press, 1951.

Hull, C. L. *A behavior system*. New Haven: Yale University Press, 1952.

Jones, Mary C. The elimination of children's fears. *J. exp. Psychol.*, 1924, **7,** 383–390. Reprinted in H. J. Eysenck (Ed.) *Behavior therapy and the neuroses*. New York: Macmillan, 1960.

King, G. F., Armitage, S., & Tilton, J. A therapeutic approach to schizophrenics of extreme pathology. *J. abnorm. soc. Psychol.*, 1960, **61,** 276–286.

Krasner, L. Studies of the conditioning of verbal behavior. *Psychol. Bull.*, 1958, **55,** 148–170.

Krumboltz, J. D. Counseling for behavior change. Paper read at the American Personnel Guidance Association, Boston, April, 1963.

Lazarus, A. A. The elimination of children's phobias by deconditioning. In H. Eysenck (Ed.) *Behavior therapy and the neuroses*. New York: Macmillan, 1960.

Lindsley, O. R. Operant conditioning methods applied to research in chronic schizophrenia. *Psychiat. res. Rep.*, 1956, **5,** 118–138.

Mowrer, O. H. A stimulus-response analyses of anxiety and its role as a reinforcing agent. *Psychol. Rev.*, 1939, **46,** 553–565.

Murray, E. J. A content-analysis method for studying psychotherapy. *Psychol. Monogr.*, 1956, No. 13 (Whole No. 420).

Murray, E. J. Sociotropic-learning approach to psychotherapy. In P. Worchel and D. Byrnne (Eds.) *Personality change*. New York: Wiley, 1964.

Pavlov, I. P. *Conditioned reflexes*. G. V. Anrep (Trans.), London: Oxford, 1927.

Peck, Ruth. The influence of anxiety factors upon the effectiveness of an experimental "counseling" session. Unpublished doctoral dissertation, University of Iowa, 1951.

Peters, H. N., & Jenkins, R. L. Improvement of chronic schizophrenic patients with guided problem-solving motivated by hunger. *Psychiat. Quart. Suppl.*, 1954, **28,** 84–101.

Rogers, C. R. *Client-centered therapy*. Boston: Houghton-Mifflin, 1951.

Salzinger, K. Experimental manipulation of verbal behavior: A review. *J. gen. Psychol.*, 1959, **61**, 65–94.

Shaffer, L. F. The problem of psychotherapy. *Amer. Psychologist*, 1947, **2**, 459–467.

Shoben, E. J. A learning theory interpretation of psychotherapy. *Harvard educ. Rev.*, 1948, **18**, 129–145.

Shoben, E. J. Psychotherapy as a problem in learning theory. *Psychol. Bull.*, 1949, **46**, 366–392.

Snyder, W .V. *The psychotherapy relationship*. New York: Macmillan, 1961.

Thorndike, E. L. Animal intelligence: An experimental study of the associative processes in animals. *Psychol. Rev., Monogr. Suppl.*, 1898, **2**, No. 8.

Thorndike, E. L. *Animal intelligence*. New York: Macmillan, 1911.

Thorndike, E. L. *The fundamentals of learning*. New York: Teachers College, 1932.

Watson, J. B. Psychology as a behaviorist views it. *Psychol. Rev.*, 1913, **20**, 158–177.

Watson, J. B. *Psychology from the standpoint of a behaviorist*. Philadelphia: Lippincott, 1919.

Whiting, J. W. M., & Child, I. L. *Child training and personality*. New Haven, Conn.: Yale University Press, 1953.

Wolpe, J. *Psychotherapy by reciprocal inhibition*. Stanford, Calif.: Stanford University Press, 1958.

Yates, A. J. The application of learning theory to the treatment of tics. *J. abnorm. soc. Psychol.*, 1958, **56**, 175–182. Reprinted in H. J. Eysenck (Ed.), *Behavior therapy and the neuroses*. New York: Macmillan, 1960.

chapter 5

E. G. WILLIAMSON | *Vocational Counseling: Trait-factor Theory*

The trait-factor type of vocational counseling consists of techniques based on an early German and French concept of personality which states that man is an organization or pattern of capabilities (Hall & Lindzey, 1957, Ch. 9). These capabilities were originally referred to as "faculties" of the mind. Of course, we have long since abandoned the concept of faculty psychology, but nevertheless, we still have factor theory of a new sort. Munsterberg, the German founder of American applied and industrial psychology, earlier spoke and wrote in similar terms, and his thinking is not foreign to or inconsistent with that of the current factor theorists.[1]

Counseling based on these views originally centered on the choice of a career by adolescents but has now been broadened to include concern for life stages of development. But the thought pattern of Munsterberg still stands, although the techniques and instrumentalities and the statistical and mathematical models as well as theory making have immeasurably increased in complexity and, one hopes, in adequacy of explanation of the phenomena embraced.

The most recent definitive restatement of this concept of vocational counseling is found in Viteles, Brayfield, and Tyler (1961). The historical development, current status, and probable future development are delineated thoughtfully. The application of this theory of vocational counseling to the cases of those who are physically disabled is found in Lofquist (1957).

Assumptions Concerning the Nature of Human Nature [2]

Let me identify a number of assumptions regarding personality, work, and society which undergird this kind of counseling:

[1] The *beginning* counselor will need to understand the psychologist's unique methods and perspectives concerning human behavior, if he is to use, fruitfully, psychometric data describing that behavior in quantitative form. An excellent introduction to the scientific method applied to human behavior is found in Brown & Ghiselli (1955).
[2] A most thoughtful and stimulating delineation of assumptions of vocational counseling is contained in Davis, England, and Lofquist (1963).

1. Each person is an organized, unique pattern of capabilities and potentialities.[3]
     a. These human capabilities and capacities are identifiable by objective
        "tests."
     b. These objective tests should be developed by research of a sophisti-
        cated, statistical design, reproducible by other research workers, and
        capable of validation in the spirit of the early German psychological
        laboratory without regard to the research worker's point of view.
     c. For most individuals, these human capacities are stable, at least after
        the late adolescent period when maturity is achieved.
2. These capacities are differently correlated with different work tasks, so
   that different capacities are significantly involved in different tasks or behavior.
     a. These differential correlations between success in work tasks and per-
        sonality characteristics should be verified by research rather than by
        casual observations, unverified inferences, or untested "intuition."
     b. Psychological interests are also correlated with different work tasks
        and are differentially characteristic of identified criterion groups of
        workers of known competence.
     c. Research-established characteristics of successful workers in different
        work tasks constitute dependable, usable, and stable vocational in-
        formation for use in counseling.
3. The task of succeeding in school curricula may be studied by research designs comparable to those used by industrial psychologists for differentiating occupations.
     a. Different training curricula may require different capacities or inter-
        ests which are identifiable prior to enrollment in these curricula.
     b. Those work and school tasks which are learned most easily and most
        effectively are those which are congruent with the individual's poten-
        tialities and aptitudes.
4. The diagnosis (by student and counselor) of potential should precede
   choice of or assignment to or placement in work tasks or in curricula. (In
   this respect, prior diagnosis in school before classification and grade placement *resembles* but is not identical with a comparable operation in the selection of workers in industry.)
5. Diagnoses of capabilities and interests before instruction facilitates learning since it is assumed that modification of instruction in terms of these
   diagnoses should be used in schools and colleges as the school's instruction
   is adjusted to the individual.
6. There is some degree of homogeneity or commonality within each occupational criterion group; therefore diagnostic tests should be composed of
   items which predominately characterize one occupational criterion group
   as compared with other occupational groups.

[3] See especially Eysenck (1959) and Cattell (1950), who have researched and theorized
extensively about the organization of individual traits and factors in the total organization of personality.

7. The highest prediction of success in work tasks and in school is obtained by a battery of unique trait tests which correlate low with each other but cumulatively high with the criterion.
8. Each individual is capable of and seeks to identify cognitively [4] his own capabilities and to organize and maintain his daily life in order to utilize these capabilities in reasonably satisfying ways of living at work and at home.

Pioneering Research

The trait-factor theory of vocational counseling is grounded on a theory of personality organization which in turn has been subjected to continuous research and refinement. We can understand the current formulation best in terms of developmental stages of the theory and research. The American psychologist, Cattell, first began the study of the organization of the "mind" and was followed by Spearman, who identified a common trait among a variety of "test" results as the G factor. European psychologists also applied the concept of unique traits and patterns of traits to the task of identifying, prior to employment, those individuals who possessed the most likely probability of success on the job. This type of test construction led to the development of the Army Alpha Test for the assignment of Army recruits to tasks during World War I. Thurstone later developed the American Council on Education Psychological Test which was used for decades for the selection of students in college. The Thurstones, using factor analysis, later developed a unique trait test battery called the Primary Mental Abilities Test. Other psychologists have contributed over the past half century to the early identification of those traits which are predictive of success in work tasks or in school. In all such research, external, objective criteria of success in school were used, such as grades earned, length of duration in curricula, and graduation. These objective measures replaced the early estimates of satisfactoriness made by teachers.

Essentially, such a research pattern involved the use of *external* and *objective* criteria of some measure of success. Against these criteria, predictive tests were correlated for the early identification of capabilities prior to instruction or employment. Research studies using aptitude tests also yielded "occupational ability" patterns or profiles in which the scores on a battery of tests were shown to be characteristi-

---

[4] Perhaps this use of "cognition" is similar to "insight" as appraised by Hobbs. But I assume, perhaps unsupported by research, that man's efforts at self-cognition are more closely related to his actual manner of living than in Hobbs' conclusion as to the role in therapy of insight.

cally and significantly different for criterion groups of successful workers in various occupations (Dodge, 1935).

This research design involved experimental research with psychometric data as contrasted with the use of data from clinical and intuitive insight of the therapists. Recently Meehl (1954) and Sarbin, Taft, and Bailey (1960) have applied a similar research design to clinical data.

E. K. Strong, Jr., (1943) developed an interest inventory using an external criterion to measure the differentiation of groups of employed workers. That is, groups of known characteristics, such as "successful" lawyers and dentists, are studied to find objective measures which differentiate the groups characteristically from men in general. By means of such differentiating items, a student can be described objectively as resembling, to a known extent, men engaged in a given occupation rather than men in general.

In a similar manner, tests of aptitude are used to differentiate those who succeed in a curriculum in a college as contrasted with those who fail. It is because of this pattern of research development that the present Differential Aptitude Test battery and others of that type have proved useful as a basic instrument in high school counseling.

It has been commonly revealed by research studies that these criterion groups are not entirely and completely dissimilar. That is, there may be some commonality or overlapping, and only relative homogeneity of measured characteristics is the rule. Therefore, counselors need to keep in mind that we are considering the identification of traits which are *relatively* different in contrasting criterion groups.

Underlying Theory of Learning

The learning theory underlying the trait-factor type of counseling embraces the development of the human personality from infancy to adulthood. It is assumed that there is a developmental pattern of progression from infancy to adulthood with respect to the emerging and maturing of interests and aptitudes. Further, it is verified by research that during adolescence many aptitudes and interest patterns, likes and dislikes for activities and work tasks, emerge and are identifiable by objectives tests. Strong's (1955) research, for example, shows that after the years twenty or twenty-five most men's interest patterns are stable.

There are, of course, many unsolved problems remaining, not the least of which is that for many individuals there is no presently identifiable unique or outstanding pattern of interest or aptitude at any time in life. These are so-called "men in general" who apparently must look to extrinsic factors rather than to work itself for basic satisfaction.

A second aspect of learning theory, integral with personality development, concerns man's cognitive capacity as applied to the task of understanding and controlling himself, profoundly and comprehensively. This aspiration for self-understanding is a life-long urge, or motive, and possibly is never fully completed. But the full meaning of life is understood only by becoming one's potentialities and understanding cognitively through this process of becoming. Therefore, man seeks to use his cognition of potentialities as a means of controlling his efforts to become himself. Such efforts of cognitive self-discovery produce basic intrinsic satisfactions which further reinforce his efforts. Thus it is that many philosophers have concluded that man's capacity to understand is his greatest capability. All education, including counseling, should facilitate this profound understanding of potentialities, preparatory to efforts to fulfill these potentialities.

Learning As Developmental Stages of Striving

It would be incorrect to characterize D. E. Super's theory of vocational development as a mere extension and updating of Frank Parsons' 1909 three-step formulation. These three classic stages of choosing a vocation are (1) analysis and identification of one's capabilities, aspirations and interests; (2) learning about vocational opportunities and the capability requirements of jobs; and (3) comparing the two sets of information preparatory to choice of career.

Many basic changes have been made in the theory which were implicit in Parsons' position. Nevertheless, Super would probably classify himself along with Parsons as a trait-factor theorist in that his theory seems more firmly anchored in this position than in others. One of the basic changes in Parsons' theory to be found in Super's (1957b) position is the "life-time continual development" idea which corrects Parsons' location of only one "decision point" of career choice in early adolescence. Without minimizing the importance of this choice point, Super relates this period to other stages of development. Super's stages are as follows:

1. In adolescence, exploration: developing a self concept.
2. In young adulthood, the transition from school to work: reality testing.
3. In early maturity, floundering or trial process: attempting to implement a self concept.

4. In maturity, period of establishment: the self concept modified and im-
   plemented.
5. In later maturity, maintenance stage: preserving or being nagged by a
   self concept.
6. In old age, decline: adjustment to a new self.

Tyler(1959), too introduces a lifetime dimension to counseling in
the form of complex patterns of choice in style of living and in form of
behavior patterns. The individual's unique grid of preferences
(choices) constitutes individuality.

Super also introduced a more sophisticated and more adequate
role for affect development in his concept of career development. But
perhaps a more complex embracing of modern theories of emotional
development through occupational living is to be found in Anne Roe
(1956). Since it is not our function in this chapter to review this
modern conception of the role of affect in vocational development, a
mere mention is made of the rounding out of Parsons' and Munsterberg's original thinking by the incorporating of modern theories of
personality. Theories of counseling today must account not only for
aptitudes, in the German concept of Wundt, but also must account for
the revolution in our understanding of personality theory resulting
from Freud's teachings and those of other psychotherapists.

Goals of Counseling

The task of the trait-factor type of counseling is to aid the individual
in successive approximations of self-understanding and self-management by means of helping him to assess his assets and liabilities in
relation to the requirements of progressively changing life goals and
his vocational career. Characteristically, the young person in our culture begins to concern himself with what he will become when he is an
adult. This query may begin early in the elementary grades and may
be facilitated by the use of autobiographies and occupational information of a general character.[5] Unfortunately for many individuals, their
characteristic pattern of aptitudes and interests have not yet emerged

[5] If Super's findings are substantiated concerning the vagueness of the pre-choice
occupational orientation of ninth-grade boys, then we may need to translate time
and motion studies of work into simple job descriptions, perhaps of a new sort, and
then upgrade and intensify occupational information courses before the ninth grade.
To be sure, I am assuming that we cannot reorganize school and society so as to
postpone until later crucial occupational and job choices. If early life choices must
be made, then we may need to reconstitute counseling, individual and group guidance courses to prepare students for them (Super & Overstreet, 1960).

when they begin to raise the question of their future career. But as soon as the counselor and the student can identify, preferably by objective means, whatever assets the individual may have, then the comparison of the possessed aptitudes with those required in work may proceed in the counseling relationship.

In the early days of Frank Parsons, when this method of vocational counseling was invented, counseling was a one-step operation. Today it is thought of as a process from infancy to adulthood in the manner described by Super (1957b). And in this type of counseling there is gradually emerging the related concept that counseling is designed to help the individual develop skill and understanding for future readjustments and changes of interest and career activity. In a real sense, counseling is for the purpose of helping the individual to approximate self-management throughout his life.

The Role of the Counselor

The role of the counselor is to help the individual learn to understand and to apply to his own self information arrived at through psychometric means, vocational information, and case study, in the context of his whole perception of himself as a unique individual. In a sense, the counselor brings external information to help the individual "measure" himself cognitively against the "known" requirements of adult tasks in school and later in occupations. To be sure, every individual has made some earlier appraisal of himself with regard to the school, which is in a real sense a large-scale "testing" experience, and the individual student knows the teacher's appraisal of that testing experience. But what the individual does not know, except in rare instances, is the amount and kind of aptitude required in future adult work tasks. That is, he does not have available sufficient *objective* and *verified* data to answer the question whether he is capable of becoming an engineer, even though he may identify his own desire and aspiration or subjective interests. But when the counselor assists him to compare his current mastery of mathematics with that required of successful graduates of engineering colleges or with freshmen admitted to engineering colleges, then he is in a better position to make a judgment as to whether he wishes to attempt such training tasks. In like manner, he has early identified his own interests, as subjectively appraised, but he does not know to what extent his interests coincide with that of men successfully engaged in such work tasks.

These external comparisons are made more complete by means of psychometric data available through counseling. To be sure, there is a

great deal of research needed before we shall know in sufficient detail
the many requirements of school and work tasks. Nevertheless, the
research methods established a half-century ago still have relevancy
and utility.

These functions of the counselor we call diagnosis, that is, the coop-
erative interpretation and identification of potentialities, as well as
aspirations and motivations. This is not an impersonal "scientific"
operation. Diagnosis rather takes the form of a series of questions or
hypotheses to be "tested" by the student by means of continued conversation and by psychometric means and other data which permit
comparisons of the individual with the requirements of the task. During the initial interview (Tyler, 1956) the individual identifies verbally his own particular questions and queries and the counselor then
helps him begin the systematic search for relevant information which
will provide some approximation to answers for his questions, queries,
or hypotheses.

The role of the counselor is not limited to helping the client make a
choice of career or of school tasks, or is it limited to the diagnosis of
difficulties encountered in school. Counseling is a relationship between
a sympathetic adult and a querying adolescent which also has to do
with value commitments as to life style and life fulfillment. In a real
sense, the basic underlying questions formulated in part, or in depth,
by each adolescent are "What do I wish to do with my life? What do I
wish to accomplish? What am I able to accomplish?" In this sense,
counseling is usually the initial stage of a life-long self-query.

In a very substantial way, counseling involves information giving
and collecting, but it is information of a profound sort having to do
with the development of a human being. It is also information with
highly personalized values since it has to do with a unique individual.

Counseling techniques are adaptable to both individual interviews
and group processes. In some counseling centers the individual interview is largely preferred, perhaps because it can be tailored to the problems of one particular person. But counseling also takes group forms,
either as organized classes on occupational counseling and information
or in temporary groups organized preparatory to individual counseling.
Stone's early research (1941, pp. 132, 145) indicated preference for a
combination of the two, with the group sessions preceding the individual interview. Hewer and Volsky (1960) have reported successful
group sessions in which common methods of information gathering are
delineated and in which certain information about occupations and
curricula is given to all individuals to be followed by personalized
interviews when necessary or requested.

Case Materials

Early forms of counseling borrowed from social work the case history method in which the individual's entire life story up to the current stage is considered relevant to an understanding of his present status and also necessary for the projection of his aspirations and ambitions into the future years. That is, the life style of the client's individual personality development was thought to be best perceived, both by the individual student and his counselor, when the psychometric and other life history data are appraised as a whole, even though the relevancy and correlation of certain data with the criterion desired, for example, the curriculum chosen or considered, may differ in magnitude. Nevertheless, the identified characteristic individuality of a student is a preferred datum in organized counseling. Behavior patterns and activities in school, home, and community, aspirations, accomplishments, difficulties, adjustments, capabilities and interest, and interpersonal relationships and satisfactions—are all thought to be important data in the counseling process. However, it is apparent that much research of a new pattern is needed to "test" the relevancy of many such case data. The following material illustrates the use of trait-factor theory in a counseling case.

Illustrative Interviews (by courtesy of Dr. Ralph Berdie)

After graduation from high school this student entered the Navy for a year and a half and then worked for a year. He then completed his University courses in pre-law with barely-passing grades and because of this borderline record and low scores on the legal aptitude test, he came to the counselor to discuss educational and vocational alternatives. Ability test scores showed wide scatter, interest test scores were not well defined, and personality test scores were essentially normal. He had adjusted rather well to a serious family problem. Counseling dealt with the educational and vocational problems, the relationship between this student and his friends, and his family relationships. He eventually received his arts degree with a major in the social sciences and completed a few quarters of graduate work with borderline success.

Interview recording. (This is not the first interview.):

1. **C.** Well, how do things stand now?
2. **S.** Well, uh—the way they stand I have investigated quite a bit, both Arts and Education.

3. **C.** Uh huh.
4. **S.** Uh—either one of the two of them, I think I can finish in five quarters.
5. **C.** In either one of them.
6. **S.** In either one.
7. **C.** Uh huh.
8. **S.** I think I've decided on education but uh—(pause) I'd like to have a little information on—
9. **C.** Uh huh.
10. **S.** The possibilities—
11. **C.** What do you have in mind in education, what sort of—*uh?*
12. **S.** Well, uh—they tell me that this elementary education is a very good field—for men.
13. **C.** For men particularly.
14. **S.** For men, yes. And that's what I had in mind uh—the major isn't really too important there—I'll just have to figure out something that I have in Junior College background.
15. **C.** Let's see, if you major in elementary, I mean, if you're going into elementary education, that *is* your major.
16. **S.** That is your major.

· · ·

17. **C.** Uh—what is there about—about education? You've been thinking the pros and cons—what were you thinking?
18. **S.** Well, I don't know, the more I think about it—the more I like it—I just think I'd like—I like teaching, of course perhaps I'm looking at the bright side of it—
19. **C.** Uh huh.
20. **S.** But uh—it seems to me that to uh—teach kids and try and—do a better job,—is interesting, I know some of the teachers I had, of course I—I went to junior high and high school during the war—we had a lot of retired teachers brought back.
21. **C.** Emergency.
22. **S.** Yeah, emergency situation. It just uh—it seems, I think it'll be very interesting and I—think I—have confidence that I could do something like that, whereas in law I don't have confidence even if I did have the ability for it, I don't have confidence in myself.
23. **C.** Is that because of the feeling you have or—
24. **S.** It's just a feeling I—it's not based on anything—it's more or less just a feeling—
25. **C.** I was wondering, does it make you feel more sure of yourself, when you're with younger people or with—
26. **S.** I usually do, yes, I feel much more sure of myself than when I'm with older people—

· · ·

27. **C.** Have you ever done any kind of work that was involved with children like Scout work or—YMCA work or that sort of thing?

28. **S.** Oh, yes.

29. **C.** What sort of work have you done?

30. **S.** I've been a camp counselor uh—but I guess I was pretty young then— I was 15—and uh—I coached uh—midget and intermediate baseball one year—got a big kick out of that.

31. **C.** When you were in high school?

32. **S.** No, that was the year after I got out of the Navy—I stayed home a year.

33. **C.** Oh.

34. **S.** I coached the uh—the DeMolay basketball team in the winter time, and I coached uh—baseball in the summer, junior baseball I kind of got a kick out of it—I enjoyed it.

35. **C.** What were the kids, what age, was it between 10, 15 or—

36. **S.** Well, on the DeMolay (sighs) I was playing coach—on that, but I—I was the only one out of high school. The rest of them were mostly juniors and seniors—of high school and uh—the baseball were—the midget group was 12 and under and the intermediate group was 15 and under—

37. **C.** So, you really had experience with people in a broad range of age.

38. **S.** That's right. And uh—well, in—in fields like that, I know uh—it's been my experience in Scout work all the way through Scout work, were all, all these—more or less on the top of the pack—all the way up and—it seems like my—my confidence is pretty good and my authority is not questioned—(laughs).

39. **C.** (laughs)

40. **S.** Whereas uh—in a group uh—of older people—I feel a little bit out-classed.

.   .   .

41. **C.** Well, let's look at some of these tests that you took, because I think they fit in pretty well with what you've been thinking about—Uh—I think the—the most significant test for this is the Vocational Interest test you took. Uh—what we do on the test, this test takes your interests, your likes and dislikes, and compares your interest with those of men who are successful in different occupations. We want to really find out if you're the kind of personality that successful lawyers have or teachers or business men or, what kind of person you are, in terms of different jobs—And you have to remember that this isn't—it doesn't have anything to do with your abilities—because you can have the kind of personality that a lawyer has, and still not have enough ability to get through Law School.

42. **S.** Uh huh.

43. **C.** But it's really an attempt to answer the question, how well will you like the job, if you *can* do it. We have a lot of experience with people

who—have plenty of ability to do work but they just don't like that kind of work, so that they are never happy. And so this is the question from that personality end of it, do you understand that?

44. **S.** Yes, uh huh. I understand it.

45. **C.** Uh, well, we—this is the way we present the scores here, it'll make it a little easier if you look at them. You see these are the—the different occupations that we use—

46. **S.** Uh huh.

47. **C.** For points of reference—and these are the scores up here. Now an A means that you—are very much like people in an occupation and C means you aren't. Here for instance you've got a score of C for an artist. That means you don't resemble a group of artists that we have studied—

48. **S.** Uh huh.

49. **C.** Neither do you resemble psychologists or architects, or physicians, or osteopaths, or dentists, and you aren't at all like engineers, or physicists, or people in that general area. And let's go down here a little bit, skip down to this group. This is the group where we have the lawyers, we have your author-journalist, you don't really resemble them very much. You are somewhat like lawyers but not extremely much. And you're somewhat like advertising men, but not—not a whole lot—but we'd say, there's a slight resemblance—that you have to lawyers but not enough to indicate that—you're going to be particularly happy in that kind of work.

50. **S.** Uh huh.

51. **C.** And uh—now let's see where you do have your greatest resemblance. That is this area right over here, these jobs—we'll now look at them. YMCA Physical Director, Personnel Directors, you don't resemble this person much, YMCA secretaries, Social Science High School Teacher, City School Superintendents and Ministers. Well, we haven't actually studied men elementary teachers but they'd fall in here, too. These are essentially those jobs where you're working with other people—uh—welfare jobs, or—where you're—you've got a different —you see the salesman is working with people too—

52. **S.** Yeah.

53. **C.** But it's a different kind of approach—than the YMCA worker.

54. **S.** Yes.

55. **C.** So, uh—that seems to be about the point where you fit best. And then there is some indication that down there in the sales group you do resemble those people to some extent too. But they're not quite as much perhaps as the people in these teaching fields—You come up here for instance, here's a Math, and Physical Science teacher, some indication there too—

56. **S.** Uh huh.

. . .

57. **C.** Do you have a hobby or interest, or hobby of music?

58. **S.** I—I like music but I—I have no musical ability, of any kind, I've never played any instrument—

59. **C.** Well, that's a good example—of how your personality can resemble those and yet—you don't have the ability—So up here I'd—I'd say that on the basis of this, it looks like there's quite a lot of evidence to show that teaching might be a pretty good choice for you. Either elementary teaching or high school teaching perhaps.

60. **S.** Uh huh.

. . .

61. **C.** I think a lot of this goes to show that—that school isn't the only place where you learn, because—

62. **S.** Oh, yes.

63. **C.** You get a lot of people who—who get high scores in tests—in courses they've never had—and then don't have to go to school necessarily—

64. **S.** Well, that's fine arts now, that's why it kind of amazed me— I don't think I've had anything in school—a little bit in humanities, very little, we didn't have any music, we had a little uh—art—not very much and that's about all.

65. **C.** How did you like the humanities course?

66. **S.** I thought it was wonderful, I think it ought to be required for everybody.

67. **C.** Uh huh.

68. **S.** Of course I had Castell and well we couldn't have a better instructor.

69. **C.** It makes a difference who teaches it (laughs).

70. **S.** (laughs) Well, on the classics I had McClusky the first quarter, he was just as good, I think except I couldn't keep up with him.

. . .

71. **C.** And you're going to be moving into the new hall?

72. **S.** Yeah, we'll be in the new hall, next year when I'm trying to study— see, there's—it's not too much uh—him talking to me—because if I want to study, I'm going to try to study—but it's somebody else comes into the room and talks to him. There's four of us see, and there's two of them talking you might say—or maybe I do the same thing to him.

73. **C.** Where are you going to do your studying—where—where you, you do most of your studying in your room now.

74. **S.** I do, yes— I never have cared much for the library.

75. **C.** Like maybe (laughs) that's one of the problems—you're out because uh—

76. **S.** It might be—study habits—

77. **C.** You can't, you can't study, I'm sure of that—when you've got two other people in the room talking—

78. **S.** No.

79. **C.** I'll agree with that.

80. **S.** But uh—this uh—new uh deal will be two guys in a room. Well, when

I'm studying if I don't want to talk it's not much he can do about it—
he's got to go (laughs) someplace else.

81. **C.** Yeah, that's right.

82. **S.** Or if I want to talk and he's studying, I've got to go someplace else.

. . .

83. **C.** Uh huh.

84. **S.** Before, it's just been last quarter—I don't recall, I mean, too much
trouble—(raises voice) I've always had a lot of trouble getting up in
the morning—but that's uh—because I'm probably one of these types
of people who are more awake at night than I am at the day time.

85. **C.** Uh huh.

86. **S.** But uh—I've never had too much trouble sleeping and I did sleep all
night until this fall—quarter I think perhaps a lot of it is due to
law—and I'd know I'm not getting it—and—I—I worried about it. I
spent a lot of time trying to drill it into myself—and my mind didn't
want to accept it, I think.

87. **C.** Uh huh.

88. **S.** (pause) That probably was the cause of my trouble (raises voice) I
think if I get into something I like—and I have the abilities for something I don't have to knock myself out to get—then I won't have any
trouble—

89. **C.** Uh huh.

90. **S.** The idea is I'm not the type of a person who enjoys knocking myself
out—it makes me nervous, and probably contributes to the non-
sleeping factor.

91. **C.** You've got to find something that you can enjoy pretty much.

92. **S.** —because otherwise I probably won't do it, that's the way I am. My
high school principal used to tell me at high school, he said, you do
all right but you enjoy taking the road of least resistance.

. . .

93. **C.** You'll worry about that when the time comes.

94. **S.** (laughs) I'll worry about that when the time comes—but if I had've
done this two years ago—I certainly would've picked education, if I
had've saw—if I had've seen—what you have just showed me that
uh—it looks like uh a possibility of enjoying it and succeeding in
it—whereas law, I don't know, it doesn't, was a possibility according
to that interest chart—it was not as strong as education, I don't think
I would've gone into law. I probably would've taken education. Because I know myself, I know that I don't (pause) I uh—was probably—It would be dumb to say, I don't like things I don't enjoy
but—uh—(laughs).

95. **C.** Uh huh (laughs) Even if you know they're worthwhile you don't
like (laughs).

96. **S.** Yes.

Interpretation

What do these excerpted interview transcriptions reveal about the counseling process? Many things are implied, and others are to be inferred. Please recall that this student initially sought counseling following marginal or minimally satisfactory pre-law courses. Thus it may be inferred that the counselor was initially sensitive to the near-failure syndrome and to the motivation of the student to avoid the probability of failure through continuance of pre-law or law courses. That is, he was searching for means of discovering, through counseling and testing, an alternative career objective which held higher probabilities of success, both academic and later on the job.

Rather than force explicit discussion and verbalization of these motivational and sensitivity factors, the counselor skirted them through cooperating in a positive search for a real promising alternative goal. This search led to the review of satisfying and successful working relationships with youngsters in camps as a sort of imaginative tryout of elementary school teaching.

In retrospect, always a posture of wisdom, it seems clear that he was a marginal student academically but one who profited from this kindly and thoughtful review of the process of identifying and assessing relevant data bearing on the choice of a college career. Perhaps there are those who would handle this type of case by rigidly enforcing initial "higher" admission standards. Perhaps so, but one reads the literature on admissions with a nagging query or hypothesis that, wherever the admission threshhold is set, there will always be a similar type of borderline case. Perhaps one can at least entertain the thought that this case illustrates the "humane" methods of the counselor in aiding these cases and others of high capability to achieve motivation through the fuller utilization of whatever capabilities they possess and thus can mobilize in the educational enterprise, as well as in the wider human enterprise. I believe such a perspective is relevant and basic to counseling as it relates to full humane and human development.

Research Evidence

As is true of all forms of counseling, and all counseling theories, the present state of theory should be perceived historically as just that—the current stage of evolution and development. All theories about human beings and human development are provisional, subject to continuous research. Since there are no completed and fully proved theories, when one searches for evidence to support the trait-factor theory, as well as any other, he finds fragments rather than a fully documented support. We shall, therefore, select a few illustrative research results to indicate the widespread and continuing attempts to improve, refine, and revise this theory of counseling.

There is first the eighteen-year follow-up study of E. K. Strong, Jr., (1955) of the tested interest of seniors in Stanford University. Amazingly, 85 percent of these seniors were engaged eighteen years later in the occupation in which they received their highest ratings of measured interest. This is a most crucial test of the stability of the early identification and diagnosis of measured interests. Research of this type is difficult and expensive to collect, and few long-range studies of this character are available.

Williamson and Bordin (1941) report a study using earned grades in college as a criterion and also one using a control group matched on the basis of sex, class, curriculum, and level of scholastic aptitude. Case judgments as to "adjustment" were made by independent judges in the type of research design employed in the early Birmingham experiment (Scott, 1936). The results are as follows:

1. Cooperation with the counselor was positively related to adjustment and those students who cooperated reached their level of adjustment in a shorter period of time than those who did not.

2. Students experiencing educational and vocational problems were more successfully counseled than were those with dominant social-personal-emotional problems.

3. Contrary to belief, the data indicate no differences in adjustment among counseling cases classified as vocational choice confirmed, altered, or undecided at the first contact. But, if vocational choice is deferred, the prognosis of adjustment is less favorable.

4. High school or previous college achievement is positively related to cooperation and adjustment, but level of ability, as measured by the aptitude test used in this experiment, is not (Williamson & Bordin, 1941).

A third illustrative type of research in support of vocational counseling involves the use of judgment (by independent judges) of the appropriateness of the choice made by the individual student as a result of counseling. Stone found the following results: Students in experimental groups tended to adjust their vocational choices to more appropriate levels (usually downgraded to more realistic levels) than students in the control groups who did not receive vocational counseling and course instruction in vocational orientation.

Such course instruction prepared the students for counseling and reduced the amount of time necessary for the resolution of both vocational and educational problems.

In addition, significant changes in social adjustment in a favorable direction resulted from this combination of counseling and course instruction in vocational orientation (Stone, 1941, p. 145).

Gonyea (1962) recently reported a pre- and postcounseling experiment in which the appropriateness of the vocational choice was determined by independent judges with regard to interests and scholastic aptitude, background information and school records. Postcounseling ratings of appropriateness of choice were significantly more appropriate than precounseling objectives. However, a year later it was found that only 29 percent of the students were still pursuing their postcounseling objective.

Still a fourth illustrative type of research concerning trait-factor theory vocational counseling was pioneered in England by industrial psychologists who turned to the problem of vocational guidance of youth. Using the method of comparing those who followed the counselor's recommendation as contrasted with those who did not follow it, independent judges found a greater degree of satisfaction among those who followed advice rather than those who did not (Stott, 1936). Using a similar research design, Williamson and Bordin (1941) found like results with a college student population. Williamson and Bordin also discovered significant differences in favor of counseled groups, both with respect to progress toward adjustment and scholarship. Using a criterion of external judgments of satisfactory adjustment, these same authors found that 82.8 percent of the arts college students and 86.2 of the general college students were rated as satisfactorily adjusted about a year after counseling. Again the degree of cooperation with the counselor was significantly related to adjustment. But adjustment was not related to whether or not the counselor confirmed the student's original choice.

An extensive review of the research literature is found in Leona E. Tyler (1961, pp. 260–286), involving a number of criteria including evaluation of the guidance program, clients' attitudes toward counseling, effects of counseling on school achievement, effects of counseling on vocational adjustments, effects of counseling on personal adjustment, and the effectiveness of different kinds of counseling. This review of the literature includes a consideration of the complicated research problem of the relative effectiveness of different kinds of counseling based on different theories of personality development and adjustment.

A fifth pattern of research designed to determine effectiveness of trait-factor theory of counseling is to be found in the research literature in industry. The research involves determining the extent or effec-tiveness or satisfactoriness, in work criteria, correlated against meas-ured aptitudes and characteristics (Viteles, 1932, p. 274). Link's (1919, p. 45) early study of two different criterion types of workers, engaged in the same type of work, illustrates this research design. In Figure 1 scores from one to fourteen correct responses on a "number-checking test," are related to time required to check the test. The regularly employed "pieceworkers" were significantly faster in test performance than were those workers employed less regularly as "day workers."

Still a sixth type of research indication of the efficiency of counseling based on trait-factor identification is found in the concept of the occu-pational ability profile or measures of the characteristics of employed workers. A standard battery of different tests of aptitudes with low intercorrelations are given to employed men who meet the criterion as to number of years of steady employment and presumably at least minimal success on the job since they retain their employment for this specified number of years. This same battery of tests is given to more than one occupational group, and then comparisons are made to de-termine the extent of similarity or dissimilarity. It is assumed that employed men or women, after the selection and elimination process on the basis of satisfactoriness on the job, will be characterized by a certain kind of test profile, on the average, which is different from the profile on men engaged in other types of work. Figure 2 presents data from the Minnesota study of employed and unemployed workers of thirty years ago and will serve to illustrate this type of evidence (Dvorak, 1935; *Guide to the use of the G.A.T.B. B–1002;* Dvorak, 1955; Green, Berman, Paterson, & Trabue, 1933). Scores on clerical

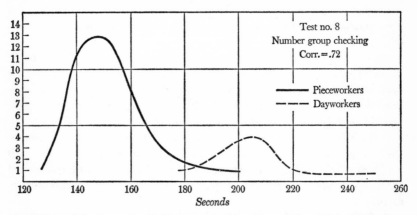

FIGURE 1. Scores on Number Group Checking Test. [After Link (1919), from Viteles (1932, p. 274).]

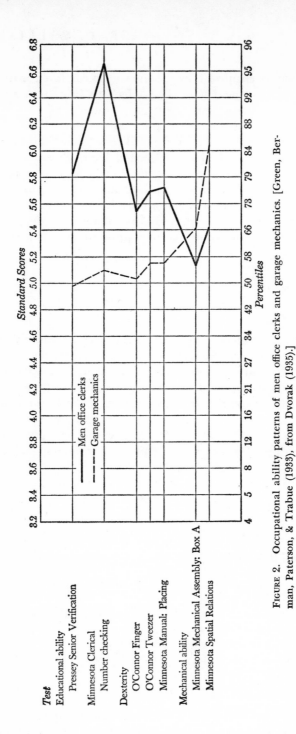

FIGURE 2. Occupational ability patterns of men office clerks and garage mechanics. [Green, Berman, Paterson, & Trabue (1933), from Dvorak (1935).]

dexterity and mechanical tests are shown for employed male clerical workers and garage mechanics. The differences in mean scores on this test battery indicates some of the required qualifications; that is, as to be expected, office clerks ranked high on the clerical test but lower than garage mechanics on a mechanical test. These findings are what one would expect on the basis of general knowledge of occupational abilities, but they are objective verification of common observation. Sometimes, of course, such research does not confirm general observation, and therefore, occupational ability information should be subjected to research verification. This kind of verified information may be used in counseling young persons prior to their choice of adult careers.

Summary

Vocational counseling, as grounded on trait-factor organization of personality with *external* criteria of satisfaction and satisfactoriness, is a highly personalized and individualized assistance to the individual in his effort, cognitively, to discover his capabilities and those opportunities in school and vocation in the mastery of which he can find success and satisfaction. This counseling is the high art of assisted self-discovery and self-understanding, of cognitive and perceptive identification of one's potentialities, and of aspiration to develop those potentialities. This form of counseling, like others, is basic to that education which is dedicated to the cultivation and development of human potentialities.

BIBLIOGRAPHY

Brown, Clarence W., & Ghiselli, Edwin E. *Scientific method in psychology.* New York: McGraw-Hill, 1955.

Cattell, R. B. Personality: *A systematic, theoretical, and factual study.* New York: McGraw-Hill, 1950.

Davis, Rene V., England, George W., & Lofquist, Lloyd H. *A theory of vocational behavior.* Minneapolis: University of Minnesota Industrial Relations Center, 1963.

Dodge, Arthur F. *Occupational ability patterns.* New York: Teachers College, 1935.

Dvorak, Beatrice J. *Differential occupational ability patterns.* Minneapolis: University of Minnesota Employment Stabilization Research Institute, Vol. III, No. 8, 1935, p. 12.

See also: Dvorak, Beatrice J. The new G.A.T.B. occupational aptitude pattern, norm structure. *Vocational Guid. Quart.,* 1955, 3 (4), 110–112.

Eysenck, H. J. *Structure of human personality.* (2d ed.) London: Methuen, 1959.

Gonyea, George C. Appropriateness of vocational choice as a criterion of counseling outcome. *Journal counsel. Psychol.,* 1962, 9, 213–220.

Green, Helen J., Berman, Isabel R., Paterson, Donald G., & Trabue, M. R. *A manual of selected occupational tests for use in public employment offices.* Minneapolis: University of Minnesota Employment Stabilization Research Institute, 1933, 2, No. 3.

The General Aptitude Test Battery was developed in the U.S. Employment Service, serving to differentially identify aptitude for work tasks in different occupations. *Guide to the use of the G.A.T.B. B-1002,* Section II: Scoring Directions and Norms. Washington: 1952. For an evaluation of available aptitude test batteries, see *The use of multifactor tests in guidance.* Reprint Series from *Personnel Guid. J.,* 1958.

Hall, Calvin S., & Lindzey, Gardner. *Theories of personality.* New York: Wiley, 1957. Chap. 9.

Hewer, Vivian H., & Volsky, Theodore. A program of group counseling. *J. counsel. Psychol.,* 1960, 7 (1), 71–73.

Hobbs, Nicholas. Sources of gain in psychotherapy. *Amer. Psychologist,* 1962, 17, 741–747.

Link, Henry Charles. *Employment psychology.* New York: Macmillan, 1919.

Lofquist, Lloyd. *Vocational counseling of the physically handicapped.* New York: Appleton-Century-Crofts, 1957.

Meehl, Paul E. Wanted: A good cook book. *Amer. J. Psychol.,* 1950, 11, 262–272.

Meehl, Paul E. *Clinical versus statistical prediction.* Minneapolis: University of Minnesota Press, 1954.

Roe, Anne. *The psychology of occupations.* New York: Wiley, 1956.

Sarbin, Theodore R., Taft, Ronald, & Bailey, Daniel E. *Clinical Inference and cognitive theory.* New York: Holt, 1960.

Stone, C. Harold. Evaluation program in vocational orientation. *Studies in higher education.* Minneapolis: University of Minnesota Press, 1941.

Scott, Mary B. Criteria used in England. *Occupations,* 1936, 16, 953–957.

Strong, E. K., Jr. *Vocational interests of men and women.* Stanford, Calif.: Stanford, 1943.

Strong, E. K., Jr. *Vocational interests eighteen years after college.* Minneapolis: University of Minnesota Press, 1955.

Super, Donald E. The preliminary appraisal in vocational counseling. *Personnel Guid. J.,* 1957, 36, 154–161. (a)

Super, Donald E. *Psychology of careers.* New York: Harper & Row, 1957. (b)

Super, D. E., & Overstreet, P. L. *The vocational maturity of ninth-grade boys.* New York: Teachers College, 1960.

Tyler, Leona E. The initial interview. *Personnel Guid. J.,* 1956, 34, 466–473.

Tyler, Leona E. Toward a workable psychology of individuality. *Amer. Psychologist,* 1959, 14, 466–473.

Tyler, Leona E. *The work of the counselor.* (2d ed.) New York: Appleton-Century-Crofts, 1961.

Viteles, Morris S. *Industrial psychology.* New York: Norton, 1932.

Viteles, Morris S., Arthur, H. Brayfield, & Leona Tyler. *Vocational counseling: A reappraisal in honor of Donald G. Paterson:* Minneapolis: University of Minnesota Press, 1961.

Williamson, E. G., & Bordin, E. S. A statistical evaluation of clinical counseling. *Educ. psychol. Meas.,* 1941, 1, 117–132.

chapter 6

WILLIAM RATIGAN | *The Place of*
Counseling Theory in High
School Programs

In high school counseling, as in all education, there tends to be a gap
between theory and practice. The professing theorist, dedicated to the
study of crucial issues, may be inclined to look down upon the school
counselor as an assembly-line mechanic performing necessary tasks
with appropriate tools but without insight regarding the real meaning
of his job. In return the practicing counselor may stereotype the theorist as living in an ivory tower on a diet of dreams, with cobwebs his
sole output.

The gap in understanding between the theory and the practice of
counseling at the high school level outwardly reflects an attitude of
superiority that in certain cases might well be traced to compensatory
reactions springing from suspicions of inferiority. Such suspicions are
often rooted in reality. Many a professing theorist would find himself
unable to meet the everyday problems of a school counselor. It is
equally true that the mechanical-type school counselor, obsessed with
time and tools and techniques, performs his stint on the assembly line
of educational mass production with little awareness of what the total
enterprise is all about.

As the school counselor becomes more oriented to the theory of
counseling and the professor to its practice, the gap in understanding
tends to be closed by mutual respect. Each begins to realize that practical success of any importance is based on sound theory and that any
theory worth thinking about has to have eventually some capability
for application or relevance for practice. In short, the most successful
practitioners are theorists as well, and the most successful theorists are
practical men (Benjamin, 1939, p. iii).

The purpose of this chapter is to explore the field of high school
counseling in an attempt to locate the influences that guide or push
counselors into the personal evolution of a theory befitting themselves,
their counselees, and the environment in which they operate.

Each newcomer counselor enters a unique situation, and he must find the answers that are most appropriate for him. Given a do-it-yourself kit, so to speak, he finds out that some of the parts are missing, nobody knows where. He is puzzled by various sets of directions that differ not only on the method of assembly and the time it takes to do the job but also on what is intended to be built. He begins to have the characteristics of the neurotic: He has conflicts, he is confused, he is concerned. But he clings to the basic faith of all counselors: "One person can help another, somehow."

Place of Personnel Services in Education

At least in many small conservative communities a still prevailing attitude toward personnel services in education is epitomized in the anecdote of the little old lady who stood on the bank of the Hudson River while attempts were made to get Fulton's steamboat under way. "They'll never start it," she predicted, shaking her head, "They'll never start it!" When the steamboat finally went into motion, the little old lady changed her words but not her basic doubts about the whole thing. "They'll never stop it," she cried forebodingly, "They'll never stop it!"

Despite the lingering doubts and a natural reaction against the proliferation of personnel services, other than classroom help is essential in education and always has been. Wherever the teaching-learning process takes place, there are attendant problems and needs. In the American secondary school such problems and needs, intensified by the excitements of adolescence, also have been multiplied by public commitment to the Jacksonian attitude of education rather than to the selective admission principle of Jefferson, which is often followed at the college and university level. "High School U.S.A." fulfills the Jacksonian doctrine as expressed by period historian Bancroft in phrases that carry a guidance personnel ring:

> Let the waters of intelligence, like the rains of heaven, descend upon the whole earth.... The prejudices of ignorance are more easily removed than the prejudices of interest; the first are blindly adopted; the second are wilfully preferred! Intelligence must be diffused among the whole people; truth must be scattered among those who have no interest to suppress its growth.... It is alone by infusing such great principles into the common mind that revolutions in society are brought about. They never have been, they never can be, effected by superior intelligence (1954, pp. 271–272).

The modern "open-door" policy of the American secondary school, reflecting both national policy and the personnel viewpoint, has made other than classroom help increasingly necessary to more learners and nonlearners, all with their unique quotas of individual differences and inalienable rights, the heart of the matter to the personnel worker, whose professional goal and reason for being is to *personalize* education.

The Case for Personnel Services

Despite growth of acceptance of his program, the personnel worker learns by experience that, if not already equipped with the characteristic, he must develop a tolerance for ambiguity. He is neither here nor there in the world of education, not on the faculty, not in administration, but plying his trade in a never-never land somewhere in between, balancing himself on a high thin wire of uncertainty. He has at least four bosses: the faculty, the student body, the administration, the community. Which should he please to succeed? Lining up too closely with any one of these factions will result in the failure of his program, the loss of his job. He must keep the confidence of the student body and yet advise the faculty, report to the administration, and inform the community. He has to accept his marginal role, which is crucial in the educational process but always vulnerable.

Although now accepted by the majority of administrators and faculty members, highly trained personnel workers may be regarded by old-line administrators as necessary nuisances or potential rivals while veteran teachers may look upon them as free-wheelers with soft jobs and no pupil load, as nonessential, as cluttering up the place, and as people who only offer services to individuals who have no business to be in school anyway. Some teachers feel threatened by personnel workers, suspecting that they hear things from pupils about which teachers are sensitive, categorizing personnel workers as undercover agents spying out faculty weaknesses. These teachers resent the fact that personnel workers know things about pupils that they won't share, that they have to defend pupils against the faculty, and that they come into a school system announcing, in effect: "This guidance-personnel work is too complicated for the classroom teacher. To do a satisfactory job, a person must have specialized training and devote full time to the program with no divided allegiances to academic subject matter."

Recognizing the possibility of arousing negative attitudes, personnel workers are generally agreed that what happens between the classroom teacher and the learner is the most important thing that happens in any school, but they insist that their own program of welfare services is what puts democracy into education. In an era when individual values are being eroded away by tremendous forces, the personnel worker realizes that the budget of personal freedom is as rigidly fixed as any economic budget, that perhaps 90 percent must be allocated to society, leaving only 10 percent to manipulate, but he is convinced that the way the individual is allowed to manipulate his precious 10 percent of independence often decides between success and failure, between happiness and grief.

Place of Counseling in Personnel Services

There is a growing tendency at the secondary level to classify guidance as one of the personnel services and to regard counseling as its basic function. Although there is no such general agreement as to what other specific services should be identified as guidance, a minimum program customarily includes individual inventory, occupational-educational and social-personal information, placement, and follow-up. After these services there is less agreement about what should be on the list. Are school activities such as orientation, career days, college nights, science fairs, or the hot lunch program a part of guidance? Agreed that counseling is the one basic service, does only the person who holds the title attempt the job? Observation replies that everyone in school, from classroom teacher to football coach to custodian, carries on some form of counseling.

In the field of personnel services the general guidance worker who had to stretch himself so thin across such a wide area that he lost identity and usefulness seems to be another vanishing American. The effective counselor is primarily a specialist, much as he may worry about Thorstein Veblen's definition, "trained incapacity," about the dangers of learning more and more about less and less, and about increasing his stock of tricks of the trade and losing his touch of empathy. Despite the preceding anxieties, most school counselors consider themselves specialists in such areas as test interpretation, occupational information, and human relations.

The trend toward specialization involves the school counselor in one of the paradoxes that plague the profession. The guidance movement, intent on the consideration of individual differences and the unique personality, was conceived as a counteracting force to the assembly-line system of mass production in education that tended to produce specialists and render the entire process impersonal, with the individual learner reduced to a number or name in a roll book. But now the school counselor, as the leading expert in guidance, finds himself a specialist in combating the evils of specialization, a contradiction that bears watching and that points toward more training in the humanities rather than in the technologies because, essentially, guidance is the business of helping man reach full development as a human being.

Another Definition of Counseling

As treated on these pages counseling may be more fully defined as the profession of helping people make intelligent choices on their way to becoming self-respecting citizens in a culture that historically places maximum value on individual development. The school guidance program is a continuing and developmental attempt to provide a healthful climate for the ultimate mental, physical, and spiritual dignity of man with his conscience and free will in oppositon to the other dominant social philosophy of the electronic age which requires the negation of the individual as a sacrifice to the growth of the state.

Every counselor faces another paradox of his own profession when he tries to follow the behavioral scientists in the belief that human behavior is caused and therefore can be predicted and controlled. If this is not so, then why is he wasting his time at impossible tasks? If this is so, then he is toiling hopelessly in a culture opposed to his efforts, a culture dedicated to the proposition that men are free and responsible for their actions rather than the captive victims of predestination.

The above paradox may be resolved by paraphrasing a message of Christ, Himself called Counselor: "Render unto Science the things that relate to Science, but to Art the things that relate to Art." Although scientific behaviorism is useful as a guideline to school counselors, counseling at the secondary level remains an art, with human values and intangible verities still the heart of what takes place between the counselor and counselee.

Counseling Theory and the National Defense Education Act

School counselors may take pride in the knowledge that counseling is one of the oldest and most honored of callings and yet so young a profession that it may be dated from the first decade of this century. From the start the "stripling" showed sturdy growth, rising and broadening from the vocational guidance-counseling movement, refusing to be swallowed up by progressive education, declining to join the mental hygienists because of reluctance to believe that everyone who does wrong is an unresponsible victim of disease (Pierson, 1961, p. 54). In 1958, on what might be called its fiftieth birthday, guidance-counseling was ranked top priority in importance by the Federal government's passage of an education act "to insure trained manpower of sufficient quality and quantity to meet the national defense needs of the United States."

Pleased by the opportunities that Federal monies would provide their profession, some counselors were nevertheless troubled by certain implications in the wording of the National Defense Education Act (NDEA). The government's intentions were bluntly stated, and a definite policy stood out in such passages as, "the security of the nation requires the fullest development of the mental resources and technical skills of its young men and women. . . . We must increase our efforts to identify and educate more of the talent of our nation."

Title V, the section of the act specifically related to school counseling, promised, in effect, to reward each state which planned "a program for testing students in the public secondary schools to identify students with outstanding aptitudes and ability . . . and a program of guidance and counseling to advise students of courses of study best suited to their ability, aptitudes, and skills, and to encourage students with outstanding aptitudes and ability to complete their secondary school education, take the necessary courses for admission in institutions of higher education, and enter such institutions."

The provisions of the NDEA, logical enough on the surface to a nation up in educational arms over Sputnik, failed to make any allowance for the bright boy who might prefer becoming a truck driver rather than a space pilot or for the gifted girl who might prefer to raise a family instead of bacteria cultures. Young people were viewed as defense weapons rather than as human beings. Ignored was the philosophy that courses in a curriculum and the careers to which they lead are the means of education and not the ends. In this light the NDEA appeared as new pressure in an old American paradox: the individual impulse toward freedom and the social impulse to restrict that freedom in the name of national interests. Clearly, large numbers of people, including educators, were willing to accept ready-made values rather than search their souls for values appropriate to themselves.

The NDEA emphasis on testing programs also seemed to reflect a national mood naïve in its trust that the way to avert unprecedented disaster was to locate the talented through standardized tests and then process them for the public welfare. Pencil and paper performance does not necessarily predict behavior or predict much needed creativity.

School counselors, reacting with schoolmen in general against the flood of testing and the "quest of excellence," soon learned that professing theorists could indeed be practical men. NDEA Counseling and Guidance Institutes acted as checks and balances against the extreme implications in the National Defense Education Act itself by training counselors to deal more effectively with students representing the total range of academic talent.

Counseling Goals in Public High Schools

One definition of high scholarship equates it with skill in pleasing teachers, by practicing orderly conduct, and by memorizing trivia that can be easily test-measured. The worthy qualities of both the creative and the nonacademic are not so glibly indentifiable. Both as guidance experts and as schoolmen, counselors face the fact that broader goals of education have revolutionized the high school program. The many must be served, not the exclusive few, and the greatest good for the greatest number is no idle watchword. Responsible for the education of more than 90 percent of all American youth fourteen to seventeen years of age, the secondary schools cannot be operated as farm clubs for colleges and universities, as nothing more than training camps for talent earmarked for higher education (Testing, testing, testing, 1962, p. 25).

Although in the American culture a college education has become increasingly crucial in determining occupational and status levels, the college-bound remain a minority, and therefore much of the high school program must be for the benefit of the terminal pupils and must be maintained so against all pressures because this majority of school citizens has equal need for approval and of assurance that achievement in areas other than the traditionally academic is commendable. The scholarship examinations that downgrade the general and nonacademic program should not be allowed to downgrade individual dignity, and the college admissions requirements that early in school life slam the doors of higher education on these classroom citizens cannot bar them from the human race (Testing, testing, testing, 1962, p. 26).

The continuing clash between the Jeffersonian principle of selection at the college level and the Jacksonian principle of admission at the high school level needs to be weighed in the balance on a scale that can evaluate traits of originality, courage, and stability, essential qualities in any era but especially required during world crisis. Such traits, generally developed and fixed early in life, are by no means monopolized by those who excel academically, and the secondary school provides the last organized large-scale opportunity for adolescents to develop these qualities of originality, courage, and stability vital to continued national existence on a moonstruck world torn between its daydreams of reaching the stars and its nightmares of falling through space (Testing, testing, testing, 1962, pp. 11, 26, 27).

The educational, and therefore the counseling, goals of the public high school seem as clear and as inclusive as the welcome extended by the Statue of Liberty to all comers, but it is obvious that the counselor who leans toward the Jeffersonian principle of selection will choose a different theory of counseling than the one who favors the Jacksonian principle of "come one, come all." In fact, *whatever the counselor's personal bias toward theory, the choice may not be his at the secondary level but dictated by the educational philosophy of his particular school situation,* as has been implied from the start of this chapter.

Although reasonable compromises seem destined at the secondary level if the counselor and the counseling program are to have any chance for growth, the counselor must resist insofar as practical the pressures in high school, including the NDEA, pushing him toward goals that are not compatible with the purposes of counseling. It is not the purpose of counseling, for instance, to recruit pupils for occupations in which they are needed, or is it the purpose of counseling to encourage bright pupils to go to college and dull pupils to go into the world of work. It is the purpose of counseling to help the pupil help himself toward goals that meet his own needs and satisfactions. If the individual is not permitted access to free choice, then he becomes a shadow of the school and of the larger society, a credit to neither of these because he has lost his own identity, the preservation and development of which is a primary goal of the democratic process. A literary reference appears in order here.

A Novelist Indicates His Counseling Theory

The following is a copy of a letter written by an American novelist to his father, a physician, who was furious at having counseled a young friend of the family only to find the counsel ignored:

> It's too bad that Edwin did not appreciate your efforts, but you must remember two things: First, West Point, though a good training physically, is none too wonderful intellectually ... Second, the boy had to decide for himself. He may not know what's best for him—but maybe you don't either. You answer, Well, then, he should have made up his mind before we took

all that trouble. That's only partly true. Are there *any* of us who decide things right off, before partly going into arrangements? ... Stop sulking at Edwin, or you'll make him feel guilty and self-conscious, and you have no right to do that. If he's shiftless—ALL RIGHT ... Claude and you and even my perfect self are too confoundedly impatient with people who haven't our sort of ambitions. Why should they have? And we have no right to ... make them feel guilty—a frame of mind in which it's much harder to get on ... Huh? ... When you say "I am thru with him for he deceived us"— hang it, the best way to make the poor devil deceive all of you is to be impatient ... you give him another chance, if you have a chance to give him a chance! (Schorer, 1961, p. 379).

A definite stand on the purposes of counseling is indicated in the above letter by the novelist who scolded and satirized his fellow Americans for their tendency to relinquish individual freedom for group security, the first American writer to win the Nobel Prize for Literature, the creator of Babbitt and other forerunners of today's status seekers and organization men, Sinclair Lewis. Is there not room for reflection here by school counselors in general, and in particular by those who feel moved by personal compulsion or by external pressure to become recruiting officers or directive agents of another kind? Whatever the response, counseling theory is plainly a process of choice and evolution, here as elsewhere.

Role Expectation of the School Counselor (*How is he seen?*)

The saying, "We see ourselves as others see us," may be turned around: Others see us as we see ourselves, as we give the appearance of being. If the school counselor has a distinct impression of his own role, the faculty, the student body, the administration, and the community will tend to accept his self-image.

All too often the school counselor has no clear-cut definition of his role. There is the story of a counselor, now a university dean, who told of having been appointed guidance director of a high school so suddenly that he had not the vaguest idea of his duties at the secondary level. Finally he decided to hustle down the corridor several times a day with a batch of papers clutched in his hand, looking as if he were going somewhere on important business. This convinced the high school people that he knew what he was supposed to do, and it gave him a breathing spell to find out.

The school counselor who fails to brief the administration on what he should do and what he should not do soon finds his responsibilities defined for him, generally in an unhappy fashion for the success of the counseling program and for the counselor's autonomy. However, if he is competently trained and skillful in action, administrators will tend to give him a free hand, consult with him about school policy and public relations, and weigh his opinions heavily.

An indication of how administrators see the role of the school counselor is evident in the fact that he may be given such titles as Assistant Principal—Guidance and Counseling, and Assistant to the Superintendent for Personnel and Counseling. By these titles the counselor is viewed as a fellow administrator, although quite evidently under the paternal system of the public schools he is in danger of becoming less a counselor and more a "Daddy's helper."

Because school counseling is regarded as a step toward the administrative level, the counselor may be seen by some faculty members as a "mouse training to be a rat," but teachers who have received the services of an adequate counselor are prone to look on him as a welcome assistant in various areas of school work and a handy man to have around in an emergency.

School Counseling and Pragmatism

In analyzing his role, it is well for every school counselor to bear in mind that in many high schools, and especially in the conservative school caricatured by the sabre-toothed curriculum, seniority and case load are what count. The teacher who, even under the ideal circumstances of facing only twenty-seven pupils in a classroom and an accredited limit of no more than one hundred and seventy during the school day, tends to be irritated by (or envious of) the apparently uncluttered life of someone who deals with perhaps three or five pupils during a clock hour and rarely more than twenty-five or thirty during a full-time counseling day. Case loads are not matters to be dismissed (or discussed) lightly at the secondary level. The school counselor's role here is the tactful one of showing respect for those carrying the quantitative burden, while at the same time gently emphasizing the essential importance of his own services to individuals.

Despite all efforts to the contrary, the school counselor may find it difficult to avoid being regarded as an authority figure by the student body. Even if he does not teach a single period, he belongs to the adult world and is therefore viewed as a potential antagonist. He may be seen as a tower of strength on which to lean or as a weakling who steers clear of discipline and looks the other way when misbehavior occurs. He may be labeled "an okay guy" or a "head-shrinker."

The student body of any high school is made up of practical people.

The school counselor must bear in mind that their philosophy is fundamental American pragmatism. Pupils care little about intentions; they are interested in results. If the counselor proves to be of some use, if he makes school more pleasant by rescheduling a slow learner, by helping a football player get back on the eligibility list, by steering an academic pupil into a college scholarship, then the student body will see the counselor as a worthwhile instrument and put him to use.

Half the girls who face the counselor will be married at the age of twenty, and it behooves him to be practical also or he will "lose" them. It is a challenge to orient girls, while they are daydreaming about kissing husbands home from work and pushing baby buggies, to the faraway fact that they will spend some twenty-five years of their adult lives at an occupation other than housewifery.

The school counselor faces many variations of the American youth. How he perceives them and how they in turn perceive him will serve to define and perhaps to change their respective roles. It is evident that *the very pupils the counselor interviews and that the teachers who work with him will bring persuasion and pressure to bear on his ultimate choice of counseling theory.*

Influence of Time on Counseling Theory

The counselor with a heavy case load, the rule rather than the exception at the secondary level, runs into his old dilemma, time. Although no rigid limit can be set to interviews insofar as satisfactory procedures and results are concerned, practical limits will be set by the counselor's schedule, and he must decide the limits applicable to his own situation. It is apparent that how he budgets his time will reflect a theory of counseling. For instance, he may feel that he is the expert who knows the answers, become didactic, and push toward the directive extreme; he may compromise (synthesize?) and become eclectic; he may borrow time from some counselees and lend it to others; he may consign time to perdition and attempt to remain client-centered with all. In any case *the pressure of the clock has influenced his choice of counseling theory.*

Depending on the philosophy of the community and the policy of the administration, the school counselor may find himself involved in functions that he does not consider part of his role. Although 98 percent of attendance problems are routine and only 2 percent of absenteeism and truancy are matters for counseling, he may be ordered to check attendance. As a result of false economy he may find his counseling time swamped by clerical chores. He may be expected to stand in for an absent principal, supervise study halls and other areas, police lunch lines, ride the spectator bus, chaperone dances, and, in short, share the myriad tasks assigned to faculty members. Although a few of these chores could be related to counseling, the rest rob counseling to pay expediency or to make the counselor appear as "one of the boys"; for time is the school counselor's dilemma, and almost every counselor has a tendency toward becoming an efficiency expert. As such, he runs the risk of changing his methods and his attitudes until, almost unconsciously, he may turn into a caricature whose business is compulsion rather counsel.

As counselors acquire sophistication in theory and on the job, there tends to be a closer agreement between their ideas on how they should spend their time and how they actually do spend it. They find in general that Darley's study (1943) of the problems of youth in the high schools of Minnesota still relate to their own situation. About 95 percent of the problems presented to counselors at the secondary level remain vocational and educational, with vocational needs somewhat more frequent. Both the vocational and educational problems are becoming increasingly complex in a rapidly changing world. The exploding population, the shifting labor market, the affluent society with its poverty pockets, the changing pattern of American life, the global revolution, the doubling of the world's knowledge every ten years—all these have focused, indeed, forced, attention on the special knowledge and training of the school counselor. Historically responsible for counseling their offspring, bewildered parents have shifted that responsibility largely to the schools, at least insofar as vocational and educational matters are concerned. They look on the school counselor as a specialist in the foregoing areas, but they do not picture him as playing as important a role in helping with the personal-emotional-social problems that make up the remaining 5 percent of his case load.

The above judgment may come as a shock to the type of school counselor who has fancied himself as dealing preeminently with the latter problems and whose mirror reflects a practicing psychologist rather than the practical counselor required at the secondary level. The typical school counselor refers to the child guidance clinic or to another appropriate source the 4 percent of the student body who indicate need of intensive therapy. Obviously these two counselors, depending on how they distribute their time among the school population, are acting from different theories of counseling; the one sees himself as a clinical psychologist, the other as an educational counselor with the conviction that the school is not a hospital.

Always the role of the counselor—how is he seen?—depends largely on how he sees himself and how successfully he projects the image.

The effective school counselor realizes that professional behavior has been achieved only when the practitioner perceives that techniques and practices are means and not ends, when he knows not only how and what but *why*. He appreciates the fact that there are as many differences *within* people as between people. He strives toward the essence of counseling described in Kahlil Gibran's *The Prophet*:

> The teacher who walks in the shadow of the temple among his followers, gives not of his wisdom but rather of his faith and his lovingness. If he is indeed wise, he does not bid you enter the door of his wisdom, but rather leads you to the threshold of your own mind.

School counselors, doubtful of their wisdom, try to offer understanding, acceptance, and love above and beyond mere information. When they come face to face with hostile reactions, they examine themselves first on the possibility that they have projected feelings, perhaps frustrations, of their own onto others.

On the basic practical level every school counselor's best hope of being accepted in his role by his peers, the student body, the community (and not least of all by himself) is the recipe for success in any other walk of life: to fill needs and offer satisfactory services in spite of pressures from the clock and the calendar.

Role Enactment of the School Counselor (What does he actually do?)

The written job description, used with success in business and industry, may also be used effectively by the school counselor. A daily record should be kept, and he should take inventory each semester to determine the relation between role expectation and role enactment.

A counselor chosen to head a program in a school committed for the first time to a formal guidance program invariably meets the universal question: "Exactly what is this fellow supposed to do?" The sequential remark, not always complimentary, as events develop, becomes: "What doesn't this fellow do?"

The special services expected of a counselor in high school may range from being able to teach at least one subject to handling every phase of the guidance program and coordinating the pupil personnel services by acting as contact man between such specialists as the school psychologist, school social worker, school health worker, and school attendance worker. The counselor's private office, if he is fortunate enough to have one, becomes a sounding board for personal problems, school gripes, occupational outlook information, career exploration,

parental confessions, and probate reports. The counselor's files hold
material relating to every pupil in school, with special data on disciplinary cases, dropouts, the retarded, the gifted, and the underprivi-
leged. His research projects examine the changing characteristics of the
school population, and he interprets this information to teachers and
administrators for use in curriculum planning and in the development
of administrative structure and regulations.

The counselor is expected to become a liaison officer between administration and faculty, a link between school and community resources. He is expected to establish better understanding between children and parents, student body and faculty, and among the pupils
themselves. He is a go-between, a negotiator, a peacemaker, an expert
in human relations and in interpersonal relations.

Even if he has a private office, the counselor tends to hold interviews
in halls, in doorways, or in a corner of the lunch room or library. He
tends to favor the dynamic rather than the formal approach, willing to
meet his counselees on the decisive spur of the moment, between
classes, before or after school, in groups, or in the classic one-to-one
situation. Despite all efforts, and perhaps because of them, the counselor is criticized for being too much of a specialist, too much of a
generalist, too nondirective and wishy-washy, or too directive and
bossy.

In brief, the school counselor wears many hats, and this tends to put
him in the position outlined in the familiar cartoon strip where a
gentleman in a derby is passing a public playground during a season
when the snow is good packing. Personalities aside, the target is irre-
sistible.

School Discipline and Counseling Theory

Because of his role as a defender and guardian of individualism, the
school counselor faces innumerable problems in interpersonal relations. No matter how strongly he may feel about not becoming involved in punitive discipline, the pressures of faculty, administration,
community, and even student body may be so strong as to force him to
conform (at least with lip service) or resign. Not to engage in what
others consider right and proper (and necessary) is a difficult task. It
requires extreme tact and diplomacy to avoid the implication that
disciplinarians are wrong or the suspicion on their part that the counselor is shirking responsibility to curry favor with pupils. An effective
counselor must, in words and in actual practice, keep on redefining his
role while simultaneously indicating acceptance of faculty roles: They

are largely concerned with the group, he is largely concerned with the individual; they are largely concerned with control, he is largely concerned with self-expression; together as a team they carry on the educational program at the secondary level.

Professors of counseling generally recommend that even the sort of discipline implied in scheduling interviews with pupils should be eliminated where possible, claiming that counselors' contacts with adolescents should be voluntary on the part of the pupil, arguing that the slightest coercion may result in loss of support and confidence. Recommended are such mechanics as leaving a box supplied with slips and pencils outside the counselor's door, bearing the notice: "If you want to see me, sign the slip, and I'll get in touch with you." In the actual working situation at the secondary level, the assignment of pupils to counselors by sex, grade, program, random selection, or otherwise results in compulsory counseling sessions as a general practice. In smaller school system the self-referral approach is more common, but even here counselors tend to use the interpretation of standardized tests as springboards for counseling.

Although there is much verbiage on such topics as "Do guidance and discipline mix?" the effective school counselor seems largely untroubled by the differing opinions, realizing what neophytes and certain of their educators may not—that discipline, if swiftly and justly administered, is a compliment seldom resented, a sign that the individual disciplined is worthy of attention. Such a counselor does *not* disassociate himself from discipline. In fact, he may even become punitive on occasion without losing the respect and trust of the student body. He recognizes, however, that his primary function is to prevent rather than to punish. He is concerned with cause rather than effect. His aim is to get at the roots of maladjustment rather than to deal with the obvious symptoms.

A step in counseling prior to punitive discipline is to explain alternatives to the student in much the same way that they are pointed out in occupational and educational matters. Just as the student must be told that unless he takes certain subjects and makes certain grades, he won't have much chance to get into certain jobs or schools of higher learning, so must he be told the consequences of disobeying rules. The school counselor must also be ready to accept the possibility that even when the consequences have been pointed out, the student may decide to disobey the rules anyway. If disobedience results, the counselor becomes neither judge nor executioner.

Irrespective of innermost feelings, he adheres strictly to professional ethics and to school policy. When the rules are flouted, the general welfare of the student body must be safeguarded. Neither an informer (except in extreme situations involving great danger to self or others) nor an apprentice principal (except when he confuses his role), the school counselor recognizes that it is the administrator's duty to carry out punishment and enforce discipline.

The counselor's responsibility is to give the administrator all available (nonconfidential) information about the individual to provide the basis for making a fair judgment for a course of action. If the administrator refers a student for counseling, the counselor's appropriate role is to attempt to help the student achieve greater self-understanding, accept the consequences of his behavior, and profit from experience (Ratigan & Johnson, 1961, p. 49).

How the counselor sees his role in discipline and in a testing situation undeniably affects his choice of counseling theory. To the counselor inclined toward the client-centered position, tests may be regarded as clouding the issue. It is common experience, however, in the supervised practicum course conducted in university counseling laboratories, for the inexperienced or unsure counselor to hide his own inadequacies behind an immediate barrage of tests. Such counselors tend toward control of the individual through other forms of discipline as well as tests, and therefore they are inclined toward a directive counseling theory.

Modus Operandi: Implications for Counseling Theory

As the school counselor sits face-to-face with the pupil who has a problem, he reminds himself to look for the *single simple* cause first, then go on to the complex. He uses the law of probability instead of playing hunches. He asks himself: "Which is most likely? What's the best bet?"

Counselors learn by experience that the original reason for seeking counsel often turns out not to be the real reason. They school themselves not to mistake symptoms for the cause, realizing that a headache is a symptom of something and that "I want to drop English Comp" is a symptom of something else. They learn to pay close attention to a typical counselee's theme song, asking themselves: "What's he harping about? What tune does he always come back to?" On the other hand, counselors also "listen" for what the counselee *avoids* talking about.

In the course of his day, the school counselor encounters a variety of problems initiated by questions or statements similar to the following: "I want to be a doctor. How much do they make?" "What am I best suited for?" "I have this interest and ability. How can I turn it into money?" "I've got to drop out of school. What can I do in the way of work?" "I guess I'll join the Peace Corps. Tell me about it." "I want to be an engineer, but my parents want me to be a minister." "I'm graduating in Commercial. What kind of a job can I get in this community?" "I want to get married, but my folks think I'm too young." "I was kicked out of math and told not to come back, but if I don't get the credits, I can't graduate, and my Dad's got heart trouble." "I'm physically handicapped and I want some kind of suitable work." "I haven't got a single friend in the whole school." "My father would like to know my IQ so he can tell whether I should be a physicist or not." "Where's there a school that learns you how to operate Diesels"? "How can I get to be a butcher?" "Look at this mark on my report card, just because I wouldn't cheat on the test, and all the rest of them did." "I've decided on nursing. Where can I get a scholarship?"

During this counseling session the school counselor avoids "thinking ahead" because it prevents understanding of the counselee's immediate feelings. After the session he spends five minutes or so going over his notes and reviewing the interview. He examines himself, perhaps probing for the reason why his thoughts went wandering at a certain point, not necessarily a sign of boredom but of higher interest in other areas. He double-checks his observation of the slightest personality changes, realizing that these progress geometrically rather than arithmetically. For example, if a shy boy mentions that he asked a girl to dance during the noon hour, this may be a sign of what might become geometric progression, whereas it is no sign in an aggressive girl-happy boy.

The way in which he goes about his daily tasks, the degree of sensitivity he displays toward counselees, the methods he uses in problem-solving, the very schedule he sets himself, all these point the school counselor toward a theory of counseling. All counselors are more alike than they are different. They vary in depth and in degree. Their choice of counseling theory is based largely on emphasis in attitude rather than on any sharp dichotomy.

Relation of Goals to Counseling Theory

There are as many goals in counseling as there are problems, but in general the school counselor keeps to the three primary purposes of the interview: to get information, to give information, and to change attitudes. He sees counseling as getting to learn about the personality of the individual and then attempting to remove the blocks preventing further personality development. His primary business is to lend his strength to support a person in undergoing attitude change.

In defining goals, school counselors are generally agreed that the pupil must make his own decisions, but they insist that the counselor may supply knowledge the pupil lacks. If adolescents have the right to fail, then the counselor has the responsibility to see that the failure amounts to a learning experience and not to a personal catastrophe.

There are implications for counseling theory in these beliefs. How much support does the counselor believe the counselee should get? How much attitude change is to be attempted? In answering these questions for himself, a counselor's theory of counseling may range anywhere from psychotherapy in depth to undiluted instruction.

The school counselor's broad goal may be summed up as a developmental process of helping the individual find himself in the present and, on the basis of apparent potential and desire, locate himself in the future. However, not to be lost sight of in the broad and lofty goals of counseling are such practical bits of business as hunting up and putting into the pupil's hand a scholarship blank or information about a job opportunity suited to his ability and needs. This simple and very obvious service may take only moments, but it might result in more geometric progression across a lifetime than the most brilliant applications of any counseling theory.

One vital goal of the school counselor is to identify and to encourage real nonconformists among the student body, not those who act differently for the sake of seeming different, but those who are truly divergent thinkers. For most of the school population they are uncomfortable people to have around but, far more than the academically talented whose very willingness to exhibit high performance is a pledge of allegiance to the status quo, these nonconformists are the potential bearers of new gifts to man's cultural heritage, and the counselor must bid them welcome, perhaps in spite of his own discomfort at their divergent ideas.

Relation of Theory to Behavior

What kind of personal philosophy does each school counselor build or borrow for himself? Is he fixated on middle-class values? Does he enjoy Buddha and Beethoven, or does he bowl every Wednesday and feel motivated by progressive jazz? Is he cosmopolitan or insular in outlook? Does he study the issues involved in his profession? Has he developed a style and a way of life that make him an individual, or is he trying to educate the young without having either an educational philosophy worth defining or a personal philosophy of life worth transmitting to others (Ratigan, 1963, p. 335)?

If each particular school counselor knows where he himself stands right now on such matters as are mentioned above, then he knows where he stands right now on counseling theory. His behavior, within the possibilities of the school situation, will tend to reflect a definite theory of counseling and to be consistent. The counselor who does not know where he stands *with himself* does not know where he stands on counseling. His behavior will tend to reflect his indecision and to be inconsistent. This means neither that the consistent counselor's stand on ways of life is an either-or manifesto nor that his stand is rigidly fixed. This does mean that a counselor's stand is a place from which to take new sightings and soundings before moving one way or another. In brief analysis the conflicts or issues in school counseling perhaps may be reduced to philosophical attitudes regarding the nature of man and the nature of the universe.

Summing up the relation of theory to behavior, there is more than jest in the conclusion that it is the relation of the chicken to the egg. Each produces the other in an uninterrupted sequence of cause and effect, but the ancient riddle remains unanswered: "Which came first—?" There is another way to illustrate the relation of theory to behavior: Evolution produced Darwin; Darwin proposed the theory of evolution.

Relation of Counselor Training to Theory

In considering the relation of training to theory, it is evident that a person generally does what his nature and training have prepared him to do. A lawyer practices law, a surgeon operates, a psychometrist gives tests. This means that a counselor trained as a clinical psychologist will tend to treat pupils as patients and turn the school into a hospital. Having been alerted to the manifestations of disturbed people, he tends to see them everywhere—and they are not hard to find (in temporary state) among a population of volatile adolescents. On the other hand, a counselor with less training in psychology but with more training in the social and biological sciences and the humanities (not to mention the school situation) will tend to look on the student body as normal and counsel them accordingly, in the faith that they are going through a period where "disturbance" and, in fact, "turbulence" are the rule rather than the exception and that almost all of them "grow out of it" thanks to no other therapy than time.

In any event the training of the two counselors mentioned above has pointed them toward different theories of counseling.

It should be stressed that because of the gap between the theory and

the practice of counseling and because of faulty communication between educators and secondary school administrators, too many counselors are being trained to perform one set of tasks and hired to perform another (Ratigan & Johnson, 1961).

The decisive element in both practice and theory, all else considered, is the counselor himself. Course work is important in counselor
education; personality is vital. No amount of "right" courses can
change the wrong personality for counseling. The head may be fur-
nished with knowledge, but empathy has to come from the heart. There
is growing conviction, however discouraging or encouraging it may be
to educators and to counselors in training, that counselors are born,
not made.

Psychotherapy in High School

As mentioned previously the adolescent commonly shows many
pseudopathological symptoms that generally disappear as he gropes
toward adulthood, but during this period there is the ever-present
danger that he might be triggered into an emotional blowup by counseling techniques not recommended in a school situation. The use of
free association, for instance, may possibly draw out primary-process-
dominated problems that secondary school counselors are not normally
trained to handle. Pointing out that the emphasis during the decade
or two around the mid-century on psychology as the core of counselor
education has been a mixed blessing, C. Gilbert Wrenn (1962, p. 182)
maintains that one crucial decision regarding counseling goals must be
made by every school counselor: "Am I a specialist for a few who are
in trouble, or am I a specialist for many with normal growth problems?"

An answer to the above question inevitably leads away from some
theories of counseling while leading toward others.

Limitations of Client-centered Counseling in Schools

Counselors have been asked to reevaluate their ideas about the client-centered approach in counseling at the high school level. They are
urged to be semicorrective because lack of direction may put the responsibility on the shoulders of an adolescent who lacks the experience
or emotional maturity to handle his problem. In other words, let the
pupil drive the car toward becoming what he is to be, but put up
enough warning signs along the road so that he cannot go too far

wrong. As a professional man every counselor has to pass judgments and make decisions regarding such matters. A Lincolnian formula applies here: "You can be nondirective with some of the pupils all of the time, and you can be nondirective with all of the pupils some of the time, but you can't be nondirective with all of the pupils all of the time."

Relation of Counselors' Training to Client-centered Theory

Most school counselors begin their training by joining the Rogerian disciples with enthusiasm. They are enchanted with "client-centered" counseling largely because Rogers gives them a tool and a rationale—acceptance of the other person clears a way to problem-solving—that seems, in the first flush of discovery, easy to learn and easy to apply. The Rogerian system with its faith in the fundamental goodness of man and in the democratic process appeals to counselors in contrast to the systems of the classic psychoanalysts who demean man's basic nature and appear Teutonically authoritative. There is also the possibility that school counselors in training, many of whom have had experience as teachers, seize nondirective counseling as part of a short-lived rebellion against the directive educational procedures with which they have been rather forcefully acquainted.

The honeymoon with the Rogerian ideal seldom ends abruptly, but it cools, and in certain cases a divorce results. As school counselors acquire more sophistication, they tend to develop doubts about nondirective counseling. During NDEA Institutes and other phases of their graduate program, they gain insight into other systems, and they hear counselor educators raise such questions as, "Realistically, how nondirective can you be? Doesn't every counselor affect the atmosphere with his personality and sense of values, and therefore even his presence is directive, right?" To which many counselors who have been so struck with the Rogerian way may now reply, "Roger!"

Reaction of High School Counselees to Client-centered Theory

There are even objections from pupils about client-centered counselors. In most of their classrooms they have been told what to do, and they want to continue to be told. Some students greet the Rogerian approach with wonder, then with delight, and take up the implied challenge to think for themselves. Others may decide that the counselor has no interest in them, that he is incapable, and they display sharp irritation at the lack of direction. They may feel rejected. They may get the idea that this kind of counseling not only is negligible but also is negligent, as indeed it may be, depending on the art of the counselor.

At a national science institute for high school juniors, participants were invited to receive counseling from graduate students taking their supervised practicum course in the counseling laboratory. As observed by the writer, most of the adolescents were pleased at the attention they received, comparing this process with what they called the "fast shuffle" that they had experienced with their own school counselors, but a strong minority reacted against the nondirective treatment. This minority obviously wanted nothing from the counselors except test interpretation and occupational information. They showed resentment against the permissive atmosphere, which struck them as dawdling and incompetent or as pressure to elicit personal problems. There seems reason to believe that the counselees in the minority here are more representative of the realistic school situation, whereas the counselees in the majority were responding to an amount of attention possible under the relatively ideal conditions of a campus practicum but not workable (or equitable) in the time-bound public schools. Whatever interpretation may be made of this, one conclusion appears clear: The attitude and the reaction of counselees will tend to shape counseling theory. The psychotherapist tends to attract certain types of patients (problems), and they, in turn, are attracted to him because of his specialization in their kind of troubles. This choice of selection, present to a limited degree in larger high schools, is virtually nonexistent in the smaller schools. The educational setting in general seems to demand a compromise rather than a position toward either extreme of the counseling continuum.

Practicum Surveys of Counseling Theory

Across a period of several years, the present writer has made informal studies of supervised counseling practicum groups on campus to get an idea of how students taking the course intended to relate theory to practice, that is, how they would use the knowledge and understanding gained in graduate work in an actual on-the-job situation.

Results of these investigations showed that although most of the prospective counselors paid lip service to client-centered counseling, they saw themselves as not using this very much (or at least not as much as they thought the counselor educators thought they should!). About 25 percent favored this theory as most effective, 10 percent favored the directive theory, and the majority stressed conviction that different pupils required the application of different theories.

There were counselors in training who felt that many pupils were so limited in basic abilities or backgrounds that the interview had to be structured rigidly if any communication was to take place. There were those who claimed that pupils who "let off steam" and used the counselor as a "sounding board" had to be restrained because the self-indulgence in talk became a luxury neither the counselor nor the school could afford since it robbed other pupils of the right to equal time.

Several of the counselors felt that a client-centered approach should be used only in the case of personal problems. The average run of responses indicated a prevailing confusion which seemed to regard a *direct* answer to a *direct* question as constituting a *directive* answer.

Two significant conclusions seem to stand out: (1) general agreement that counseling theory should be suited to the pupil and (2) that it should not clash with the counselor's personality, i.e., the counselor who remains himself and does not try to put on an act is more convincing and effective than the counselor who tries to use a theory which is not characteristic of him.

Tradition of Directive Counseling in High School

The strong tradition toward directive counseling in the schools, based on the didactic method of instruction and the protective principle of custodial care, has been carried forward by the fact that typical school counselors have emerged from the teaching ranks. In their role as teachers they become accustomed to telling pupils what to do, and in their role as counselors they continue to tell pupils, convinced that this is probably best and certainly quicker. There seems little argument that in a school setting the directive counselor can operate with greater *efficiency* than the nondirective counselor, but the vital issue depends on which one can operate more *effectively*. The question the strongly directive counselor has to answer in the watches of the night when self-doubts take place of dreams, is: "How would you like it if everybody you ever gave advice to had gone on to take it?"

Eclectic Theory in High School Counseling

Much confusion exists among high school counselors as to what constitutes an eclectic theory of counseling. Is it the weaving of odds and ends of other theories into a crazyquilt? Or is it being Adlerian at nine in the morning and Rogerian at three in the afternoon, with role-playing of Ellis, Sullivan, Mowrer, Williamson, Bordin and others sandwiched in between to suit other pupils of the day?

Eclecticism is as much in tune with the American way of life as pragmatism. The former has been called "the bane of our national life and either responsible for, or a rationalization of, the contradictions, inconsistencies, illogicalities, and opportunistic compromises that figure so prominently in our personal and institutional behavior" (Hartmann, 1942, p. 180). The spirit of compromise *is* strong in America. Complete ideas and extreme opinions (except in matters that become labeled "national interests") are repellent to the prevailing philosophy. When this republic was a young upstart among nations, de Tocqueville observed the American disposition to form associations on any pretext and for whatever purpose; and in this century Sinclair Lewis (himself a would-be joiner) rose up to satirize the national habit. Perhaps in the light of this history an association of counseling theories is inevitable in the public schools.

Analysis of Counseling Theories

In considering the suitability of counseling theories at the secondary level, there are four crucial variables that must be balanced in reaching any decision: the nature of the counselor, the nature of the pupil, the nature of the problem, and the nature of the school situation. Little differentiation need be made among the various theories of counseling. They have a variety of styles but interchangeable parts, most of which can be made to operate in any of the systems once the semantics are overhauled.

Counseling theories are more striking for their similarities than for their differences. Jung is on record as being an early "Rogerian":

> The psychologist has come to see that nothing is achieved by telling, persuading, admonishing, giving "good" advice. He has to relate to the individuality of the sufferer.... The deeper the doctor's understanding penetrates the patient, the weaker become the meanings of the principles based on general experience that the doctor first applied (1957, p. 95).

Freud himself could be nondirective. While a student of Freud, Theodor Reik (1948) bumped into the master on his daily walk along the Ringstrasse in Vienna and walked home with him. Freud inquired about Reik's plans, and Reik told him of his problems, about choosing a profession and a marriage mate. Freud counseled:

I can only tell you of my personal experience. When making a decision of minor importance, I have always found it advantageous to consider all the pros and cons. In vital matters, however, such as the choice of a mate or a profession, the decision should come from the unconscious, from somewhere within ourselves. In the important decisions of our personal life, we should be governed, I think, by the deep inner needs of our nature.

Art Related to Counseling Theory

The arts, particularly the art of writing, always have been close to counseling. Psychoanalysis has followed the example of the great playrights and novelists in attempting to reach the depths of behavior rather than the superficial layers. A story has to have a beginning, a middle, and an end; so does counseling. A novel predicates character change; so does counseling.

All artists study the methods and the formats of the masters. Just as an artist has to learn the principles of perspective before being able to create an effective illusion, so would it appear that a counselor must learn conformity to certain systems of counseling before being able to encourage freedom of expression in a way of his own. All art earns liberty through discipline. Not until the rules have been learned does the artist gain the insight to understand when and how they may be altered or avoided to suit his purposes. The very restrictions of the sonnet form encourage greater ultimate freedom of expression than the unrestricted license of free verse. Free verse is permissive; the sonnet is a challenge that calls upon the poet's ultimate resources. When a poet cannot contain his ideas within the framework of a sonnet, however, he does not break the framework or sacrifice his inspiration; he moves toward another form of expression. There seem to be guidelines here for counselors in quest of theory.

Flexibility of Counseling Theory

As far as holding fast to one system of counseling and forcing the counselee to fit into the framework of that system, it may be recalled that Freud deprecated all "systems" including his own in the words, *"Moi, je ne suis pas un Freudiste."* Jung (1957, p. 112) has been more explicit, declaring that since there is no nag that cannot be ridden to death, all theories of neurosis and methods of treatment are a dubious affair. He always found it amusing when businesslike doctors and fashionable consultants would claim that they treated patients along

the lines of Adler, Kunkel, Freud, or Jung. He said there simply was
not and could not be any such treatment.

> When I treat Mr. X, I have of necessity to use method X, just as with
> Mrs. Z, I have to use method Z. This means that the real and effective
> treatment of neurosis is always individual. If it has become evident any-
> where that there are not so much illnesses as ill people, this is manifestly
> the case in neurosis. . . . I myself have long discarded any uniform theory of
> neurosis, except for a few quite general points like disassociation, conflict,
> complex, regressing, *abaissement,* which belong, as it were, to the stock-in-
> trade.

Summary Statement of Counseling Theory in High School

The school counselor works in a setting where the primary goal is
not rehabilitation but education. He is trained to refer seriously disturbed pupils, not to treat them. The problems brought to him are
largely vocational and educational. Counseling theory at the secondary level rests on a basic idea in counseling and in educational philosophy, the idea of individual differences. No one theory of counseling is
suitable because no single theory can allow for individual differences,
not only of the pupil but of the counselor himself.

A theory of counseling suitable for application in high school must
conform to principles laid down by artists and top level leaders in all
walks of life. It must be flexible rather than rigid and, like the democratic process itself, adaptable. Call this eclecticism or call it a compromise (synthesis), the fact remains that every life, and every theory in
life, faces a continuing adjustment between a world of possibilities
and the world of reality.

The beginner in the field of secondary school counseling either
tends to become erratically eclectic, piecing together remnants of
theory, or he allies himself with a particular theory and clings to it,
whether suited to himself and pupil needs or not. Instead of bending
his theory or moving along the continuum, he inclines toward breaking the pupil into the mold.

An effective counselor usually begins practice by selecting a theory
of counseling that attracts him as being suited to his personality and
concept of counseling. As time goes on in his school situation, he
discovers that this favorite theory has to be revised constantly to ac-
commodate individual differences in pupils and also the changes
within himself. In due course the initial theory may become so altered
as to defy analysis of its origin.

In effect, a skillful counselor works out a theory of his own, but he does not start from scratch; he starts from Tyler or Williamson or Rogers or Thorne or someone else with whom he can identify, until in the fullness of experience he becomes his own man, thus fulfilling the ancient inscription said to have been inscribed on the temple of Apollo at Delphi—γνῶθι σεαυτόν—which is the goal of all counselors and of all counseling: *Know thyself.*

Or as that very directive counselor Polonius told his son:

> This above all: to thine own self be true,
> And it must follow, as the night the day,
> Thou canst not then be false to any man.

BIBLIOGRAPHY

Bancroft, George. As quoted by Joseph L. Blau. *Social theories of jacksonian democracy.* New York: Liberal Arts, 1954. Pp. 271–272.

Benjamin, Harold. (author's introduction to), John S. Brubacher. *Modern philosophies of education.* New York: McGraw-Hill, 1939. Pp. xiii.

Darley, J. G. *Counseling in the high school.* Chicago: Science Research, 1943.

Hartmann, George W. *NSEE 41st yearbook, part II.* Chicago: University of Chicago Press, 1942. p. 180.

Jung, C. G. *The undiscovered self.* Boston: Little, Brown, 1957.

Pierson, George A. Results and achievements to date: The failures and successes of current guidance practices. *J. N. Y. Acad. Sciences.* New York: 1961, Fall Number.

Ratigan, William. Conflicts within counseling and guidance: In broad historical perspective and in contemporary professional focus. Unpublished Ph.D. dissertation, Michigan State University, 1963.

Ratigan, William, & Johnson, Walter F. Do guidance and discipline mix? *NEA J.,* December, 1961, 47–49.

Reik, Theodor. *Listening with the third ear.* New York: Farrar, Strauss & Cudahy, 1948.

Schorer, Mark. *Sinclair Lewis: An American life.* New York: McGraw-Hill, 1961.

Testing, testing, testing. Washington: Joint Commission on Testing, American Association of School Administrators, Council of Chief State School Officers, National Association of Secondary School Principals, 1962.

Wrenn, C. Gilbert. *The counselor in a changing world.* Washington: American Personnel and Guidance Association, 1962.

chapter 7

E. G. WILLIAMSON | *The Place of Counseling Theory in College Programs*

Some college programs of organized counseling develop out of the concept or theory of counseling held by the organizers. Such concepts may range from a very simpleminded notion that counseling is an effort at "helping the individuals with their growing up problems," to the restriction of a confidential relationship with the counselor's clientele, and to an elaborate, and sometimes rigidly held, doctrine or theory of the nature of autonomous human development. A good deal of illumination will be focused on our discussion of theory, if we identify a number of these concepts as to their general characteristics.

But first, we note that it is readily observed that the actual counseling practice in any college will not be determined by any single theory held by a single counselor, not even if he were the initial organizer. Rather, the prevailing practices in most counseling centers will be the resultant of many vector forces. We shall discuss in a later section whether this dictum implies that there should be an officially adopted orthodoxy of theory or whether there may be a toleration within any one counseling center of a variety of theories or even some deviation from a consensus of orthodoxy.

Variations of Counseling Program Role Expectancies

We begin our discussion with the naming of some of the institutional determinants of counseling theory, apart from each counselor's own preferences for a given theory or theoretical persuasion. One may identify the following variations in the role expectancies held by students, presidents, deans of students, and counselors themselves in an organized counseling center in a college or university.

1. There may be generalized vague ideas, notions, or concepts. Since organized counseling programs have become rather universal, the gen-

eral theory behind a program may be as simple as *keeping up with the Joneses.* Or it may very well be that the college has been nudged by the representatives of an accrediting agency whose report forms call for evaluation of any identifiable organized counseling centers. It is to be regretted, of course, that there may be such low level stimulus for theory and role determination; but, hopefully, once a good counseling staff is employed, its members will bring with them the urge for more sophisticated theory making and role expectancies.

2. Counseling centers may be thought of by some students as playing a *repair station* role. Years ago a dean of engineering told me that his students did not need counseling since they "knew what they wanted to do." He ignored the fact that many of them failed in their first quarter of doing what they thought they wanted to do. In addition to the strategy of preadmissions counseling in this college, some students could have been salvaged, no doubt, if they had been examined in a remediation clinic with respect to study habits and skills, motivation, and similar repair functions of counseling. Unfortunately the role expectancy resulting in going to a counseling center only when "something goes wrong" is very common but often results in action too late to bring effective results.

3. Traditionally, organized vocational guidance has centered on the *reasoned choice of a life career early in adolescence* in the pattern of Frank Parsons, the originator of modern organized counseling. And it is a rare freshman today, enrolled in a college, who has not at least given some consideration to the choice of a career appropriate to his interests and hopefully to his abilities, too. College catalogs increasingly invite students to seek counseling in the choice of career and curriculum before they choose and enroll, when a choice of alternatives is possible. Fortunately, in most institutions, we have long since abandoned the notion of "try out" as a counseling method *without* some prior appraisal of probabilities of "success."

4. Some counselors may be of the persuasion that counseling is entirely *a friendly, sympathetic "listening" to troubled and perplexed students.* Such a counseling role expectancy may range from the faculty advising pattern of friendly, sympathetic, intimate relationship of an encouraging sort to a more profound psychotherapy. That is, counseling may take a form similar to private pratice with full responsibility to the client-student and with minimal or secondary institutional responsibility in the manner of the recommendations of the Committee on Ethics, chaired by Nicholas Hobbs (1953, pp. 42 and 169).

5. No doubt every campus also has its *negative role expectancy,* its *verboten* practices. In one institution I heard the chancellor instruct the counselor that he did not want any counseling discussion of sex

between the male counselor and girls. On other campuses there may be a negative expectancy centered on the notion that counseling creates overdependence. One dean of women asked, "Don't you think counseling deteriorates the students' moral fiber?" Those who do not understand the strengthening process with regard to moral fiber, through the cultivation of confidence in one's own competence, often are resistant to the introduction of the counseling relationship as a relevant function of higher learning.

6. On an increasing number of campuses, the counselor and the counseling center are *perceived as research stations on technique and accomplishment,* somewhat in the pattern of the revolution in medical practice resulting from the Flexnor-Carnegie study of 1910. Research is becoming, hopefully and increasingly, a normal part of the work of college counselors. Counseling is thus viewed in this role expectancy as a not yet completed profession, requiring every (?) counselor to contribute to increased understanding of human development as well as to perfection of technique. It would be our hope that this research function will develop beyond technique and evaluation to basic research on the developing adolescent. That knowledge is the foundation needed for the perfection of technique of the practitioner. I believe that we are some decades away from this stage of professional development in most institutions.

7. Happily, in many institutions the counseling center and the counselors are viewed as *potential contributors to professional graduate training of new counselors,* thereby integrating didactic training with the practicum. This may be viewed as one indication of a real advance in professionalization of counseling, but it requires that the counseling staff be qualified for graduate school appointments, which probably means that they must do research themselves comparable to that of the academic faculty, and they must also be qualified to supervise theses and other research.

8. We are at the beginning of a still higher level of sophisticated professionalization. After five or six decades of pragmatic search for technique, we are now organizing our experience for the *matured intellectual task of theory making.* As for me, at its highest level a theory underlying counseling is a theory of personality organization and development (Hall & Lindzey, 1957).[1] It is an intellectual (cogni-

---

[1] The reader will be greatly aided in theory-building and theory-thinking in counseling by reading Chapter I, The Nature of Personality Theory, in *Theories of personality.* He will find more advanced appraisal of theorizing and theory building in the writings of Professor Herbert Feigl, who replied to my query as to the differences between a theory and a philosophy in these words: "You can do something with a theory but you can only talk about a philosophy." I have accordingly reserved de-

tive) structure on the nature of thought underlying a professional practice and thus requires high intellectual capacity. It would be expected that counselors would vary with regard to theory making in interest, desire, motivation, and competence. But insofar as theory is an intellectual exercise, in fact freshening daily practice, counselors should attempt theory making just as counselors should be research workers, in this manner searching thoughtfully for a closer approximation to understanding the human phenomenon of developing adolescence.

Balancing expectancies. There may be many program role expectancies found on many campuses. But it seems clear that on each campus *the actual practice of counseling in a college center is a compromise or balance of many vector forces which seek to focus the major content and emphases of counseling practice.* That is, the counselor himself is not entirely a free agent in defining his counseling role or roles. To be sure, some counselors would seek to permit the student himself to define his own counseling expectancy on the grounds that it is his hour to do with as he will and wishes. But even this degree of openness has some outer limits, if for no other reason than that one counselor's competence may not embrace the full range of expectancies of a diversity of students and their problems. When a counselor holds to a rigid role expectancy, even open permissiveness, he must expect some students to be dissatisfied when their expectancies do not coincide with the counselor's competency. That is, many students come with one expectancy only to find limited competence, and they may thereafter reject organized counseling because it does not satisfy their self-perceived desires and so-called "needs."

This calls to mind the fact that the counselor's reputation, or perceived theory and role, is a factor determining whether students volunteer for counseling. If they perceive counseling as something they do not wish or need, then they will not volunteer for the counseling relationship. Such a role perception diverts those who do not want the kind of service arising from the perceived counseling theory. It should be noted that some students who do not volunteer for counseling still may actually be in need of that which they do not desire. This situation poses a perplexing problem as to how to aid the "right" student

---

ductions about assumptions underlying theorizing about counseling for the last section of this chapter. Perhaps the reader will understand why I am now toying with, for me, a "new" theory of theory; theorizing is a delightful intellectual exercise in the search for hidden but intrinsic assumptions or deductions and implications of a point of view systematically summarizing one's interpretations about related observations and experiences.

to seek the "right" relationship with the counselor in terms of his own psychological adjustments and readiness for counseling.

That is, the doctrine of *voluntarism* confuses much of our thinking about the desirable nature of the counseling relationship. According to this doctrine, only those students who request and wish *voluntarily* to enter into the counseling relationship would be counseled. Hobbs's committee recommended that clients, presumably including students (?), should be free to enter into and to terminate the counseling relationship at will. Such a doctrine (ethic) applied to the school or college clientele would raise puzzling questions in the case of scholastically failing students called in for counseling, foreign students needing but not requesting counseling, and cases of discipline which could profitably be appraised by counselors as to causes of misbehavior and steps to be taken in rehabilitation. If counselors are to fulfill significant role expectancies in these and other instances, perhaps the doctrine of voluntarism may need to be examined as to possible modification without destroying the essential nature of the counseling relationship.

Diversity of programs of counseling services. In addition to the variety of theory orientations and commitments of counselors which determine the nature of counseling service and role expectancies, there is still another dimension of this diversity. Some counselors prefer to organize an interviewing service as a full centralized and complete counseling program. Still others follow the early model of the universities, such as Northwestern University (Lloyd-Jones, 1929) in which organized and professional counseling is but one of many coordinated personnel services and indeed is also but one of many counseling services. That is, either as part of one organization or with parallel organizations, some campuses provide reading and remediation services, vocational and educational counseling, rehabilitation counseling, counseling of foreign students, study skill remediation, admissions testing and, in some cases, the scholastic aptitude testing of high school seniors—all as one master program of services. In a very real sense the desired and planned scope and diversity of the counseling and allied services and their cooperating and coordinating functions determine the perceived and actual role expectancies and, therefore, the form of the organized counseling service. That is, counseling may be organized as a separate and unrelated professional service, or it may be closely related, for example, through staff conferences and case consultations, to many other organized services for students in the health service, the admissions office, the dean's office, and even the discipline office. Again, the role expectancies are closely related to the functions covered in the services.

Concepts of Human Nature Determining Counseling Theory and Practice

Since counseling has as its end goals to help the individual understand his potentialities and achieve the "best" development (Williamson, 1963) of those potentialities, within the spirit of Western education, each counselor should continuously and thoughtfully reformulate his own theory of counseling in terms of four basic philosophic queries. Each counselor should philosophize about the human situation as integral to his theorizing about the counseling relationship. Counseling theory should thus evolve in a matrix of a philosophy of Western civilization. There would seem to be at least four basic philosophic queries which each counselor should examine and thoughtfully consider as he seeks to perfect his effectiveness in the techniques of the counseling relationship. In complex ways, each counselor's formulation of answers to these basic queries about human development will exercise significant influence on the counseling theory entertained by the counselor and also will determine, in conjunction with the above noted role expectancies held by personnel of the institution, the counseling techniques adopted by each counselor as his own *style* of counseling relationship (Williamson, 1962). The four basic philosophic queries follow:

1. What is the nature of human nature? Good, evil, neutral? Should a counselor maintain an optimistic expectation of the human enterprise? Should he be doubtful but hopeful?
2. What is the nature of human development? Is the individual capable of being autonomous, or does he need the interaction and mutual helpfulness of other members of his group to become fully human? Is "natural" man "best" or is civilized man the "best" of his potentialities?
3. What is the nature of the "good" life? Plato said that the good life consists of "contemplation of the good," as contrasted with an active life style. Concerning each student, we should have some notion of what are the desirable characteristics of the kind of life he wishes to construct. To be sure, he is morally free to become whatever he desires, but what can and should a counselor do and be to aid him to want to become the best of his potentialities? There will not be unanimity with regard to the nature of the good life, and perhaps this diversity is to be expected within Western civilization. But counselors need to consider: What is the relevance to counseling of the ancient Greek concept of areté (excellence) in all modes of one's living?
4. Who determines the nature of the "good" life? Parents, each individual for himself, or society? It may be that a counselor will conclude that perhaps human development is a product or resolution of all these vector forces.

To repeat, these queries are basic to the formulation of each counselor's theory and techniques of counseling. Each counselor, as well as each student, needs to formulate, at least provisionally, answers to these basic queries. Since such answers will determine the counseling theory and technique adopted by the counselor, they are therefore leading questions of great importance in clarifying one's concept of counseling.

To concentrate only on perfection of technique of counseling without thoughtful and sincere but provisional formulaton of these philosophic queries is to operate at the level of a skilled tradesman or as a participant in a tribal ritual incantation of magic. There is much to think about concerning theory of counseling in Allport's exhortation for us to strive to develop in our client, paradoxical though they are, "tentativeness of outlook" and "firmness of commitment." He could well have applied this same admonition to the counselor himself, for these superficially contradictory but basically supporting values should be part of the counselor's character (Allport, 1962).

The Role of Value in Counseling Theory

For me, a good theory orders a hierarchy of values to identify the forms of the good life to be sought in the human enterprise. Such a striving to attain a desired stage of development is called teleological in philosophy, and telos gives purpose and meaning to living. Some optional values which may be explicated in a theory of counseling include the following aspects of the "good" life *for both student and counselor:*

1. The fullest possible development of one's potentialities (Dewey, 1916, p. 142)
2. Doing some "social good" or making some contribution to human betterment (Dewey, 1916, p. 142)
3. Striving for "full humanity" (Pusey, 1955)
4. Decency in conduct and relationships with others
5. Taste in behavior, aesthetics, speech, dress, etc. (James, 1960, p. 285)
6. Ethics of conduct (Conant, 1953, p. 184)
7. Treating other persons as ends in themselves and not as means to ends, according to Kant's categorical imperative

These values or others may well serve as unifying guidelines in the counselor's efforts to work out his own notion of how he may aid his clientele to appraise possible goals in their daily living. As such, they then give meaning to the counselor's task and serve as basic foundations to his theory of counseling.

It bears constant repeating that in Western civilization each individual, student, *and* counselor possesses and should *exercise* his moral right to choose that hierarchy of value commitments which he defines as essential to his own conception or philosophy of the good life.

The quest of meaning. Perhaps implicit in all theories of counseling is the concept that the function of counseling is one of aiding students to strive to achieve full, humane potentiality. That is, life for the student is a quest for the deeper meaning of life. It is also a search for a hierarchy of value commitments which serve as guidelines to pull him into full humanity, utilizing his full potentialities. This teleological function of theory is in contrast with the learning theory which looks to the origination of action in such sources as the search for reduction of visceral tension or the satisfaction of psychological "needs." In the philosophic realm a life goal or theory of life, as defined by the individual in terms of his own hierarchy of value commitments, literally pulls him forward into full development. And counseling may well prove to be that kind of human relationship which aids in clarifying one's thoughts about the meaning or goals of living and thus facilitates one's development in the direction of desired forms of life style.

Counseling Theory in College and High School

There are many aspects of a theory adequate for college counseling which differ from counseling theory appropriate in other educational institutions. In naming these peculiar characteristics of the college scene, I do not speak disparagingly of other educational levels, but rather I seek to highlight the fact that it is possible to do some things at the college level because of our collegiate traditions and because of the age and maturity of our clientele which cannot as easily be done at the high school level. Not the least of these important differences is the voluntary enrollment of students in college as contrasted with the required enrollment in high school. In this connection I spoke earlier of the doctrine of voluntarism of the counseling relationship. Such a voluntary relationship is easier to establish in the college than in the high school. And this difference has many modifying influences on one's theory of counseling.

The college counseling scene is privileged in many other respects, not the least of which is the fact that most college counselors have obtained the doctorate level of professional preparation, whereas most of the high school counselors are still at or near the masters' level. A half-century in the future there undoubtedly will be more doctorates employed in the high schools, and, therefore, one can anticipate that the level of theory exploration and formulation will be stepped up at this school level. Incidentally, the fact that one is trained at the doctorate level frequently means that one has available more relevant knowledge and that one has also experienced certain intellectual exercises which make possible a different kind of conceptualization or theory making. Thus we need to appraise the possibility that counseling theory is related at least in part to the amount and complexity of professional preparation.

Other factors making for differences between high school and college theorizing include the following.

(1) Differences from institutional function. The prototype for American colleges, as distinguished from the American university, is Plato's academy in which dialogues and conversations were the instructional methods used to examine ideas and concepts, as well as to learn content or knowledge. We need to keep in mind that this prototype has had a profound effect on the traditions and the programs of colleges and in certain respects universities, too. Attending Plato's academy required more than lesson getting because there were no organized curricula as of today. Indeed, education was designed to train the cultural and political leaders in the art of contemplation and thoughtful examination of the nature of the good in preparation for playing their role as political city leaders and rulers. The curriculum, therefore, was made up of exercises in philosophizing about the true, the beautiful, the good, and the just. Since American higher education is an extension of Greco-Roman-Hebraic civilization and thought, educational theory making is built into the tradition of the colleges and universities. When, in the nineteenth century, the German model of research as a university function was introduced, as opposed to contemplation, theory making became scientific and not merely contemplative. That is, today theorizing continues as a high level of conceptualization, but it now employs data from the direct empirical study of nature, in the spirit of Bacon's *Novum Organum.*

(2) Differences from presence of philosophers. There is another difference between the high schools and colleges in theory-making that arises from the fact that in colleges there are more philosophers skilled in theory making and in the examination of theories and concepts than in the high school faculty. That is, there are not only more doctorates in psychology and in education, but there are more advanced philosophers in the philosophy department, in the humanities,

and elsewhere. There are also more scientists who are skilled in theory making, that is, in ordering facts resulting from research into grand schemes of thought. College counselors, possessing advanced education in graduate schools, have undoubtedly become acquainted with some of these theory makers and philosophers and have therefore observed theory in the making. It is to be expected that they would therefore be somewhat advanced in their conceptualization of the theory of counseling.

(3) Differences from tradition. There is also deeply imbedded in the collegiate tradition the method of critical inquiry and examination of assumptions and implications of points of view and theories about human existence. There is also the tradition of innovation of theories through research. These traditions make for a community of scholars who are constantly reexamining old assumptions and trying to reformulate them into more adequate conceptions. These examinations and inquiries take place in the seminar pattern of discussion of topics and their implications. But the inquiry also takes the form of conversations, of reading, of debates, of dialogues, of thinking, and of contemplation in Plato's manner.

(4) Differences from student problems. It is further to be expected that theory making at the college level of counseling would differ from that at other levels of education because the students being counseled are at a more advanced stage in knowledge, in maturity, and in ability to think for themselves about their own existence. The students being counseled exhibit certain kinds of problems, critical decisions, and certain questions and queries which may be more complex than is sometimes the case of the younger-aged clientele. The college student may have played out to a more advanced stage his search for a theory of human existence, and this, in turn, invites the college counselor to aid in the search for a more advanced and complex stage of personal theory making or personal cosmos (Hobbs, 1959).

(5) Differences from faculty diversity. There is another difference between the college scene and other stages of education. There are more kinds of experts and advanced thinkers in the college than there are found elsewhere. This situation is true not only of formal education, but it is true of other disciplines which have relevancy to theory making about counseling individuals at all stages of maturity. That is, there are experts in sociology, anthropology, medicine, psychiatry, education, the humanities, philosophy, and other bodies of knowledge which go to make a very rich mixture of relevant information, thought, and theories about human development available to stimu-

late the college counselor. It would be expected, therefore, that the counselor in the college scene would not be limited to theorizing about the immediate day-by-day problems of his clientele. He would, in fact, be encouraged by conversations with these available experts to bring to bear their knowledge and expert thinking in his search for an understanding of both the counseling process and the objectives or end goals of human development sought through counseling.

(6) Differences from research tradition. Still another source of theory making in the college counseling scene is the long-established tradition that research is a part of the normal expectation of those who work in the college and university. It is expected in many colleges and therefore in many college counseling centers that the staff members will use part of their day to think and rethink and to collect data for testing hypotheses (theory) about counseling. This is defined as part of their normal work load; that is, college counselors are not service workers, trained only to perform a routine task repetitively day after day. To be sure, they are supposed to do this in counseling, but they are also expected to "think differently" as a result of research and critical inquiry. In contrast, in the high school for the most part, we have not yet reached the stage of professionalization achieved in higher levels of education where research on established counseling techniques, concepts, and theories is part of the daily task and is rewarded accordingly. Usually, the high school and elementary school counselor who does research and publishes is subsequently encouraged to seek a college instructional or counseling position. This promotion scheme further drains away those who can do research or innovate in theory making and thus concentrates such individuals in the college scene. In the decades ahead research will doubtlessly be expected of counselors in all educational institutions, but presently, unfortunately, research is considered a disagreeable chore to be completed for an advanced degree and then to be avoided. Such a tradition is not becoming to a profession dealing with so many unsolved questions and problems of human existence.

A creative scientific environment should encourage counselors in college centers to theorize and test their assumptions in terms of dialectics as well as in terms of experience, practice, and research. One would expect that in a college environment one would find great individual differences but much productivity in theory and theory making. It would be an interesting research to see whether this is true, that is, whether more systems or theories and more elaborate systems of theories for describing and analyzing counseling emerge from college counselors than from high school counselors.

Concerning the locus of theory making, I believe that counseling theory should differ at various levels of education. Although there are desirable continuities and commonalities in the nature of human development through the medium of education at all ages, there may yet be some essential differences because of the factor of increasing maturity and capacity for approximating self-management with age growth. In line with this concept, the higher learning is assumed to enhance individuality and styles of living more than is possible at earlier stages of maturity in primary and secondary education: Nevertheless, it is interesting that the efforts of the progressive educators to free the individual child in Rousseauean style from the rigid conformity of the surrounding context began and succeeded most evidently at the elementary level of education while only partially succeeding at the secondary level and is only slowly being imported into higher learning (Sanford, 1962).

To be sure, the stage of the growth curve of human development is undoubtedly related to the capacity and readiness of the individual for progressive exercise of control of his own development. This is not to say that self-management suddenly emerges at some mysterious stage in the transition from dependence to independence, but rather counselors should theorize in terms of dictum of the American Civil Liberties Union, the "college is also committed to daily, progressive withdrawal of its authority" (1959). The growth curve of self-management would seem to be a very important factor at different stages of development, both with regard to intellectual behavior and with regard to emotional and moral behavior. Thus a theory of counseling needs to take account of the attained level of maturity of clientele.

(7) Differences from institutional diversity. There is another important distinction between a theory of counseling at the secondary level and one at the higher level of education in American education. That is, it is a very firmly established tradition that institutions of higher learning are unique and diversified in definition of historical mission and concerning the nature of the curriculum. To a greater extent, secondary schools and primary schools have much more in common, although no doubt there are many significant differences among separate schools. But it is by no means a negligible factor in the definition of a theory of counseling within education that professors in colleges are more highly individualistic in their intellection and that academic freedom was first established in the higher learning and

is only now becoming an accepted characteristic of certain phases of secondary education.

For example, the effects of standardizing agencies and forces on the curriculum are much more powerful at the elementary and secondary levels than at the higher levels. Therefore, counseling theories will probably be correspondingly more diversified and much more explicitly different than would be true at the earlier level of education.

(8) Differences from visibility. Another important factor is that, administratively, counseling is more widely organized as a separate clinic or service in colleges than is yet true in many high schools. One exception to this generalization is the organizational model of the child guidance clinics which were originally set up as separate clinics, apart from the instructional programs. But for many decades and no doubt in many high schools, counseling will be an integrated student personnel service rather than a separate clinic as presently organized at the higher levels. This has both advantages and disadvantages, but it probably, again, encourages more diversity in theoretical positions and postures and thought patterns among college counselors.

Some Tentative Assumptions Derived from Theories

A good theory for use in a college counseling program or elsewhere should be based on identifiable assumptions which are testable in practice and experiment. More elaborate theories are based on a variety of assumptions, some of which may prove to be contradictory and others false or at least unnecessary to explain the phenomena of human life. We may exemplify this *heuristic* characteristic of theory by means of a few examples of assumptions (Williamson, 1960; Williamson, 1959).

1. Counseling assumes that man is a rational being capable of using intellectual thought and scientific discovery of cause and effect in furthering his own development and the progress of the human enterprise. Bruner (1961) calls this "the arts of inquiry," and defines "discovery" (creative thinking) in these words: "... a matter of rearranging or transforming evidence in such a way that one is enabled to go beyond the evidence so reassembled to additional new insights."

This viewpoint may be contrasted with the assumption of certain forms of psychotherapy in which intuitive insight as to the meaning of human nature and the meaning of the universe is a basic assumption and indeed yields the basic datum of understanding. In respect to this assumption, counselors need to avoid confusing and completely identifying education with therapy, and counseling psychology with clinical psychology.

2. A second assumption, common in many systems of counseling, refers to the diagnosis of human potentiality by objective measurement, with a minimum of error originating in the agent or measurer so that there can be an objective description of human potentiality. This assumption seems to have emerged in the nineteenth century in both industrial psychology in Europe (Viteles, 1932) and in the psychological measurement of Binet and Simon. The search for objective measurement continues, and it has yielded much illumination in the search for meaningful matching of vocation and each individual in terms of job requirements and capabilities and aspirations.

3. A third assumption of counseling is that the pursuit of happiness as a human goal or the attainment of success and satisfaction is a function, at least in large part, of the degree of congruity between an individual's potentiality and the requirements of school, work, and community. This assumption is related to the Protestant ethic which assumes that the individual can help to create that congruity himself rather than passively accept, in a resigned manner, whatever transcendental fate or heredity assigns to him.

These three examples will suffice to illustrate the point that a good theory is capable of being examined in search of implicit assumptions. The intellectual task of the counselor becomes one of explicating assumptions and examining them experimentally and experientially in an effort to make the counseling relationship one that facilitates human development as well as one that refines theory.

Summary

We have now identified some of the functions and utility of counseling theory which underlie and give direction and form to college counseling. Such theory is not entirely derived from cognitive and creative thinking by the counselor but is determined in part (1) by the views of the function and nature of counseling held by faculty, administrators, other student personnel workers, and by the student clientele itself; and (2) by the role expectations held for the counselor by these significant others in his professional life space. Counseling theory is further influenced by the consultative relationships expected of counselors by foreign student advisers, dormitory directors, admissions officers, and others who need assistance in understanding students' problems and motivations and also assistance in aiding them with these problems.

Counseling theory in the college is also influenced by the counselors' and the students' value commitments and their provisional answers to certain philosophic queries as to the nature of human development and the nature of the good life. Finally, college counseling theory is greatly influenced by the long tradition of college teachers in theory making of a complexity not usually present in the preceding stages of education. No doubt in the decades ahead, counseling as an educational profession will saturate counseling techniques with more complex and hopefully more adequate theories of human development through education. Such theory making will then be "testable," both through the counseling relationships and through formal research experiments.

BIBLIOGRAPHY

Academic freedom and civil liberties of students. New York: American Civil Liberties Union, 1959.

Allport, Gordon W. Psychological models for guidance. *Harvard educ. Rev.,* A Special Issue, *Guidance—An examination,* 1962, 32 (4) 378–379.

Bruner, Jerome S. The act of discovery. *Harvard educ. Rev.,* 1961, 31, 21–32.

Conant, James Bryant. *Modern science and modern man.* Garden City, N.Y.: Doubleday, 1953.

Dewey, John. *Democracy and education.* New York: Macmillan, 1916.

Hall, Calvin S., & Lindzey, Gardner. *Theories of personality.* New York: Wiley, 1957.

Hobbs, Nicholas. Science and ethical behavior. *Amer. Psychologist,* 1959, 14 (5), 217–225.

Hobbs, Nicholas, et al. *Ethical standards of psychologists.* Report of the Committee on Ethics, Division of the American Psychological Association, 1953. Washington.

James, William. Democracy and the college-bred. In George B. DeHuzzer. (Ed.) *The intellectuals.* New York: Free Press, 1960.

Lloyd-Jones, Esther. *Student personnel work at Northwestern University.* New York: Harper & Row, 1929.

Pusey, Nathan M. The exploding world of knowledge. *Fortune,* 1955, 96–97.

Sanford, Nevitt (Ed.) *The American college.* New York: Wiley, 1962.

Viteles, Morris S. *Industrial psychology.* New York: Norton, 1932.

Williamson, E. G. The uses of the counseling interview. *Current status and future trends in student personnel.* Report of a Conference of City School Superintendents, Principals, Directors of Guidance and Counseling. Kansas State College of Pittsburg, Nov. 11–12, 1960, pp. 31–43.

Williamson, E. G. The meaning of communication in counseling. *Personnel Guid. J.,* 1959, 38, 6.

Williamson, E. G. The counselor as technique. *Personnel Guid. J.,* 1962, 41, 108–111.

Williamson, E. G. The societal responsibilities of counselors. Illinois Guidance and Personnel Association. *Newsletter,* 1963, 7–14.

chapter 8

BUFORD STEFFLRE | *A Summing Up*

Having examined four current counseling theories and the place of such formulations in counseling settings, we may now be ready to make some observations regarding their similarities and differences. An unexpected similarity may lie in the extent to which they fail to qualify as "theories" by any rigorous definition of that term. They attempt to account for relatively few of the phenomena observed in the counseling relationship, and their explanations are characterized by little precision and certainty. Perhaps, a more accurate designation of these statements would be "counseling systems" or "counseling positions" or "points of view on counseling." However, the value of boggling at strained terminology is not great, so, theories or not, let us proceed to a consideration of their usefulness, likenesses, and uniqueness. And, as we do so, it is but honest to acknowledge a frankly relativistic bias which militates against ever actually finding the Holy Grail, while it continues to point out promising hiding places. A bias against the question "Which theory is best?" and for such questions as "Who will feel most comfortable using which theory?" and, "Which clients and problems are most apt to be helped by which procedures?" The true believer will not be comforted by such a view, but true believers find their comfort in other ways.

The substantive elements expected in a theory of counseling, as specified in Chapter 1, will establish the framework for a summary comparison of the theories.

The Nature of Man

Although no clear philosophical or theological beliefs about the nature of man are found in the theories, some plain implications emerge. Although unstated assumptions may be difficult to clarify, several differences are apparent.

One way of categorizing these differences is found in Ford and Urban's *Systems of Psychotherapy*, in which they refer to conceptions of man as a "pilot" and conceptions of man as a "robot" (1963, pp. 595–598).

The pilot conception sees man as capable of determining his course and assuming responsibility for his voyage. The externals of wind, reefs, and currents are secondary to his subjective decision to select and make for a port of his own choosing. The client-centered position seems most completely to embody this view, although a case could also be made that the trait-and-factor theory is built on the implicit assumption that given the necessary data (facts about the self and occupations), the individual is capable of wisely charting his course.

Those who are said to view man as analogous to a robot believe that he only appears to be self-directing while, in fact, his behavior is determined by the nature of his mechanism and perhaps by the signals emanating from a power outside himself. Focus is on the field of forces—events, situations, other people—that call into motion those responses that occur from among all those that are theoretically available but do not occur. Theorists subscribing to the robot view of man attend to ways in which behavior becomes acquired, selected, and generalized. Proponents of this position include those espousing the psychoanalytic and behavior-theoretical views.

Unfortunately, this neat dichotomy is mussed by further examination. The pilot described by those of the client-centered persuasion appears to choose a port but in reality sails to the only available harbor compatible with his phenomenal chart of the world and his conception of himself as a captain. He selects the choice that seems most self-enhancing as surely as a computer calculates the sum of squares on command. It is only from our external frame of reference that he looks as if he were choosing, and indeed it may *look* the same to him, for he adopts our framework in describing himself to us as an actor. Beck (1963, pp. 66–70) has done an excellent job of considering choice as a pseudoconcept in phenomenology.

Conversely, the psychoanalytic and behavior-theoretical students, although agreed that past and present actions are determined, seem to be working toward a situation in which greater choice is possible. By relieving the hiccupping effect attendant upon anxiety with its ineffective and damaging repititions and by providing the client with lessons in psychological map reading, they imply that the individual will become less a robot and more a pilot.

Not surprisingly, none of the theories have been able to unravel one of mankind's oldest, most snarled Gordian knots—free will versus determinism. They explain behavior in robot terms, while they hope for future adventures in piloting.

Another dimension to be examined in determining the nature of man is his basic trustworthiness. Left to his own devices, will man woo Lilith or Eve? The client-centered theorists posit a fundamentally "reliable," "constructive," and "good" man. They say that when nature takes its course, good results are obtained, for human beings are to be trusted. A gyroscopic self-enhancing mechanism enables man to do the right thing for himself and his fellows. An ethical phototropism is innate in all of us, and counseling is designed to remove the deterrents to the proper functioning of this characteristic.

The psychoanalytic schools, particularly the Freudian, are less sanguine about man's basic nature and have less difficulty in seeing the skull beneath the flesh. Evil is seen as not only something done *by* man but as something natural *to* him. Counseling, then, has the function of the proper housebreaking of the part of man's nature which loves to romp. One goal becomes awareness, acceptance, and control of primitive drives so that they serve both society and the self.

Later psychoanalytic thinkers, as well as advocates of the trait-and-factor and behavior-theoretical positions, seem to see man as having a wider repertoire of responses and as possessing much talent for both good and evil. This more neutral view of man suggests that he has in common with the little girl with the little curl right in the middle of her forehead a tendency when he is good to be very, very good, and when he is bad to be horrid. Counseling may then release potentialities of all kinds, though; since it is given within a societally defined structure, it should tend to shape behavior in a way that permits and acknowledges the presence and rights of others.

How Behavior Is Changed

Counseling is a form of purposeful intervention into the lives of clients. The purpose of the intervention includes the changing of behavior—in the broadest sense. Such change may replace a vague uneasiness regarding a choice of classes with greater certainty regarding the decision. It may replace panic and anxiety about the purpose of life with greater focus and acceptance. The client as well as the counselor expects differences to result from the counseling, although the client's overt desire for change may be unexpressed and minimal. Being concerned with changing the ways in which the client behaves, the counselor will presumably act from some theoretical base which includes a point of view on how change is best accomplished.

The trait-and-factor theorists suggest that behavior changes when new information is made available to the client. The emphasis, then, becomes one of providing facts about the individual (largely through test information and a consideration of past events) and facts about the world of work (largely through information about occupations and the style of life accompanying them). The notion that people behave rationally leads to concern for providing facts which they will take into account in guiding their behavior. Behavior is changed by information and thinking.

The client-centered theorists suggest that behavior is changed by the restructuring of the phenomenal field that takes place when an individual is placed in a setting of maximum security and minimal threat. Under such conditions the client can reexamine his views of himself and his world and let the self-enhancing tendencies inherent in him be operative. Behavior is changed by creating a situation where it can change itself. The counselor does not act directly on the behavior in order to change it but establishes a climate conducive to the self-actualizing and at the same time societally valued behavior which is the natural expression of man.

Behavioral theorists have the most clear and explicit plan for changing the behavior of clients. They diagnose the situation to determine the responses to be extinguished and those to be encouraged. By a form of conditioning, they set about systematically to induce more appropriate responses. Most self-conscious and aware, this position knows what it is trying to change and how it hopes to accomplish its goals. Behavior is changed somewhat in accordance with classic Pavlovian conditioning that rewards responses which are desired, places in contiguity unconditioned and conditioned stimuli to link the latter with a response occasioned naturally by the former, and punishes to extinction, or permits to occur until extinction, undesired responses. Their concern with changing behavior is focused on problems of anxiety which are seen as primary blocks to sensible, successful instrumental acts. The nature of the behavior change for this school will be in the form of less anxiety and therefore freer and more effective responses.

Similarly, the psychoanalytic theorists are clearly committed to a reduction of anxiety in the belief that more flexible and discriminating behavior will result. Counseling is needed when much energy is being used in intrapsychic conflict caused by forces blocking the immediate—and often socially unwise—discharge of primitive forces. Verbalization in counseling leads to the substitutive discharge of controllable quantities of energy. Pent-up feelings are thus recognized, accepted, and canalized. Behavior is changed in that it becomes less feared, blind and restricted. A clear commitment to change behavior is a hallmark of this theoretical position.

In various degrees these four counseling systems recognize that the counselor is a change agent. Some hope to induce change by accretion of information, some by providing a client with maximum opportunity for change, some by explicitly specifying areas and direction of change, and some by sensitizing the client to the depths of his nature and thus inducing change. All would seem to be committed to furthering change, although the client-centered advocate finds it more difficult to openly accept the responsibility that accompanies this function.

Goals of Counseling

The general goals of counseling are sometimes phrased at a rather high level of abstraction. Client-centered: The client is more congruent, more open to experience, less defensive. Psychoanalytic: Ideally the number of cues to which the patient may respond is multiplied. His restrictions on both perception and response are minimized and are subjected eventually to an altered and increased conscious control (Snyder, 1963).

The trait-and-factor counselor seeks, "To aid the individual in successive approximation of self-understanding and self-management..." while the behavior-theoretical practitioner removes anxiety so that the client may function more effectively and less blindly. Little disagreement is evident in these statements of general goals—all seek liberation from the forces of darkness and ignorance so that rational, flexible, and satisfying behavior can result. That the model of psychological health varies somewhat for different theorists, however, is suggested by Glad who contrasts values related to the psychoanalytic and client-centered view by suggesting that the former strives for an individual who is an "internally organized, emotionally controlled, parent-like person" and the latter for an "internally articulated, comfortable selfhood, prizing his own individuality, and democratically understanding the individuality of others" (1959, p. 62).

When these high-level abstractions are traced to specific referents, some contradictions and confusions may eventuate. That is, when we ask the question "How can we tell if the client is better off than he was?" we get less unanimity regarding the answer. (This question, incidentally, is not the same as "How can we tell if counseling helped?" an even more difficult query which will be discussed later.)

Behavioral manifestations of having been helped might include such diverse outcomes as educational and vocational achievement (measured by such criteria as grade-point average, attendance, staying in school, money earned, promotions received, etc.); different and more pleasing behavior as viewed by friends, teachers, and employers; establishment of vocational goals seen as more "suitable" by judges;

absence of apparent symptoms previously present. The difficulty with such criteria is that for any one individual any single criterion might be completely inappropriate and misleading. For example, educational achievement in the aggregate is desirable, but perhaps Mary is investing too much time in school and not enough on other activities. Pleasing others is often desirable, but Riesman's concept of the consequences of extreme other-directed behavior and Fromm's concern with the "marketplace" aspects of some nonproductive orientations would suggest that *not* pleasing others may sometimes be more healthy. A panel of judges might well have viewed Gauguin's decision to leave a fine job in banking for the vicissitudes of art as clearly "unsuitable." Perhaps for such reasons "goals" tend to be stated in mystical, sonorous ambiguities, and research tends to turn to investigations of process rather than outcomes. The consideration of the extent to which counseling goals are achieved is perhaps at a stage parallel to that of considerations being given to the extent to which teaching goals are achieved. Judgments need to be suspended until we know more about the practitioners' characteristics and the practitioners' behavior (process). Estimation of effectiveness must be preceded by (1) descriptions of behavior, (2) judgments and consensus regarding which behaviors manifest effectiveness, and (3) studies of the relationship among characteristics, behavior, and accepted evaluative criteria (Ryans, 1963).

Role of the Counselor

The counselor, regardless of the theoretical framework he favors, may be met by expectations from the client similar to those faced by counselors of other and differing persuasions. The client's expectations will vary with his sophistication and current needs but will rarely if ever be completely fulfilled as originally presented to the counselor. The expectations themselves may change as the client enlarges his view of himself and the presenting problems; the counselor's uniqueness will preclude his fulfilling precisely the preconceived role expectations; finally, the counselor's greater professional knowledge will usually result in behavior unforeseen and unexpected by the client. In spite of the literally unique nature of the interaction between any one counselor and any one client, there are counselor role expectations common to the theoretical positions considered, although the patterns of role fulfillment will vary with the counselor, the client, and the hour on the face of the sociopsychological clock that measures their changing relationship. More clearly, what the counselor does is a function of (1) his own personality, including knowledge, skills, and needs, (2) the client as perceived by the counselor, (3) the instant in the history of their relationship in which the counselor is acting, and (4) the counselor's notion of what he *should do* which is a value related to his total theoretical position on counseling.

Tests. Although the client may approach counseling expecting that tests will be prominent in the experience, the type of tests given and the centrality of their use to the total experience will vary with the orientation of the counselor. The trait-and-factor theorist is most apt to make use of cognitive measures because of his greater emphasis on this aspect of problem solving. The use of "objective and verified data" to permit greater self-understanding and exploration is a hallmark of this position in which measures of interests and aptitude are particularly prominent. The adaptation of the client-centered method for school and college settings, in which educational-vocational concerns are frequent, makes room for the use of tests, and excluding the most orthodox doctrinaire, counselors taking this stand will give tests at least occasionally. Here, however, tests are apt to come late in counseling and are rarely used routinely. The other two theories seem to view testing as largely a phase of diagnosis rather than of solution. Consequently, the tests used may more generally be of a projective nature than of the kind associated with the work of the trait-and-factor adherent. Again, however, the use of tests late in counseling to help with educational-vocational matters does not appear to be specifically excluded but rather is peripheral to the counselor's main purposes.

Case histories. Although perhaps varying in completeness and focus, case histories appear central to the conception of the trait-and-factor, psychoanalytic, and behavior-theoretical views. Especially in the latter two they would serve to provide information to enable the counselor to decide whether his skills, orientation, and institutional responsibilities are such that he should undertake to counsel the individual who has presented himself. The focus of the case history would likely be personal adjustment and perhaps cover such areas as family relationships, peers, attitudes toward authority, and emotional expressiveness and appropriateness. The trait-and-factor orientation would seem to call for more attention to educational-vocational successes, failures, and perceptions although other aspects of life might well be included. The client-centered formulation leaves no place for case-history taking but does raise the problem of which clients should be dealt with, and a solution to this problem would seem to rest in part on information gleaned from the case history. This formulation might be said to (1) do no diagnosis because it might interfere with a desired structure of the relationship or (2) diagnose everyone who appears for counseling as someone who could benefit from the client-centered approach as practiced by the counselor he happens to see. In view of the laxness in licensing laws and the absence of realism in some counselors' self-evaluations, Grummon's concern that counselors have knowledge and training in psychopathology and supervised experience in working with the severely emotionally disturbed before they undertake to counsel such people independently is well founded.

Values. The once widely held belief that the counselor's position on values should be eunuchoid was generally and effectively shattered for many by Murphy's 1954 address to the convention of the American Personnel and Guidance Association in which he said, "... while no one knows enough to construct a philosophy of life, nevertheless, if he who offers guidance is a whole person, with real roots in human cultures, he cannot help conveying directly or indirectly to every client what he himself sees and feels, and the perspective in which his own life is lived" and went on to call for an emphasis in counselors on "... sound, rich, generous, and wise personality" rather than "tricks of the trade" (Murphy, 1955).

Now the usually held view is that the counselor's values are not only present and consciously held but constitute an important part of his armamentarium. The debate has shifted from the question "Should the counselor's values be apparent to the client?" to the question "Should the counselor have in mind values which he will attempt to implant in the client?" The affirmative position is clearly stated by Williamson in his chapter on trait-factor theory and elsewhere (1958).

A persuasive case against counselor neutrality toward values is made by Samler who writes,

> One can list a set of troubles, the therapies of choice and their underlying orientation:
>   For the demanding and infantile—assumption of responsibility;
>   For the vocationally disorientated—assumption of a working role congruent with the picture the client will develop of himself;
>   For the guilt ridden—tolerance for himself and life's reality;
>   For the unloved and unloving—self acceptance and kindliness;
>   For the achievement and power-ridden—appreciation of the rich resources in human beings;
>   For the highly controlling—reduction of anxiety and a more trusting and optimistic outlook (1960).

The negative position on the implanting of values has come to be associated with the client-centered counselor and is characterized by a belief that the client must freely accept or reject the moral and ethical values of the counselor who would leave to such social institutions as the church, the family, and the school the teaching of values (Patterson, 1958).

While only Williamson elaborates his position on this matter, it would seem that the psychoanalytic and behavior-theoretical counselor would be closer to the trait-and-factor than to the client-centered one. Because there is agreement that the counselor's intervention is a stimulus that affects the client and because the nature of the intervention must be a consequence of the counselor's values system, some *rapprochement* would seem possible. The apparent difference may lie in the client-centered counselor's lesser reliance on societally constructed signposts in finding viable values. That is, the value communicated may be a consequence and a meriting of personal standards to a greater extent than is true with other theories placing greater (although, of course, not exclusive) reliance on social consensus. If so, it follows that recognition must be given to the fact that personal responsibility, self-determination, and freedom to reject the counselor's values are themselves a value commitment, and the counselor's behavior may be designed to inculcate this position in the client.

Group procedures. All but the behavior-theoretical positions have some history of group counseling activity. The trait-and-factor position has been used in high school classes—variously labeled "occupations," "vocational problems," or "orientation"—designed to learn about aptitudes and occupations. Analytically orientated group therapy and client-centered therapy provide models for group counseling sometimes supplemented by individual sessions. The purposes of behavior-theoretical counseling would appear to be so specific that group procedures would not be feasible. However, conditioning plays a large part in the rationale for group counseling; because of his responses, the client is enabled to act out new ways of behaving and achieve reinforcement from the other group members. He learns that it is possible to say things which previously he has suppressed, to think thoughts which previously he has rejected, and to perform in new ways with support from group members and success in maintaining their regard. It would appear, then, that the behavioral-theoretical position has in it room for group methods of counseling. While obvious modifications are called for in moving from an individual to a group procedure the theoretical framework would seem to hold and to provide clues for the counselor's behavior.

Research support. The discouraging state of research support for the notion that people are helped by talking is most forcefully presented by Eysenck, who, after a review of the literature, concludes that, with the possible exception of treatment of the behavioral-theoretical type, there is no evidence that people get better as a result of therapy (1961). (In discussing the difficulties of obtaining objective consideration for such research, he includes a delightful quotation, "To some of the counselors, the whole control group idea ... seemed slightly blasphemous, as if we were attempting a statistical test of the efficacy of prayer ...")

In reviewing three years of counseling research Callis writes that, "Trends in the data indicate that experienced counselors may produce better results than neophytes and that most experienced counselors choose their methods to fit the task rather than a stereotyped school of conviction" (1963).

Such a conclusion gives little optimism to those who have been attempting to find research support for their favorite counseling theory especially since in this same article Callis adds, "In many instances, the outcome against which counseling was evaluated was not the intended goal of the counselor but an incidental by-product."

Patterson seems to agree that there is little present and unassailable evidence of the value of counseling but believes that the situation stems not from the basic worth of counseling but from inadequacies of research design.

From the analysis of the deficiences of current research, a number of suggestions or recommendations for future research are apparent:

1. Consideration must be given to the goals and objectives of counseling and guidance services and to the criteria relevant to the attainment of these goals and obejctives developed and used in future studies.

2. Attention must be given to specifying and to defining the nature of the treatment variable in order that studies may be replicated and in order that one may know to what variable what results may be attributed. Study of specific, defined methods or services in terms of specific criteria will lead to knowledge of what leads to what and will enable investigators to select methods or approaches that will lead to desired criteria or outcomes.

3. An adequate test of the effects of counseling, especially when criteria of personality changes are used, must provide counseling services that are sufficiently extensive and intensive to provide realistic expectations for such changes. It is unreasonable to expect superficial one-interview counseling to have such effects.

4. Any adequate test of the influences or effect of counseling must be based upon the use of counselors who are trained and experienced and who have competence in the methods or approaches they use.

5. Although it is of interest to study the effects of counseling on unmotivated clients or on clients who do not apply or volunteer for counseling, the primary concern is with individuals who are interested in or desirous of receiving counseling. Studies using involuntary clients are not a test of the effects of counseling in a normal counseling situation.

6. Long-term follow-up is necessary to ascertain the nature and persist-

ance of effects. In some instances, there are delayed effects; in others, there may be superficial effects immediately following counseling which will not persist.

Controlled experiments which meet these requirements are difficult and expensive to conduct, not only in terms of experimental design and controls, but also in terms of time, including the duration of the experiment and the follow-up. It would appear that, as in other areas of research, an adequate study requires more than the resources of a single investigator. The time is ripe for an extensive, long-term investigation with adequate financial support, in which existing knowledge may be applied to the conduct of meaningful research on the effects of counseling and guidance services (1963).

An evaluation of the state of counseling research, particularly as it applies to educational settings, indicates that we are far from definitive answers (Stefflre, 1963).[1]

The present relationship between research and practice in counseling is much like the relationship between research and practice in other areas of education. If we did in the name of counseling only those things which research has proved to be worth doing, we should have a good deal of free time on our hands.

Present knowledge in counseling can be divided into three categories. There is a very small category of knowledge which we know to be true as a result of sound research evidence. There is an extremely large category of "knowledge" which we "know" from common sense or scholastic revelation; such knowledge may be said to be a part of the "conventional wisdom." Finally, there is a category of knowledge, which is growing rapidly, that indicates what we do not know! Well-designed research in counseling typically results in transferring "knowledge" from the second category to the third one. The most common conclusion reached as a consequence of carefully designed research in counseling is the verdict "Not proved."

To be more specific with regard to our present situation, let us take a look at the research which deals with the value of counseling. In reviewing this research, the most defensible conclusion is that there is no solid evidence that counseling helps its recipients. An optimistic reaction to this same evidence is contained in the article "Counseling Theory" in the *Encyclopedia of Educational Research* (1960, p. 347), in which Leary and Harvey are quoted as follows: "The steady growth in prestige of . . . (psychotherapy) in the teeth of these two obstacles— its unscientific status and its inherent threats to the conscious ego—is a remarkable testimony to its basic effectiveness or to the capacity of otherwise intelligent professional workers to deceive themselves" (1960, p. 347).

---

[1] Much of the remainder of this section is adapted from this article by the author.

Regardless of our interpretation of the lack of proof of the value of counseling, the fact remains that such proof is not now existent. The difficulty of gathering evidence in this field is tremendous, inasmuch as the goals which we might evaluate are not the same for all classifications of individuals. In short, we are not always certain of what we are trying to accomplish in counseling, but it seems clear that we are trying to achieve different ends with different clients. In some cases, we are trying to make an individual more free in the expression of his impulses; in others, we are trying to make him more controlled and more subject to the dictates of society. In some cases we are trying to get him to be more "realistic." Thus, counseling programs are now found in schools and colleges not because of sound research evidence of their value but rather because it is the considered opinion of specialists, teachers, students, administrators, and community members that counseling is a worthwhile educational activity.

Essentially, the same conclusion is inevitable when we consider the value of systematic high school counseling programs. The best research in this area is reported by Rothney and Roens (1950) and Rothney (1958).

These studies both come to the conclusion that some value (although much less than was anticipated) probably accrues to the high school student who receives counseling. While these are the most definitive attempts to illustrate and prove the value of high school counseling programs, the findings cannot be interpreted in any clear-cut fashion. The first study separated students into experimental and control groups on the basis of matching rather than randomization, and of course we cannot be sure that the crucial variables were taken into account. The second study does not spell out exactly what the treatment effect was that the experimental group received, that is, the reader does not know what "counseling" meant in this context. The most defensible conclusion to be drawn from these two studies is that doing something is generally better than doing nothing. The results of both research studies, while not at all clear-cut in favoring the counseling group, can best be explained by the so-called "Hawthorne effect," which was discovered long ago in industry and is instinctively understood by the physician who supplies his patient with a placebo in the expectation that attention will succeed where more verifiable science falters.

To illustrate further the present state of counseling research, we can point to the fact that our nomenclature is so ambiguous that we are not even certain how many counselors there are working in the United States, or how many schools have counseling programs, exactly what a counselor does, or how many counselors we still need. There is no clear and agreed upon job description for school counselors; they are, in fact, engaged in a variety of tasks as Ratigan so well points out in his chapter, "The Place of Theory in High School Programs." Some function almost as psychologists, some as quasi-administrators, some as disciplinarians, some as liaison men trafficking in college admissions, some even as heavy-handed advice givers and soothsayers—and this list is not exhaustive. Because of this lack of agreement with regard to the counselor's role, his education neither fits his present function nor reflects precisely what the universities training him think he should do. Research has not helped us describe the function we are talking about, the specialist who is performing the function, or the purpose for which he was hired.

Furthermore, there is a large hiatus between practice and the research that has been done. Practice seems to move by instinct and inertia, while researchers talk only to each other and sparingly at that. An example of the lag between research and practice is the present expansion of elementary school counseling programs. All over the country, administrators are seeking and hiring elementary school counselors. There is as yet, however, no research evidence indicating that these people will be helpful. Certainly there are those who believe fervently that if guidance is good, it is good at all levels. There are also those who think that if it is difficult to cure "maladjustment" it is better to prevent it, and the way to prevent it is to work with students at the youngest possible age. Such reasoning may or may not be logical, but it is certainly not based on research. Again, then, we find the field moving on the basis of faith, hope, and "expert judgment," but not on the basis of research evidence.

In view of the present state of affairs, how can research be used to aid guidance practice and, in turn, the total educational activity of the school? First, we need, as a profession, to come to some agreement with regard to what we mean by such terms as "counselor," "pupil personnel services," "therapy," and "guidance." Until we have done this job of thinking through and defining, it seems unlikely that we shall make any significant progress in research in this field. What counseling most needs at this time is a Linnaeus!

Second, we need much research that is local and descriptive. That is we need much study of the process of counseling rather than of an ultimate product. Such studies are best done by local school counselors and do not involve any ultimate proof of the value of their work but rather describe for us what they are doing. Such local research obviously should not be done without a careful consideration of its effects on the setting because it may intrude on the personal values of the professional staff or the community, it may offend certain groups or

alter their relationship within the school, and it may use time which
we can ill afford for such purposes. Before beginning such research,
counselors should carefully consider who should be consulted and
whether the results will be worth the effort. Once such consequences
are considered, however, there still might be much room for research
studies which tell us how a counselor spends his day, what the perception of the community is in regard to the guidance program, what
teachers see as their responsibility for guidance, and other practical
"bread and butter" questions.

Third, we need to recognize that knowledge of human behavior is
not confined to the quantitative sciences. Certainly there is much more
to be learned about the nature of adolescence from reading Salinger's
The Catcher in the Rye than from reading the most recent issue of the
Journal of Consulting Psychology. Too many counselors like other
workers in education have blinded themselves to the humanities as a
way of understanding behavior. We have leaned too long and too
heavily on numbers. Do we learn about old age only by reading journal articles on gerontology, or can we not also learn by studying the
self-portraits of Rembrandt? Before counseling can make significant
contributions to education, it must turn again to the sources which traditionally have both satisfied and aroused curiosity about the human
condition. These sources are the literary and visual arts, and while they
do not dispel the need for more systematic statements, they certainly
should supplement our exercises in the quantitative and the minute.

Fourth, we must recognize that along with a human need to "know,"
we have an equally human need "not to know." Some of our most
supersophisticated research designs grow out of the latter need. The
insistence on complete randomization when we know that it is impossible to achieve, the use of very involved statistical manipulations for
data which do not merit such careful treatment, the obsession with
assumptions underlying statistics when their violation sometimes does
not really alter the conclusions—all are evidences of our need not to
know. Such a need, perhaps stemming from the guilt of some unresolved academic voyeurism, needs to be brought out into the open and
clarified if we are going to make progress in research in counseling.
Absolute, ultimate answers—free from the pedant's attack—will not
soon be found in counseling research.

Fifth, we must be more concerned about illuminating ends and less
concerned about examining means. Certainly the kind of clarification
offered by Barry and Wolf (1957) helps us sort out the purposes of
counseling programs and is much needed.

We cannot expect any dramatic breakthrough in guidance, or for
that matter in education, until we have thoroughly thought through

what it is we are trying to do. We could make a plea, then, for less correlation and more conceptualization.

Sixth, in some cases we ought to delay research and substitute demonstration projects. In elementary school counseling, for example, it seems that there is no general agreement as to what the program should involve. Since we know very little about the field, perhaps our "research" should deal with the evolving of theory rather than its testing. Demonstration or pilot projects would permit us to try out various approaches to this new field. One school, for example, might hire an elementary school counselor who behaves and is trained much like a secondary school counselor. Another could have a psychologist who might serve as a resource person on child growth and development. A third might hire a social worker to carry on therapy with children. There are many other possibilities within this field. Trying out several methods in schools is one way to begin to decide what is the best use of the elementary school counselor and to determine what problems evolve from various approaches. Such research, which would be essentially theory building, is much needed in guidance.

Now let us look at some promising research which does offer us a brighter horizon for the future. Major longitudinal studies, such as Flanagan's Project Talent and Super's Career Pattern Study give us much hope. These studies promise no immediate answers to our questions, but they will provide us with a basis of data which will permit sounder research and study. They may well do for our understanding of counseling what Terman's study did for our understanding of the gifted student.

A second kind of study which has much promise is exemplified by Coleman's *The Adolescent Society* (1961) which examines the values and attitudes of schools and their impact on the learning and behavior of youth. Coleman has pointed to the importance of considering not only the individual but also the context in which the individual learns. Such studies may constitute a major advance in understanding the behavior of adolescents and the levers instrumental in changing it.

A third kind of research is illustrated by Jahoda's *Current Concepts of Positive Mental Health* (1958), in which she does a splendid job of classifying the definitions of mental health and helping us see that before we can work for mental health, we need to agree on what it is. This kind of taxonomic conceptualization is badly needed in the whole field of counseling.

These three kinds of research seem to be the sort that will lead guidance out of its present state into a more promising future. They have in common a strong belief that counting is not a substitute for thinking! Too much counseling research has been concerned with the manipulation of figures, too little of it with the manipulation of ideas. The future depends on the clarification of concepts more than it depends on the calculation of figures.

In summary, then, the present state of counseling research is not reassuring. We are not able to demonstrate the value of what we are doing, or are we even able to agree on who is doing it or what should be done. As a result, we make radical moves, for example, in increasing the number of elementary school counselors before we have any clear understanding of why we are doing what we are doing. We need clarification of concepts, we need a return to the importance of the humanities, we need local descriptive studies, we need to understand why we act, as well as how we act, and most of all, we need to know when we do not know. We must unmask easy answers and reveal that they are often but fraudulent substitutes for hard questions.

Crucial Determinants

The practical consequences of commitment to a given theoretical position continue to be unclear. Relevant studies are concerned with frankly psychotherapeutic activity and may not be generalizable to counseling. In an important early study Fiedler (1950) found that experienced psychoanalytic, client-centered, and Adlerian therapists tended to resemble each other in their behavior more than experienced therapists of any one of these orientations resembled inexperienced therapists of the same orientation.

Fiedler also speculated that knowledge of theory helped a practitioner feel more secure and hence released him to attend to the patient's needs in ways that experienced practitioners would tend to regard as effective. Strupp (1955a), however, found sharp differences in the types of responses given by the client-centered as opposed to psychoanalytically oriented therapists, although with greater experience and with personal analysis, the client-centered workers' responses become more similar to those of the psychoanalyst.

In another study, Strupp (1955b) found support for Fiedler's finding that greater experience leads to a diversification of technique.

The present state of research would, therefore, suggest that intensive training, personal therapy, and experience are greater determinants of counseling behavior than are stated theoretical positions. It is possible, however, that familiarity and comfort with a counseling theory is a necessary but not sufficient condition for the emergence of a relationship between the counselor's background and his counseling behavior.

Common Elements

At the risk of some violation of niceties within the four schools of thought let us search for common elements as a corrective against the possible magnification of differences. This consideration does not constitute a synthesis but rather a recognition that "counseling," of whatever style, is apt to use bricks which are basic and solid regardless of the esthetic principles advanced by the architect. Ten facets of counseling which seem both crucial and common will determine the structure of our examination of commonalities.

(1) *Flexibility*. Although counseling procedures are most clearly seen in extremes approaching caricature, they are apt to be used by any one counselor along several continua—from active to passive, directive to compliant, cognitive to affective, etc. The hallmark of the experienced counselor seems to be the ability to fit his style to the unique character of the client and the relationship at any one time. All schools imply that some variation in style is advisable, although they differ in their emphasis on this matter. No theory advocates fitting a client to a mold, all presuppose reasonable flexibility in the application of theoretical principles.

(2) *Motivation*. While not always made explicit, it would seem that the several theories are agreed that the clients who want counseling are more apt to profit from it than those who don't. The unmotivated client may be dealt with, but the likelihood of success is felt to be minimal. The school or college which drags the reluctant client to the counselor's door will find little optimism in the counselor's assessment of his chances of being helpful. Motivation for counseling would appear to be a necessary condition for behavior change and counseling "success." Research which has not taken this crucial variable into account is open to much criticism.

(3) *Relationship*. From time to time one theory or another tries to claim the concept of "relationship" as its personal discovery, and all are agreed that it is a most important element. Some might say it *is* counseling; all, with the possible exception of the "direct" behavior-theoretical advocates, would agree that it plays a crucial role in counseling. The concept includes, but goes beyond, the notion of rapport to take in (1) improved interpersonal relationships as a goal of counseling, (2) practice in relating to another person during the interview, and (3) relationship as the base on which the entire structure of counseling must be built. To attempt to create a relationship is to give an earnest of caring; to establish a relationship is to make counseling possible; to continue a relationship is to permit growth and change.

(4) *Respect.* Again, respect for the individuality, humanness, and wonderful complexity of the client is shared by all counselors. This respect for the other grows with self-respect and an appreciation of the command to love others as you love yourself. For the counselor to appreciate the client, he must first appreciate himself so that out of his self-acceptance, out of his deep understanding of his virtues and weaknesses, and out of the recognition and control of his own needs comes the skill, the wit, and the love to respect another in a way that makes counseling result in growth.

(5) *Communication.* Whether through words or nonverbal cues, through symbolizations or plain speaking, through physical arrangements or limited time, the counselor and client must communicate, and all four theories are concerned with this problem. The sensitivity and objectivity of the counselor will greatly determine the extent and accuracy of communication. If the counselor with his "third ear" can hear and understand the story of the client's personal world, if he can help find a Rosetta stone to aid in the translation of the client's private language and symbols, and if he can detect the presence and meaning of nuances of tone, word choice, and bodily gestures, then communication and counseling become possible. The greatest sensitivity needed by the counselor, however, may be that reserved for his self-understanding. Why does he press testing onto the client or alternately blind himself to the service it may sometimes perform? Does his silence mean support, approval, or anxiety? Is his restraint in the face of client provocation the result of maturity shown by the control of impulses in the interests of work to be done or is it the result of that narcissism, that higher smugness, expressed as an angelic air of patience and forbearance which has been called the vocational disease of counseling (Wyatt, 1948)?

Sensitivity to self and sensitivity to the client is a necessary condition for the kind of communication required in counseling.

(6) *Learning.* Although the psychoanalytic adherents may tend to be skittish about the use of the term and the trait-and-factor adherents to embrace it too fervently, the concept of learning is present in all four theoretical formulations. Basically the client learns more about himself and his world and, therefore, performs better. The explanation of why he learns may vary from the client-centered emphasis on the climate for emotional learning to the trait-and-factor belief in the value of the structured lesson and plan. The fact that this learning has so often defied measurement would seem to be related to differences in subjects being taught (information or release), in teachers (counselors), in readiness (motivation and maturity), and in the tests used to measure the results of counseling. However, all counselors face and

answer, openly or covertly, the basic pedagogic question "What do I want this person to learn?" (Sometimes, of course, it is expressed— "How do I want him to be different after counseling?" or "What is the justification and purpose of my intervention into his life?")

(7) *Direction.* Although once serving as a psychological litmus paper thought capable of clearly differentiating types of counseling, the concept of direction of the client by the counselor is now more frequently seen as an omnipresent aspect of all counseling. All but the client-centered group have recognized and consciously used their capacity for direction. The client-centered have, on the contrary, resisted the view that their presence or behavior in any way directs the client. (The term "nondirective," as noted in a previous chapter, was originally used to label the point of view in which the client-centered roots are found.) The consideration of the counselor's responses as a stimulus in a conditioning sequence has resulted in an extensive literature. After a review of such literature, the conclusion is reached that the majority of studies demonstrate that such responses as "mmm—hmm," or "I see" do positively reinforce the making of affective statements (Krasner, 1958).

Concern now shifts from the presence or absence of direction to the extent, method, and purpose of direction. Some direction may be explicit and clear (trait-and-factor and behavioral-theoretical), some subtle and tentative (psychoanalytic), and some intuitive and unrecognized (client-centered), but most would agree that it is always present. Perhaps the struggle should shift to the arena of social direction. Perhaps we should ask—Does the counselor direct the client's attention to societally established (external) or personally derived (internal) sign posts? Answers to such a question result in much overlapping among the theories (for like most dichotomies this one is unstable) but directs the dialogue to a more meaningful level of disagreement.

(8) *Support.* The presence, interests, and activity of the counselor are seen by theorists of all schools as supporting the client. The counselor gives the client support by acting out for him such messages as "You are deserving of my time and concern," "We can talk and by doing so can 'touch' and teach each other," and "You will be able to cope with the decisions, crises, and problems facing you." The openness and form of the support would likely vary with the personality of the counselor and the perceived needs of the client as well as the moment of interaction more than with the theoretical orientation of the counselor. By cultural definition the counselor is one who provides support, but he may do so unconsciously and incidentally or deliberately and directly.

(9) *Rewards.* The counselor rewards the client for his presence

and for some of his behavior. (For the argument that the counselor rewards all the client's behavior equally, or perhaps not at all, as suggested by the client-centered practitioners—see Direction, number 7 above.) Such consequences may go beyond support as discussed in the previous section to the kind of conditioning mentioned previously. An aspect of reward sometimes overlooked, however, is the reward received by the counselor from the client. If he does not understand the basis in his own need system for the rewards he feels, the counselor may be in danger of exploiting the client out of insatiable psychic greed. The counselor who refuses to recognize the limitations of his training and role and therefore undertakes to counsel those whose needs are beyond his training to deal with is probably best explained by his failure to be significantly cognizant of the nature of the rewards that have "hooked" him.

All four theories have room in them for an explanation of the mutually rewarding nature of the interaction between the counselor and client, although the psychoanalytic system is most explicit about the genesis, dangers, and function of this reward. The superior status of the counselor and the counseling relationship is so unmistakable that the client would have to be completely outside our culture not to be affected by it. This status is active in direction, support, and reward. It cannot be cast off: It can only be consciously used, partially neutralized, or blindly denied.

(10) *Purposes.* The discussions of counseling goals show us many elements of commonality among the systems with regard to this dimension of counseling. All seek a free, informed, responsible person conscious of himself—his strength and weaknesses, his sickness and health —and capable of viewing the world unblinking and unafraid; capable, too, of making decisions for himself in harmony with his unique nature and at least minimal societal requirements. It is not true, as their enemies may contend, that the client-centered counselor seeks anarchy, that the psychoanalytic counselor seeks an orgy of impulse gratification, or that the trait-and-factor and behavioral-theoretical counselors seek a brave new world of controlled robots.

Conclusion. The beginning counselor may need to remind himself that, although theories are best separated by concentrating on their differences, successful counseling is best accomplished by attending to their similiarities. What they have in common needs to be learned and put into practice before fine doctrinal disputes distract us from the core activity, which is helping the client to find his identity in a culture that like the human condition itself is both baffling and beautiful.

Theory is needed to help us conceptualize the interrelationship of data, to help us temper intuition and rigidity, and to help us examine the efficacy of our actions. Reasonable freedom from theory is also needed if we are to overcome the smugness of the "in" counselor, if we are to free the individual to add himself to the counseling equation, and if we are to be capable of making that higher synthesis which results in better and more inclusive theories. The learning of theory may be likened to the learning of the descriptive rules of grammar. Only after they are known, understood, examined, and evaluated may they be safely breached.

BIBLIOGRAPHY

Barry, Ruth, & Wolf, Beverly. *Modern issues in guidance—Personnel work.* New York: Teacher's College, 1957.

Beck, Carleton. *Philosophical foundations of guidance.* Englewood Cliffs, N.J.: Prentice-Hall, 1963.

Callis, Robert. Counseling. *Rev. educ. Res.,* 1963, **33** (2), 184–185.

Coleman, James S. *The adolescent society: The social life of the teen-ager and its impact on education.* New York: Free Press, 1961.

Encyclopedia of educational research. (3rd ed.) New York: Macmillan, 1960.

Eysenck, H. J. The effects of psychotherapy. In *Handbook of abnormal psychology.* New York: Basic Books, 1961. Pp. 697–725.

Fiedler, Fred E. A comparison of therapeutic relationships in psychoanalytic non-directive and Adlerian therapy. *Journal consult. Psychol.,* 1950, **14.** 436–445.

Ford, Donald H., & Urban, Hugh B. *Systems of psychotherapy.* New York: Wiley, 1963.

Glad, Donald D. *Operational values in psychotherapy.* Fair Lawn, N.J.: Oxford University Press, 1959.

Jahoda, Marie. *Current concepts of positive mental health.* New York: Basic Books, 1958.

Krasner, Leonard. Studies of the conditioning of verbal behavior. *Psychol. Bull.,* 1958, **55** (3), 148–170.

Murphy, Gardner. The cultural context of guidance. *Personnel Guid. J.,* 1955, **34** (1), 8.

Patterson, C. H. Program evaluation. *Rev. educ. Res.,* 1963, **33** (2), 222.

Patterson, C. H. The place of values in counseling and psychotherapy. *J. counsel. Psychol.,* 1958, **5** (3) , 216–223.

Rothney, John W. *Guidance practices and results.* New York: Harper & Row, 1958.

Rothney, John W., & Roens, Bert A. *Guidance of American youth: An experimental study.* Cambridge, Mass.: Harvard, 1950.

Ryans, David G. Assessment of teacher behavior and instruction. *Rev. educ. Res.,* 1963, **33** (4) 415–441.

Samler, Joseph. Change in values: A role of counseling. *J. counsel. Psychol.*, 1960, **7** (1), 36.

Snyder, Benson K. Student's stress. In Terry F. Lunsford (Ed.), *The study of campus cultures.* Boulder, Colo.: Western Interstate Commission for Higher Education, 1963, p. 28.

Stefflre, Buford. Research in guidance: Horizons for the future. *Theory into practice,* 1963, **2** (1), 44–50.

Strupp, Hans H. An objective comparison of Rogerian and psychoanalytic techniques. *J. consult. Psychol.,* 1955, **19,** 1–7 (a).

Strupp, Hans H. Psychotherapeutic technique, professional affiliation, and experience level. *J. consult. Psychol.,* 1955, **19,** 97–102 (b).

Williamson, Edmond G. Value orientation in counseling. *Personnel Guid. J.,* 1958, **36** (8), 520–528.

Wyatt, Frederick. The self-experience of the psychotherapist. *J. consult. Psychol.,* 1948, **12,** 83–87.

Name Index

Abt, L. E., 87, 89
Adler, Alfred, 94, 238, 240, 272, 277
Allport, Gordon W., 248, 256
Angyal, A., 35, 86
Anrep, G. V., 191
Aristotle, 102n.
Arlow, Jacob A., 99, 119, 137
Armitage, S., 164, 191
Aronson, E., 146, 190
Assum, A. L., 65, 86
Axline, Virginia M., 65, 86

Bachrach, A. J., 138
Bacon, Francis, 250
Bailey, Daniel E., 196, 213
Bancroft, George, 216, 241
Bandura, A., 154, 173–175, 190
Barker, J. C., 164, 190
Barrett-Lennard, G. T., 56, 86
Barry, Ruth, 270, 277
Bartlett, M. R., 65, 71, 86
Baura, M., 96, 137
Beck, Carleton, 258, 277
Beethoven, Ludwig van, 232
Bellak, Leopold, 134, 137
Benjamin, Harold, 215, 241
Berdie, Ralph F., 28, 201
Bergmann, G., 141, 190
Berman, Isabel R., 210, 211, 213
Bessenius, C. E., 190
Binet, A., 255
Bingham, Walter, 13
Bixler, R. H., 80–82, 86
Bixler, Virginia M., 82, 86
Black, John D., 20–22, 27
Blakemore, C. B., 164, 190
Blau, Joseph L., 241
Bobbitt, R., 135, 137
Bone, Harry, 10, 28
Bordin, Edward S., 14, 22, 28, 80, 81, 86, 208, 209, 214, 238
Brady J., 164, 190
Brammer, Lawrence M., 8, 13, 17, 28, 29, 81, 89
Brayfield, Arthur H., 193, 214
Brenner, Charles, 95, 133, 137
Brower, Daniel, 86, 89

Brown, Clarence W., 193, 212
Brown, J. S., 145, 148, 149, 160, 190
Brubacher, John S., 241
Brunner, Jerome S., 254, 256
Bryan, W. L., 140, 190
Buber, Martin, 30
Buddha, 232
Burton, A., 8
Butler, J. M., 51, 55, 65, 86, 87
Byrnne, D., 191

Callis, Robert, 266, 277
Campbell, Norman R., 3, 8, 28
Cannon, W. B., 147, 190
Carlsmith, J. M., 146, 190
Cartwright, D. S., 62, 73, 87, 88
Cattell, R. B., 194, 195, 212
Chance, J., 65, 87
Child, I. L., 148, 192
Cofer, C. N., 65, 87
Coffey, H. S., 135, 138
Coleman, James S., 271, 277
Colm, Hanna, 107, 138
Combs, A. W., 13, 39, 89, 147, 190
Conant, James Bryant, 248, 256
Conway, C. G., 164, 190
Copernicus, Nicolaus, 4

Darley, J. G, 226, 241
Darwin, Charles Robert, 233
Davis, Rene V., 193, 212
DeMeyer, M., 164, 191
Dewey, John, 51, 248, 256
Dodge, Arthur F., 196, 212
Dollard, J., 141, 144, 146, 148, 151, 154, 159, 189, 190
Dunlap, K., 164, 190
Dvorak, Beatrice J., 210–213
Dymond, Rosalind F., 65, 87, 88

Ebbinghaus, H., 140, 190
Ellis, A., 238
England, George W., 193, 212
English, Ava Champney, 12, 16, 28
English, Horace B., 12, 16, 28
Evan, Sarah, 138